The political
responsibility of
intellectuals

The political responsibility of intellectuals

Edited by

IAN MACLEAN
Fellow and Praelector in French,
The Queen's College, Oxford

ALAN MONTEFIORE
Jowett Fellow and Tutor in Philosophy,
Balliol College, Oxford

PETER WINCH
Professor of Philosophy, University of
Illinois at Urbana–Champaign

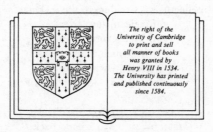

The right of the
University of Cambridge
to print and sell
all manner of books
was granted by
Henry VIII in 1534.
The University has printed
and published continuously
since 1584.

CAMBRIDGE UNIVERSITY PRESS

Cambridge

New York   Port Chester

Melbourne   Sydney

Published by the Press Syndicate of the University of Cambridge
The Pitt Building, Trumpington Street, Cambridge, CB2 1RP
40 West 20th Street, New York, NY 10011, USA
10 Stamford Road, Oakleigh, Melbourne 3166, Australia

First published 1990

Printed in Great Britain at
the University Press, Cambridge

British Library cataloguing in publication data
The political responsibility of intellectuals.
1. Society. Role of intellectuals. I. Maclean, Ian, 1945– .
II. Montefiore, Alan.   III. Winch, Peter.
305.552

Library of Congress cataloguing in publication data
The political responsibility of intellectuals / edited by
Ian Maclean,
Alan Montefiore, Peter Winch
p.   cm.
'This volume results from two meetings held at the Institut für
die Wissenschaften vom Menschen, Vienna' – P.
ISBN 0–521–39179–2
1. Intellectuals – Political activity – Congresses.
2. Intellectuals – Conduct of life – Congresses.
I. Maclean, Ian, 1945–.
II. Montefiore, Alan.
III. Winch, Peter.
HM213.P65   1990
305.5'52 – dc20   89–77385   CIP

ISBN 0 521 39179 2 hardback
ISBN 0 521 39859 2 paperback

CE

This volume results from two meetings
held at the Institut für die Wissenschaften
vom Menschen, Vienna.

Contents

Notes on contributors

ERNEST GELLNER was born in 1925 in Paris, and was educated in Prague and in England. He was on the staff of the London School of Economics from 1949 to 1984, from 1962 onwards as Professor. He is currently Professor of Social Anthropology in the University of Cambridge. His books include *Nations and Nationalism, The Psychoanalytical Movement, Muslim Society, State and Society in Soviet Thought* and *Plough, Sword and Book*. He is at present working on the current developments in the Soviet Union.

ELEMER HANKISS was born in 1928 in Hungary and educated at the University of Budapest. Since 1965 he has been engaged on research work within the framework of the Hungarian Academy of Sciences, and is at present Director of the Centre for the Sociology of Values, affiliated to the Institute of Sociology for the Hungarian Academy of Sciences. He has lectured widely both in Europe and the United States, and has published several books and collections of essays. His latest book is *Kelet-európai alternatívák (East European Alternatives)* (Budapest, 1989).

JERZY JEDLICKI was born in 1930 and is a Professor at the Institute of History in the Polish Academy of Sciences in Warsaw. His publications cover the fields of the economic, social and cultural history of the Polish lands in the nineteenth century, especially during the period of the Russian partition. His most recent book is *Jakiej cywilizacji Polacy potrzsebuja? (What Sort of Civilization do Poles Need?)*. He is also an essayist and writes a column for (what were until recently at least) two opposition periodicals in Poland.

JACEK KURCZEWSKI was born in 1943 in Edinburgh and educated at the University of Warsaw where he took the degrees of MA (1965), PhD (1972) and Habitation (1982), all in Sociology. He has authored, co-authored or edited ten books and about one hundred articles or chapters of books in sociology, mostly in the sociology of law and sociological theory. In 1979 he was a member of the Polish Government Commission of Experts on the abuse of alcohol; in 1980/1 a member of the Advisory Council of the Central National Commission of Solidarity; in 1985 a member of the Polish Government Committee on the Prevention of Drug Abuse; in 1988 a member of the Citizens' Committee under Lech Wałęsa; and in 1989 a member of the Tribunal of State, appointed on behalf of Solidarity. He is currently Director of the Institute of Social Prevention and Resocialization at the University of Warsaw, and co-editor of the independent monthly '*Res Publica*'.

J.-J. LECERCLE is Professor of English at the University of Nanterre, where he teaches linguistics and literature. He is the author of *Philosophy through the Looking-Glass* (London, 1985), *Frankenstein: mythe et philosophie* (Paris, 1988) and *The Violence of Language* (London, forthcoming).

DAVID J. LEVY was educated at Stowe School, Christ Church, Oxford, and the London School of Economics. He is Senior Lecturer in Sociology at Middlesex Polytechnic, and is the author, *inter alia*, of *Realism: An Essay in Interpretation and Social Reality* (1981), *Political Order: Philosophical Anthropology, Modernity and the Challenge of Ideology* (1987) and *Voegelin* (forthcoming).

GRAHAME LOCK was born in 1946, and studied at University College, London (BA), King's College, Cambridge (PhD), and the Ecole normale supérieure (rue d'Ulm, Paris). He was Lecturer in Political Theory at Leiden University from 1972 to 1982, and since 1982 has been Professor of Political Theory at the Catholic University of Nijmegen. From 1990 onwards he will also be acting as Faculty Fellow in Philosophy at the University of Oxford. He is the author of *The State and I* (Leiden, 1981) and of a number of books in Dutch. He has published articles in the fields of political philosophy, analytic and European philosophy, psychoanalytic theory and opera.

IAN MACLEAN is a graduate of the University of Oxford, who has taught in the University of Leeds and (since 1972) at The Queen's College, Oxford. He has published books on French literary history and the history of philosophy, and is presently working on the interpretation of law in Northern Europe in the late Renaissance.

MIKLÓS MOLNAR was born in 1918 in Budapest, and studied in Budapest (Licence en philosophie, 1956) and in Geneva (Doctorat en science politique, 1963). While still in Hungary he worked as a journalist and literary critic. He left Hungary at the beginning of 1957 and settled in Switzerland, and is now a Swiss national. He is Emeritus Professor of History and International Relations at the Institut Universitaire de Hautes Etudes Internationales in Geneva and Honorary Professor of the University of Lausanne. He is the author or co-author of numerous books. These include *Budapest 1956: A History of the Hungarian Revolution* (London, 1971), *Marx Engels, et la politique internationale* (Paris, 1975), *A Short History of the Hungarian Communist Party* (Folkestone, 1978) and *Fanaticism: A Historical and Psychoanalytical Study* (together with André Haynal and Gérard de Puymège; English edition, New York, 1983).

ALAN MONTEFIORE was born in 1926 in London and was a student at Balliol College, Oxford. After having taught for ten years in the University of Keele, he returned in 1961 to Balliol as Fellow and Tutor in Philosophy, where he still is. His books include *A Modern Introduction to Moral Philosophy* (1958), *British Analytical Philosophy* (co-edited with Bernard Williams, 1961), *Philosophy and Personal Relations* (editor, 1973), *Neutrality and Objectivity: The University and Political Commitment* (editor and co-author, 1975), *Philosophy in France Today* (editor, 1983) and *Goals, No-Goals and Own Goals: The Description and Explanation of Goal-Directed Behaviour* (co-editor with Denis Noble and co-author, 1989).

EDWARD SHILS is Professor of Social Thought and Sociology at the University of Chicago. He was reader in Sociology at the University of London (London School of Economics) and Fellow of King's College and Peterhouse, Cambridge. His writings include *The Intellectual between Tradition and Modernity: The Indian Situation, The Torment of Secrecy, Tradition, The Intellectuals and the Powers, Towards a General Theory of Action* (with Talcott Parsons). He is founder and editor of *Minerva: A Review of Science, Learning and Policy* and deputy chairman of the advisory board of the Institut für die Wissenschaften vom Menschen, Vienna.

JERZY SZACKI was born in 1929 in Warsaw. He received his undergraduate degrees from the University of Warsaw, where he is now a Professor of the History of Social Thought. He has written several books in Polish as well as *The History of Sociological Thought* (1979), which was published both in the United States and in Great Britain. Since 1984 he has also been affiliated with the Institut für die Wissenschaften vom Menschen in Vienna.

G. M. TAMÁS, after spending many difficult years outside the official institutions of his country, has just been re-appointed as a Reader in Philosophy in the Faculty of Jurisprudence at the University of Budapest. He is one of the leaders of the Hungarian Liberal Party, the Free Democratic Alliance. His most recent book is *Les Idoles de la Tribu* (Paris, 1989).

PETER WINCH is Professor of Philosophy at the University of Illinois at Urbana–Champaign and Professor Emeritus in the University of London. He is also a corresponding member of the Institut für die Wissenschaften vom Menschen in Vienna and was Visiting Fellow there in 1986. His books include *The Idea of a Social Science* (London, 1958), *Ethics and Action* (London, 1972), *Trying to Make Sense* (Oxford, 1987) and *Simone Weil: 'The Just Balance'* (Cambridge, 1989).

Editorial preface

ALAN MONTEFIORE

The papers in this collection are the outcome of a co-operative project developed under the auspices of the Institut für die Wissenschaften vom Menschen (Institute for the Sciences of Man) in Vienna, one of the prime purposes of the Institute being, indeed, to foster co-operative intellectual work between East and West in those senses of the terms according to which 'East' refers to the countries of Eastern Europe and 'West' to those of Western Europe and beyond, 'beyond' including most notably the continent of North America. During the course of the project two main meetings were held in Vienna, at which successive drafts of papers were intensively discussed; after each meeting they were taken back for revision in the light of the discussions that had taken place. In addition many of the participants worked together for longer or shorter periods in smaller groups. The papers as they are now published are not, then, conference papers in the normal sense of the term, papers that are prepared in advance of the conference at which they are to be presented and not in general very substantially amended in the light of the discussions that have there taken place. These papers, though of course the immediate responsibility each of their own author, are nevertheless the outcome of a great deal of sustained collaborative interaction.

It is worth stressing the fact that the number of very full and active participants in the project, either throughout or at one stage or another, was substantially greater than that of those whose papers now go to make up this volume. The value of their contributions to the discussions that went on is truly reflected in the papers that appear here. It should also be recorded – with a real sense of regret – that the practical constraints involved in the

xv

putting together of a volume of publishable length and coherence turned out in the end to make it impossible for the editors to include even all the completed papers that had been presented. Their non-appearance here should in no way be construed as a value judgement upon their intrinsic worth; those responsible for the project have cause to be immensely grateful to all its participants, whether their names appear as authors of the particular papers included here or not.

By the time this volume finally appears several years will in fact have elapsed since the project from which it emerges was first initiated. It goes without saying that much has changed within Europe and the wider world during these years, and changed moreover in ways and with a rapidity that virtually no one would then have predicted; indeed, as I write these words in August 1989, both the pace and unpredictability of change seem, if anything, to be increasing. Inevitably, this may give a slightly dated air to some of the references to what were then very current and on-going states of affairs. But the fact that the situation in Poland, for example, is, at the moment at which I write this preface, very different indeed from what it was when the papers that here make reference to events in Poland were actually written, surely takes away nothing of what is truly interesting about them. (In any case, for all that anyone may now know, the Polish or even the whole East European situation may have changed radically once again, by the time that this preface is actually published.) In a different perspective, there has been, since the period during which the main discussions of the project took place, a great deal more information made public and even more renewed public debate about the roles played by certain leading intellectuals during the time of the Nazi domination of Europe. But if one tried, in a project of this sort, to keep up with even the most important new developments as they arise in one part of the world or another and to adjust one's overall judgements accordingly, it would be impossible ever to bring the project to an end. In short, neither the project as a whole nor any of the contributions to it should be thought of as seeking to provide any sort of ongoing commentary on current affairs as such.

Even from the outset the project was likewise conceived within another set of limits. Much though we might have been tempted to try and do so, we knew only too well that we could not possibly attempt to deal even with all the most pressing ways in which intellectuals might be called upon to acknowledge or to face political responsibilities. There is nothing here, for example, about the question of how intellectuals should react to calls for the cultural or academic boycotting of one country or regime or another, even though this was already a very live and controversial question. The question of how intellectuals should relate or react to the values and demands of one politically powerful religious authority or another also presents, of course, among the oldest and most painfully familiar of issues; but the recent irruption of the Salman Rushdie affair has brought it back to the very forefront of current preoccupations, and the absence of any direct discussion of it here may likewise serve to mark the date of this particular project's conception. (Not that there are not many other contexts in the world today in which the demands of one powerful and powerfully emotive religious authority or another face intellectuals with pressing challenges and choices.) The flowering and (for the time being at any rate) repression of the democracy movement in China similarly belong to a period subsequent to that of the working through of the project. It is in any case true, however, that, in spite of initial hopes to the contrary, it in the event never proved possible to enlarge the scope of the project to the point at which we might have been able to engage in serious and sustained discussion with intellectuals from third world countries of the differences and similarities between the problems of political responsibility that they face as compared with those faced by their colleagues of the different countries of Eastern and Western Europe.

All of which amounts not so much to an apology as to a straightforward recognition and explanation of the fact that the project from which the papers that follow were born had the scope and limits that it had. It would in any case be an absurd pretension to hope to touch on *every* leading aspect of the topic of its concern within the confines of just one such project. Our hope in publishing these papers is simply that they may make a worthwhile contribution to the wider debate.

A word should be said about the order in which the papers here appear. One can imagine readily enough a number of different principles according to which they might have been gathered together in more or less appropriately contrasting sections: the more theoretical as compared with the more sociological or historical, those written by authors coming from countries of Eastern Europe as compared with those written by authors coming from the West, and so on. But none of these principles could in fact be applied so as to produce as clear-cut a distinction as one might have supposed, and each would present its own difficulties and disadvantages. In the end, then, we have decided to settle, with two exceptions, for a simple alphabetical order of authors' names. The first of these exceptions concerns the introduction by Peter Winch, which comes first, as any introduction should, before all the papers which it sets out to introduce; the other concerns the paper contributed by Edward Shils, which, though it was not originally conceived or written as such, in fact constitutes a happily personal retrospective survey of the ground through or within which the preceding contributions seek to thread their paths. It thus seemed very appropriate to place it last.

Finally, it should be stressed that, although Ian Maclean, Peter Winch and myself have ended up by appearing as 'editors' of this volume, many other people have also put a great deal of work into it. In particular our most grateful thanks are due to Professor Jerzy Szacki, whose repeated help in all manner of matters of substance as well as of detail has proved quite indispensable, as well as to Dr Krysztof Michalski, Director of the Institut für die Wissenschaften vom Menschen, for all the hospitality and support which he, through the Institut, has provided; and to Christine Huterer of the Institute, without whose constant and constantly cheerful practical resourcefulness nothing would have been possible.

I

Introduction

PETER WINCH

The papers in this collection are, as Alan Montefiore has explained in his Preface, the outcome of a co-operative project, initiated by Alan Montefiore of Oxford and Jerzy Szacki of Warsaw and developed under the auspices of the Institut für die Wissenschaften vom Menschen (Institute for the Sciences of Man) in Vienna. The contributors are scholars from a wide variety of different intellectual fields: sociology, social anthropology, economics, psychology, linguistics, political science, law, legal history, history, international affairs, philosophy. As is to be expected, therefore – and, indeed, as was intended – they have approached the subject from different directions and treated it in different ways; they do not even all have quite the same conception of what the subject is. The result of this might easily have been that their papers simply talked past each other. But in fact, somewhat to my surprise, it seems to me that this has not been the case. (I say this from a position of some impartiality since, although I have been associated with the Institute for a long time, I did not myself become involved in this particular project until the final general conference of the participants in September 1987, at which I took the chair.) Largely due, no doubt, to the amount of intensive discussion and mutual criticism there has been, the meeting of so many different points of view and intellectual methods has resulted in real cross-fertilization rather than sterility.

In this Introduction I shall mainly try to plot some of the interconnections between the various discussions, as I see them. That last qualifying clause is important. For more reasons than one it would be absurd and impertinent for me to pretend to be pronouncing judicially on the contributions *de haut en bas* as it

1

were. Obviously I do not agree with everything that is printed between these covers: no person consistently could. Where I disagree in a way that seems to me important I have not hesitated to say so; but of course my own opinion has no greater claim to authority than anyone else's. The only difference between my own Introduction and the other papers is that my remarks are deliberately formulated with a view to bringing out connections between the discussions of the rest of the contributors. Furthermore, my own primary interest is in philosophical questions; and it seems to me that the philosophical issues raised in a general way by Alan Montefiore's paper are relevant to the subjects discussed in most of the other papers as well. I shall frequently refer back to this paper in the course of my remarks. I do this in part because the abstraction of its argument may cause difficulty to some readers who are more at home with the more concretely historically and sociologically rooted discussions which predominate and I hope I may help to show the relevance and importance of that abstract argument if one is to come to terms with the historical realities.

The phrase 'political responsibility of intellectuals' suggests that there is something about the character of intellectual work which in a special way tends to thrust those who engage in it into the political arena. Montefiore's paper is an attempt to analyse that tendency. I distinguish the following elements within it.

1 An explication of the way in which intellectual work involves a concern for such norms as truth and validity.
2 A discussion of the way in which the realization of these norms presupposes a certain mode of interaction within a culture on the part of those engaged in such work.
3 A discussion of some of the ways in which such a mode of interaction may typically be threatened by socio-political forces.
4 The articulation of a moral demand on those engaged in intellectual work to defend the conditions which make their work possible against such threats.
5 A philosophical argument which seeks to derive this moral demand from, or ground it in, the very nature of intellectual work.
6 The suggestion that every human being is, in some measure, an 'intellectual', that is, engages in intellectual work and is there-

fore (by virtue of the argument in (5)) subject to the moral demand articulated in (4).

In Montefiore's paper these elements are intertwined in a multitude of complex ways. I have deliberately tried to isolate them from each other in what is, admittedly, an artificial way, because I believe I can thereby bring what I want to say in this Introduction into better focus. I want, first of all, to indicate some of the ways in which elements (1) to (4) above are treated in this volume as a whole. Then, in conclusion, I want to evaluate Montefiore's argument and to devote particular attention to the elements (5) and (6), which perhaps constitute his most distinctive contribution.

The phrase 'socio-political forces', which I used in my formulation of element (3) above, immediately brings into prominence the ways in which the power of the state serves to shape the cultural milieux in which intellectuals work. Elemer Hankiss discusses some of the ways in which such changes may have been brought about and their repercussions on the attitudes to responsibility of intellectuals in post-Second World War Hungary. His paper opens up certain interesting questions without really answering them. For the extent to which the statistical correlations relating to Hungary that he cites can be reliably taken to indicate 'causal' connections must wait on detailed comparisons with similar material from other societies. Edward Shils' paper is a magisterial historical and sociological survey of the multitudinous variety of forms intellectual influence can take and of the conditions that have given rise to very different responses to such influence.

Between the extremes of subservient acceptance of responsibility for the purposes of authority and the insistent claim to arrogate responsibility for guiding and counselling if not actually ruling, between the extremes of utter indifference to any responsibility for the wellbeing of society and the rancorous and aggressive rejection of any responsibility and indeed a hatred which would obliterate any sense of responsibility towards the prevailing society, there is a large and various set of attitudes and actions.

Particularly interesting in Shils' paper, it seems to me, are the discussions first, of the changes that have been wrought in the position and attitudes of intellectuals by the two great revolutions of our time (the French and the Russian); secondly, of the roles played by intellectuals in the new states of Asia and Africa; and thirdly, of the fairly recent radical politicizing of the social sciences. Of this last development Shils comments laconically: 'It is a view widely asserted that objectivity or "evaluative neutrality" is impossible. Of course, this view is incompatible with the scientific aspirations of many social scientists but such has been the force of current opinion that they affirm the view to which they do not adhere in practice.'

Shils' discussion concentrates attention on intellectuals working, roughly speaking, in the academic humanities and the social sciences; and the same is true of most of the other papers here. Given the enormous preponderance in financial support given by governments and other bodies disposing of funds for work in the natural sciences and technology, it is useful to be reminded that workers in these fields have as good a title to be classed as 'intellectuals' too, and that their activities create their own special problems of responsibility. David J. Levy, for example, concentrates on these.

In this connection it is worth noting the important general point that responsibility has two aspects: it is not only an admission of accountability but a claim to power, and these two aspects may be so interconnected that an admission of accountability in some cases can *amount* to a claim to power.

This is a point which crops up again and again throughout this collection. It is particularly important, for instance in Jacek Kurczewski's account of the role of intellectuals as 'specialist advisers' in the context of both the Gierek regime and Solidarity. He suggests that the deepest lesson to be learned from those two Polish experiences is the common will to power on the part of experts as well as those whom they advise. 'Even Gierek's failed experts were surrounded by an aura of power for those outside the arena, though they themselves explained their failure in terms of lack of power.' His paper also includes a fascinating excerpt from the proceedings of the National Co-ordinating Committee of Solidarity, in which the precise weight to be given to the opinions of specialist advisers concerning, for instance, strike action is a subject of vigorous and intensive discussion, a discussion which is all the more pointed for being immediately focussed on a pressing practical issue. Kurczewski warns against the pretensions to power to which intellectuals are prone: 'being "experts" only gave them the right to speak on the same level as Commission members, a formal right to speak, that is to persuade, that is to influence, but not a substantive right to say anything that was authoritative *per se*'. And again: 'There are no specialists on strikes except those who have organized them while, at the same time, to have organized a strike does not mean that you will know what to do next time. Changeability of context, contextuality of situation, situational character of decision making – all this speaks against the assumption.'

One particular version of the pretensions of intellectuals to power is to be found in the claims, familiar enough, that tend to be made by the 'intellectuals of technology' to be in a singularly superior position to undertake 'objective' and well-informed decision making. Levy's paper is not in fact concerned with evaluating claims that the contemporary technologist's ways of thinking might offer the key to our problems. On the contrary it presents the fruits of those ways of thinking as themselves constituting precisely the biggest problem facing humanity. It is concerned with a particular fundamental respect in which the advance of technology impinges on human needs in ways which a narrowly instrumental view does not accommodate, namely through its transformation of the human environment. We have reached the point where that environment cannot be taken for granted, as a *given* sphere in which human beings act and which their actions may, marginally, modify. In the modern world human beings are forced to take responsibility for positive measures to preserve the environment as one in which they can live: 'while other animals are attuned to survival in a given ecological niche, human beings are responsible for the creation and maintenance of an equivalent space in nature in which their continued existence becomes possible'. Full acceptance of this responsibility would, he argues, require the adoption of a different heuristic approach to our relations with nature: the replacement of Bloch's 'Prinzip Hoffnung' by an 'heuristics of fear'.

This, of course, raises further questions, not treated in Levy's paper, concerning the shape such a replacement might take in the institutions which, in our culture, control technological development and concerning the role to be taken in such institutions by technologists themselves.

That last point brings me back to one of the central issues raised in Montefiore's paper: that of the relation between an intellectual's concern with the standards and values inherent in his or her own professional work and a wider political, or quasi-political, responsibility. Whereas Montefiore's own principal concern is to establish a conceptual connection between these, several of the contributors are struck by the tensions which may develop between them.

Consider Ernest Gellner's paper on Julien Benda's celebrated book, *La Trahison des clercs*, from that point of view. Benda complained of the allegedly disastrous socio-political consequences of the tendency amongst intellectuals to abandon faith in the primacy of absolute, universal standards of reason. Gellner's discussion rests on the assumption that the most basic responsibility of an intellectual must be, with as good a faith as one can muster, to pursue one's investigations wherever the argument seems to lead them and then to conduct oneself accordingly. Gellner shows very elegantly the power of the considerations which led those at whom Benda's complaints were directed to conclude that reason, being a natural human faculty and therefore itself just one element in a natural order of things, cannot validly claim any hierarchical predominance *vis-à-vis* other such elements. The intellectual duty of those who reached such a conclusion in good faith would be to proclaim it and stand by whatever practical consequences they perceived it to have. It would then, argues Gellner, be a 'treason' to suppress that conclusion on any pragmatic socio-political grounds, as did Benda.

The naturalistic conception of reason required by Gellner's argument against Benda is in conflict with the more 'transcendental' conception to which Montefiore, at least in his more Kantian vein, is attracted. Gellner's argument naturally leads to a certain diffidence regarding one's position as 'intellectual'; more particularly, perhaps, to a reluctance to claim any special social responsibility for intellectuals as such; and this too is in sharp contrast with Montefiore's position.

G. M. Tamás voices such a reluctance from the point of view of a somewhat more sombre concession to what he sees as our contemporary 'Pyrrhonism' than Gellner's measured scepticism:

I think that if a standard of excellence in *litterae humaniores* cannot be established, a strong doctrine of political responsibility is at best presumptuous. But the search for such a standard seems to run counter to the spirit of the age. One cannot speak of this kind of responsibility except in the name of some truth acquired, taken into possession.

This too, of course, runs strongly counter to Montefiore's argument. It need hardly worry Montefiore, however: his reaction might well be (as, for the record, would be mine): so much the worse for 'the spirit of the age'; such an abdication (as Gellner too would surely agree) would constitute the worst sort of intellectual 'treason'.

J.-J. Lecercle's piece of 'Textual responsibility' is, if anything, even more strongly at odds with Montefiore. He casts doubt on the very sense of the idea that a speaker's or writer's words are his, an idea which, of course, is the source of Montefiore's whole argument. Lecercle's problem is that the notion of an author's responsibility relies on a theory that the meaning of what he says springs from his intention, a theory which is in conflict with the insight that language, as a cultural and historical structure, may endow his words with a meaning that he never intended.

I think it is important to see that, in so far as there really is a problem here, it would undermine the notion of an agent's responsibility for *anything* that he does, not just his words. A great deal of world literature, after all, explores cases in which the significance of people's acts is at the mercy of historical contingencies. There is even a popular proverb that the road to hell is paved with good intentions ...

The importance of this should not be underestimated. It would, however, be a confusion to suppose that it places the whole concept of individual responsibility at risk. What we should conclude from it is rather the need for care in deciding just *what*, in particular circumstances, an agent (and *a fortiori* an author) may fairly be regarded as responsible for. It is salutary to be reminded how much more difficult this often is than meets a hasty glance. And no doubt there are special difficulties attaching to an author's responsibility for the sense that is found in his text and for the further social or political consequences this may lead to. Lecercle's discussion of cases like those of Ezra Pound and Robert

Brasillach certainly highlights the difficulties and suggests that in certain cases a final resolution of them, and hence a final decision as to responsibility, will hardly be on the cards. But we should lose the moral altogether, so it seems to me, were we to conclude that, because of such difficulties, we cannot rightly hold an individual responsible for anything.

There is a paradox worth noticing when we juxtapose the contributions of Lecercle and Montefiore. The very intertwining of the author's own utterances and intentions with the responses of others, both to him and to each other, all of which, taken together, constitute a very large part of what 'language' consists in, is appealed to by Lecercle to undermine the author's responsibility and by Montefiore to give a very strong account of it. While, as I shall try later to show, I think that Montefiore tries to extract rather too much from his argument, I have little doubt that the direction he takes on this matter is the one to be preferred. The sense of our ways of talking about responsibility is to be found in the ways in which we *do* talk, not in some *a priori* theory about the link between responsibility and intention.

The importance of this point is apparent in Jerzy Jedlicki's lucid discussion of a *prima facie* quite different subject: that of collective and inherited responsibility. Here too scepticism springs from a reluctance to acknowledge that a person can be responsible for any state of affairs which is not a more or less direct result of his own intentional action. As Jedlicki persuasively argues, the responsibility which an individual acquires by inheritance, or through membership of a certain nation or of some other grouping, is to be understood not as a liability for punishment or blame, but as the bearing of obligations. This is an idea that gives us little difficulty in ordinary life: 'For the principle that the debts and obligations of the testator fall on the heir to a legacy is not inconsistent with the principle of individual justice.'

It is implicit in his argument that an individual's sense of his own identity is largely shaped by the traditions, national, social, cultural, family, etc., groupings to which he belongs. This 'belonging' may have something of a brute fact about it with which the intentional acts of the individual in question have had little to do. However, there is also something about it which is not just a brute fact; the heritage is given to us, and on us only depends what we do with it. One of the things which depends on us is our *acknowledgement* of our membership or participation: 'The historical "we" is an admission – conscious or unconscious – of solidary participation in the life and values, in the glories and declines of a multigenerational community.' Such an acknowledgement brings with it commitments of one sort and another, whose particular nature will depend, amongst other things, on a history in which we as individuals have played a part. A similar point may be made, for example, with respect to the influence which a particularly strong teacher may have on his or her pupils or students. Here too one may say, with Jedlicki: the heritage is given to us, and on us only depends what we do with it; and again one of the most important things that depends on us is the nature of our *acknowledgement* of that heritage. The influence of A on B involves B as much as it involves A; assessment of the character of A and of B, and of the relation between them, moreover, has an inescapably ethical dimension. 'Acknowledgement' is itself an ethical act which affects the character of the relation and hence the nature of the responsibility of the one or other party to it.

The issues raised by Lecercle and Jedlicki all have to do with the nature and extent of an individual's responsibility for words or actions which in one way or another are due to other people or to general cultural or linguistic conditions. Grahame Lock is concerned with a closely related problem in his discussion of an intellectual's relation to the political life of his or her times: a matter that he approaches by exploring difficulties in Plato's discussion, in *The Republic*, of the political role of the philosopher.

On the one hand, Plato was hostile to the idea that the philosopher could 'represent' the demands or opinions of other sectors of the population (regarded by him as a form of 'imitation'). Lock illuminatingly compares this posture with G. A. Cohen's attempt to demonstrate an incoherence in the idea that one might hold a belief by virtue of one's occupying a certain social role (though, in considering this comparison, we perhaps need to be more careful than is Lock to distinguish the case of *holding* a belief from that of *expressing* it). But on the other hand, in ascribing to the philosopher a duty to tell 'noble lies' for political purposes, Plato does seem to acknowledge that to be a philosopher is to fill a certain social role requiring one to say things which are contrary to what one personally believes. Lock observes that the contemporary social world is very much a Platonic 'theatocracy' in which opinions tend to be influential by virtue of the prestige of the person uttering them rather than by virtue of their content. 'For we now live in a theatocracy . . . Where, in this configuration, is the place of the intellectual? One does not need to be a Platonist to answer: in any case, in the refusal to play the same game; that is to say, in the refusal to play the part of imitator of the masses.'

Lock's paper can very usefully be considered alongside Ian Maclean's scholarly discussion of legal interpretation. The role of the professional lawyer, whether advocate, judge, legislative draughtsman, academic commentator, seems to commit one to arguing a case as *persuasively* as possible whether or not one believes in its *veracity*. Lock's comment on this point is that the judge (for example) 'tells us what, as he – honestly and personally – believes, is the state of the law with respect to some point'. That is, perhaps, an attractive ideal, but it is one which Maclean's paper shows to be fraught with difficulties. Those concerned with exegesis of the law, he says, are enjoined 'to act humbly as servants of the text' but, because there is 'no absolute guarantee of meaning', interpretation in fact is, perhaps more often than not, anything but a humble process and interpreters constantly threaten to become masters rather than servants. Maclean does not pretend to give any easy solution to this difficulty and is cautiously pragmatic:

A commitment to seriousness and to truth-telling may not be susceptible to adequate codification, but an explicit recognition by interpreters of the historicity of their role may go some way toward reducing the authoritative claims of any act of mediation, even if this seems to compromise their allegiance to concepts such as justice, equality, fairness and so on which are often held to be universals.

There is some hint of a tension here with the strong defense of the intellectual's responsibility for such 'universals' developed by Montefiore. The tension is stretched further in Maclean's (surely not entirely mischievous) suggestion that bad faith in interpreting the letter of the law, which the judicial process leaves open to, and to some extent even invites from, both advocate and litigant may not be as morally and politically calamitous as one might think, since it forces greater clarity on legal draughtsmen: 'The constant testing of linguistic meaning by argument in this way is a feature of an "open" society which recognizes the potential disjunction of truthfulness and meaning in its members, but monitors this by continuous inquisition.'

Two writers who do not question the reality of the intellectual's responsibility for the extent to which his or her work respects standards of truth and validity are Jerzy Szacki and Miklós Molnar, both of whom explore further the relation between this sort of responsibility and political activity. Szacki distinguishes between what he calls the 'political' and the 'cultural' intellectual. The former is distinguished by his or her characteristic behaviour in seeking political influence or power, rather than by professional competence. The danger of this posture, Szacki points out, is that

if you enter the political market-place where there is no place for culture values as such, you inevitably submit to its laws. Making politics more scientific turns out to be making science more political and nothing more; making politics more moral turns out to be making morality more political, etc. Hence the great act of creating a new culture easily turns in the end into an act of self-destruction.

But there are difficulties in the 'cultural intellectual's' posture too. It may seem to depend on a belief that cultural values are independent of politics and, as already remarked, that belief has been considerably undermined in our own times. Moreover, such a posture has been made *politically* difficult by recent totalitarian regimes (witness the case of Boris Pasternak). However, to be *forced* into the political arena in this way is importantly different from making activity in that arena a central point in one's conception of the intellectual's role. That is why, says Szacki: 'it seems very sophistical to say that an intellectual should be political because he cannot escape from politics. This is indeed sometimes difficult, or even impossible, but from this it does not logically follow that he should give up the fight for absolute culture values.'

It is this point in the argument that Molnar's paper takes up. It tries to display how the (cultural) intellectual's conception of his duty of 'reserve' *vis-à-vis* politics can be fulfilled without his turning his back on politics; and it does this very effectively by way

of thumb-nail sketches of the careers of three Hungarian intellectuals, Kazinczy, Széchenyi and Eötvös, who confronted this
dilemma. Finally, I want to return as promised to Alan Montefiore's paper
and to scrutinize what I take to be a key point in his argument. In
discussing the other papers I have noted from time to time how
some of the views expressed by contributors come into conflict
with certain important claims which Montefiore presupposes.
Alert readers may have noticed that, while in most cases I
suggested that these opposing views need cause him little trouble,
in one important case I was silent. I am referring to Gellner's
argument concerning the implications of the 'naturalistic' conception of reason held by the intellectuals whom Julien Benda had
accused of 'treason'. I noted that this conception 'is in conflict
with the more "transcendental" conception to which Montefiore,
at least in his more Kantian vein, is attracted' and left it at that. It
is clear, though, that to accept such a naturalistic conception and
to accept Gellner's claims concerning its consequences would
involve a thoroughgoing rejection of some of Montefiore's most
important contentions. For according to Gellner a reason which is
just one element in a natural order has no title to exercise precisely
that kind of ultimate authority over other elements in human
nature that Montefiore wants to ascribe to it.

Now I certainly do not wish to commit myself to a full-blown
naturalistic theory, of the sort described by Gellner, since to do so
would be to commit myself to all sorts of further metaphysical
implications about which I should certainly not be happy.
However, the warning that such a theory suggests – to look most
carefully at any claims (on the part of reason or anything else) to
'ultimate authority' – is one worth observing. It is worth bearing
in mind, for example, at the point where Montefiore, having in
his discussion of Havel's *The Power of the Powerless* articulated a
clear and compelling moral position concerning the responsibility
of intellectuals to work for the preservation and improvement of
those conditions which make intellectual activity possible, then
says that in our contemporary society 'there are many who might
feel less than wholly confident about such direct appeals to the
moral' and goes on to try to accommodate such people by trying
to provide his moral position with a sort of metaphysico-
epistemological underpinning.

I think there can be little doubt that for Montefiore himself 'the appeal to the moral' is persuasive enough in itself. It is so for me too; and I think, moreover, that *not* to accept it as ultimate, by trying to 'prove' it, distorts the conceptual situation. Of course, one's intellectual responsibility is to avoid such distortion; and furthermore, so far from strengthening the moral case, it weakens it; since, when the weakness of the argument becomes apparent, there is serious danger that this will be (mis)interpreted as a weakness in the moral position itself.

A key point in Montefiore's case is that, since 'an intellectual' is 'anyone who takes a committed interest in the validity and truth of ideas for their own sake, . . . everyone must be considered, to some small extent at least, to have something of the intellectual in them'. Taken by itself, this extended application of the word 'intellectual' need be regarded as no more than an innocent eccentricity. But the argumentative weight that Montefiore lends it makes it necessary to inspect it with a cold eye.

I acknowledged that the moral case for the sort of responsibility Montefiore (following Havel) ascribes to the intellectual is a powerful one. Now a large part of its power, it seems to me, derives precisely from the fact that an 'intellectual' (in the normal sense of the term) is one who has, in a sense, chosen a certain life: one which involves a commitment to certain values and which, therefore, if those values come under attack, demands that they be defended. If such a person tries to evade that demand, he or she invited the rejoinder: 'Look, you chose to live this life; now accept the consequences of your choice.' The (desired) effect of Monte-fiore's extension of the term 'intellectual' is that *everyone*, simply by virtue of *living a human life*, is subject to the same demand. But now, can it be plausibly maintained that every human being 'chooses to live a human life' in anything like the sense in which one may choose to live the life of an intellectual? I should say no; but let me be clear about what my denial amounts to. I do not wish to deny that a powerful moral appeal can be made to anyone, intellectual or not, to defend the values of truth and intellectual honesty when they are under attack. I want to say only that such an appeal can have nothing but its own two (moral) feet to stand on; and, in my view, these suffice.

Let me look briefly at the argument by means of which Montefiore tries to attach this special intellectual responsibility to every human being as such. It runs, as he says, 'through the theory of the conditions of self-awareness or through that of language and meaning', 'theories' which he articulates in his discussions of Kant and Wittgenstein. Crucially important is his treatment of Wittgenstein's demonstration that an individual can say something meaningful only in a context in which certain kinds of response on the part of others to what he or she says are made room for. Montefiore's gloss on this is that the publicity of linguistic norms requires that one who intends to produce meaningful utterances is thereby committed to an intention to uphold those conditions under which such utterances are possible, i.e. consistencies of use in both oneself and others: 'each has ... to conduct himself as individually responsible, for and to himself, for sustaining the meaningfulness of his own discourse – for sustaining it, precisely, through his (not necessarily, of course, invariable but nevertheless paradigmatic) recognition of his discursive responsibility to others'. In other words, everyone has a responsibility for truthfulness and to truth which is rooted in 'our capacity for language and discourse'. 'It is not possible to abandon it altogether without abandoning the realm of human discourse as such.'

It will be good to retrace the steps of this argument a little more slowly. First, it is not required by the argument of Wittgenstein's to which Montefiore is appealing that one who speaks meaningfully must *intend* to uphold the conditions which make his activity possible; all that is necessary is that those conditions should in fact exist. Montefiore reminds me here of those who try to convict socialists who have their children privately educated of inconsistency; but, however one may judge such conduct morally or politically, there is no *inconsistency* in taking advantage of conditions so long as they exist while working for their destruction. *A fortiori* there is no inconsistency in acting in a way which is only possible if certain conditions continue, while not being prepared to exert oneself for their continuance. Furthermore, it is by no means clear that the continued existence of the conditions which make ordinary human communication possible actually does depend on the sort of militant or watchful attitude on the part of speakers that Montefiore has in mind. Nor does he argue this. What he does argue (and this is much more plausible) is that the maintenance of a certain sort of desirable *quality* in human communication depends on such an attitude. But the fellow citizens of the greengrocer so graphically described by Havel seem not to care over-much about the maintenance of such quality, preferring to settle for a quiet life. One may indeed deplore this. But it is surely preposterous to suggest that such people are, in Montefiore's phrase, 'abandoning the realm of discourse'.

His argument here is obviously a Kantian one: in fact it is closely modelled on the treatment of the 'false promise' in Kant's exposition of the Categorical Imperative in *Grundelgung zur Metaphysik der Sitten*. But Wittgenstein, for all that many have claimed and that Montefiore implicitly suggests, was no Kantian; and his very explicit refusal to say, in contexts like this, that this is how we *must* behave, in favour of pointing out that such and such are the ways in which we *do* behave, is one important indication of how he and Kant part company.

Montefiore is indeed entitled to (and does) say that an existence such as Havel describes is not 'truly human'. But the natural sense of that is: 'not worthy of a human being'; and if it *is* taken in that sense it is clear that we have not got beyond that 'appeal to the moral' which the argument is supposed to underpin. The same goes for the in itself perfectly acceptable claim that the ideological ritual pervading the Czechoslovakia which Havel describes 'helps the greengrocer to conceal from himself the low foundations of his obedience, at the same time concealing the low foundations of power. It hides them behind the façade of something high'. Here the moral appeal involved in the use of 'high' and 'low' is obvious.

Havel, in the essay which Montefiore discusses, himself insists on this in his account of the kind of political resistance that is possible in contemporary 'post-totalitarian' societies:

If living within the truth in the post-totalitarian system becomes the chief breeding ground for independent, alternative political ideas, then all considerations about the nature and future prospects of these ideas must necessarily reflect this moral dimension as a political phenomenon. (And if the revolutionary Marxist belief about morality as a product of the 'superstructure' inhibits any of our friends from realizing the full significance of this dimension and, in one way or another, from including it in their view of the world, it is to their own detriment: an anxious fidelity to the postulates of that world view prevents them from properly understanding the mechanisms of their own political influence, thus paradoxically making them precisely what they, as Marxists, so often suspect others of being – victims of 'false consciousness'.[1]

In fact Havel seems to me to get the conceptual relationships exactly right. He does not deny that the moral attitude of 'living within the truth' is connected with an understanding of the human reality; but he does not speak of it as *derived from* such an understanding; on the contrary, when the greengrocer stopped servilely displaying the political slogans provided by the authorities, voting in meaningless elections, etc., he 'was a threat to the system not because of any physical or actual power he had, but because his action went beyond itself, because it illuminated its surroundings and, of course, because of the incalculable consequences of that illumination'.[2] That is, we can speak of such actions 'revealing reality as it is', but the revelation comes only to someone who is struck by the moral significance of those actions.

It is for this reason that I regard it as a mistake to try to accommodate those who, to repeat Montefiore's phrase, 'feel less than wholly confident about such direct appeals to the moral' (a lack of confidence extending beyond those Marxists to whom Havel refers in the first of my quotations). Their confusion lies precisely in the sources of their lack of confidence and needs to be treated at that level.

[1] Vàclav Havel *et al.*, *The Power of the Powerless*, ed. John Keane, New York: M. E. Sharpe, Inc., 1985, p. 45.
[2] *Ibid.*, p. 40.

2

La trahison de la trahison des clercs

ERNEST GELLNER

The most celebrated sermon concerning the responsibility of
intellectuals is perhaps Julien Benda's *La Trahison des clercs*.[1] Its
argument is articulated against an uncritically assumed background of Platonic metaphysics and universalistic ethics. A realm
of values binding all men alike is simply presupposed. The 'clercs'
are rebuked for abandoning these, and for whoring after local and
particularistic idols.

    As an account of much that had come to pass in the nineteenth
and twentieth centuries, no doubt this was accurate enough. The
monotheism which had dominated Europe for so long was both
exclusive and universalist in its claims: one truth and one only was

---

[1] Julien Benda (1867–1956) wrote this work between 1924 and 1927 and
published it in Paris in 1928. It is the response of this celebrated essayist and
political commentator to what he perceived to be a severe crisis in European
culture. The book takes the form of an essay in historical sociology. Benda
asserts that up to the late nineteenth century, there had been two broad
classes of men, the 'clercs' and the 'lay people': the latter were involved in the
practical running of society and the application of thought and science to it;
the former were those who were not active in the pursuit or support of
practical aims, but who stood aside from their society and argued for non-
immediate, non-material, disinterested values. The 'treason' of the 'clercs' of
the late nineteenth century was manifested in their involvement in practical
political life, and in their acceptance that intellectual activity could be
harnessed to political, nationalistic and racial ends. This gave to the dis-
creditable ideologies of 'lay people' the respectability of a systematic and
coherent doctrine, lending them enhanced credibility and authority. Benda
predicted that separation of function of 'clerc' and 'lay person' was crucial to
the survival of European civilization, and his diagnosis of the breakdown of
this division of roles prophetically pointed to the holocaust and other tragic
events of the Second World War. (Ed.)

17

there for all and binding on all. Those who deviated from it were wrong, and those who deviated from it out of a loyalty to local and specific idols were traitors to truth. The theologians who codified the theory implicit in this faith did so roughly speaking in Platonistic terms, even if they happened to be nominalists. The truth was unique, incorruptible and authoritative because it was transcendent.

The task of literate intellectuals was to preserve, communicate and impose the truth which was in their keeping, and to which they had privileged access. The access was made possible both through Scripture and a Special Institution linked to the point of Revelation, and with the Reformation, these two methods of validation came into open conflict. But they were at one in presupposing and proclaiming a single and universally binding truth. The position differed from Platonism proper, of course, in personalizing the Transcendent, and in possessing a narrative account concerning the manner in which the Transcendent communicated with the world and by stressing the role which the Transcendent played, not merely in providing a yardstick, but also in actually creating the world. But these details apart, the background picture, the contrast of a towering Normative Other and a subordinated Here-Now, was genuinely Platonic. It engendered a tension between Transcendent and Authoritative Other and the earthly Here-Now, and turned the scholar–cleric into an emissary and agent of the Other on earth.[2]

The Reformation, paradoxically, re-affirmed the universality of the message, by stressing symmetrical and equal access to it: yet it also contained the seeds of fragmentation. Its stress on the vernacular and on literacy jointly paved the ground for the employment, and eventually even the authority, of local cultures, in other words for nationalism. Its stress on autonomy of interpretation prepared the ground for a relativism as opposed to a universalism.

The Enlightenment challenged the Revealed truth and its institutional guardians, but once again did not really challenge the metaphysical idiom in which the faith had been codified. The

---

2 See S. N. Eisenstadt (ed.), *Axial Age Civilisations*, Albany: State University of New York, 1986.

preachers of Enlightenment took that for granted, and merely
elaborated a counter-doctrine roughly in the same terms, and
endowed with the same universalist pretensions.[3] If there was a
conflict between their characteristically naturalistic views, and the
universalism rooted in a now obsolete transcendentalism, they did
not properly face it, or supposed they could find a logical way of
making them compatible. (Cognitive functions *within* nature
could be expected to vary, like all natural organs; so why should
there be a single truth for all organisms, biological or social? Yet a
unique truth *about* nature was assumed to obtain!) They remained
guardians of a universal and unique truth, even if the content of
the message had been transformed. In fact, they saw themselves
primarily as the messengers of a secular but unique Revelation,
and made themselves into its very vocal propagandists.

It was the Romantic reaction to the Enlightenment, on the
surface an attempt to return to some earlier, pre-Enlightenment
forms of life, which in reality repudiated something that both the
Enlightenment and the theological age had *shared*: the universalist
assumption. Emotion and cultural specificity, joined to a denial of
the primacy of a universal, cosmopolitan Reason, became fashionable. This was the beginning of the treason of the clerics, so
vociferously denounced by Benda.

My main point is going to be simple: *La Trahison des clercs* was
itself a case of 'la trahison des clercs'.

Let me illustrate this by means of an example. Assume, for
instance, the truth of a naturalistic theory of knowledge. This is,
after all, by no means an absurd assumption. It might even be
considered a necessary truth: rational inquiry presupposes that the
world constitutes a single, orderly system, in other words a
'nature'. Hence creatures within nature cannot claim exemption
from its laws: what each of them considers 'knowledge' cannot
possibly be a relationship between it and something eternal and
transcending the system. It can only be an inevitably selective,
functional set of adjustments between its own *specific* nature and
its variable environment. The adjustment can only be validated by
its functional effectiveness, not by conformity to some universal

[3] C. L. Becker, *The Heavenly City of the Eighteenth Century Philosophers*,
New Haven: Yale University Press, 1952.

Norm. It is inescapably tied to transient circumstances. The relativity of the functional adjustment of each organism follows from the incorporation of all organisms, however diversified, in a single Nature.

In other words, some kind of pragmatist or functionalist theory of knowledge is presupposed by the very notion of Nature. Nature in turn can plausibly be seen to be an inescapable corollary of the idea of Reason. Reason operates symmetrically and in an orderly way: hence an orderly, rule-bound impersonal system, in other words Nature, is the shadow it casts on the world. So a rationally investigated system inevitably acquires certain formal properties, which are projected onto it by the style of investigation itself. Hence it cannot be cognitively stratified; no part of it may constitute specially weighty evidence, and claim to be a point at which Revelation alters Nature and trumps ordinary, unhallowed faith. So no part of Nature can be sacred – literally or colloquially. In this way, as in some others, Reason cuts its own throat. It demotes itself from the status of a Secular Revelation to one-style-amongst-others. Its conclusions preclude the attribution of a special status, which at the same time it also claims for itself.

But knowledge whose criteria of validity are basically those of adjustment, of pragmatic effectiveness, is therefore inescapably relative. What is functional for one organism in one set of circumstances is not so for another organism in another set. Where is universal truth and universal obligation now? Yet their repudiation was the consequence of working out the implications of ideas or ideals – Nature, Reason – which in themselves seemed impeccably universal and un-opportunistic. They seemed eminently eligible for endorsement and support by a loyal, non-treacherous guild of clerics, which had merely substituted a natural object of reverence for a transcendent one, but had hoped in other ways to carry on As Usual.

In his book, Julien Benda does not offer any real vindication of a Platonic-universalist metaphysic of binding eternal values. The argument, ironically, is implicitly rather pragmatist: unless intellectuals act as if such a metaphysic were indeed valid and binding, and unless they display conspicuous loyalty towards it, certain dire social consequences follow and have already become sadly manifest in modern Europe. If you need proof, says Benda

pointing at inter-war Europe, look around yourself, *circumspice*.
A most powerful and persuasive argument, this. Murderous political ideologies are supported, shamefully, by treacherous intellectuals. Unfortunately, the argument also happens to be a *prag-*
matic one. It appeals to the practical consequences of holding or
failing to hold certain views, rather than to their congruence with
eternal truth. So we end up with the paradox that he who preaches
against the treason of the clerics also commits it in his very
sermon; whereas he who preaches that same treason may do so out
of an unflinching loyalty to the very values which he is criticizing.
It is just because he respects truth, he endorses the conclusion that
truth is specific, pragmatic, variable, tied to particular communities or classes. If naturalism and pragmatism are valid, is not a
loyal searcher after truth obliged to say so with candour?

This is a fundamental and important point: many of the natura-
lists, pragmatists, romantics, irrationalists, relativists, who
abound so conspicuously in the history of nineteenth- and
twentieth-century thought reached their conclusions in an impeccably rational, absolutist, universalist spirit. It was *because* they
were so loyal to the old transcendent principle of impartial objectivity that they uncovered something which undermines those principles themselves. Because they were so devoted to the rules of
clerkly procedure, they loyally reported their findings. Some, like
Nietzsche, fully understood the irony of their own condition.

It is entirely possible to reach the kind of conclusion they
reached, to end with a reverence for the particular, the relative,
the functional, the instinctive, and to reach that end-point by a
path which partakes of none of these traits. It is not only possible
but, in the context of the intellectual situation of the age, enormously in character. Those who preached *la trahison* did not
commit it: whereas those who preached against it, did.

If the thinkers of the Enlightenment on the whole failed to
perceive the strain between their naturalism and their universalism, some of the thinkers of the nineteenth century were aware of
it. So as to understand their predicament, let us be the naturalistic
devil's advocate. The case can be argued in at least two spheres –
that of morals, and that of knowledge. These are in fact the two
most important intellectual arenas. Take morals first.

A thinker might well argue as follows. We know now that man is but an animal. We should not be surprised at the vigour of his instinctual drives. Nor should we fail to recognize that it is only these which endow him with vitality, vigour and health. Only the satisfaction of his instinctual needs gives him a genuine gratification. Have puritan and repressive thinkers fulminated against these dark forces within the human psyche, and preached the authority of higher, purer values? Be not deceived. Within the human psyche, there is no counter-force to the dark drives. That which would thwart them in the name of something Higher, is but a devious, disingenuous, twisted form of those very drives themselves, cunningly camouflaged. The dark Will has turned in upon itself. It is no purer than the more candid expressions of our animal nature. It is only more tortured, twisted, cunning, self-thwarting, and more pathogenic. By this argument, the old truths of Romantic literature were fused with the inevitable corollaries of the new information about mankind, relayed by Darwinian biology.

What is the point of upbraiding a thinker of this kind by stigmatizing his doctrine as an instance of the treason of the clerics? The charge only has any force if, first of all, it has been established that what he is asserting is false. And that is by no means obvious. On the contrary: he is only spelling out what seems implied in the evidence before him.

Take the parallel case in the theory of knowledge. American Pragmatism has none of that affinity to Dark Romantic literature which characterizes some of the more sombre philosophy of nineteenth-century Europe. It is, on the contrary, sober and polite and perfectly *salonfähig*. Its case can be stated roughly as follows. Those large, elegant, abstract cognitive structures, associated with transcendental visions, are but the preferred indulgence and joy of genteel souls, sheltered in some cosy rectory. William James said as much, almost in these words. Real, frontiersman knowledge – whether it be on the literal or on the cognitive Frontier – is quite other: rough, piecemeal, untidy, experimental, specific, transient. There is nothing permanent, let alone eternal about it. The Pragmatist diagnosis of the transcendental illusion is quite different from the Dark-Gods' denunciation of puritan rectitude; but the basic underlying point is similar. Jamesian Pragmatism castigated grand abstract simplicities in the name of complex tangled earthly realities: an appreciation of the latter was, precisely, its one grand abstract principle! A real practising pragmatist does not elevate his pragmatism into a formal principle: it takes a sincere love of abstract truth to do that.

I have offered simplified versions of the Nietzschean account of morals, and of a Jamesian account of knowledge. Now it would be absurd to pretend that either Friedrich Nietzsche or William James were corrupt servants of some sectional or regional interest, who had betrayed universal values out of some kind of venality of spinelessness. They were unquestionably seekers after truth; one of them was an inwardly tormented one. They were eager to work out what morality or knowledge were or could be, given a naturalistic universe. They followed out the implications of their insights with courage, candour and consistency. If their *conclusions* appear to be in conflict with the universalistic-Platonist picture, their *practice* was an implementation of its requirements. They were inspired by the very ideal whose authority they were undermining. Are we to prohibit such conclusions? Are we to place an interdict on honestly following the wind of argument wherever it may lead? Is prohibition of a given type of conclusions, or of a given type of reasoning, to be an example of respect for truth? In a fascinating footnote in the *Trahison*, Benda half recognizes all this. He observes that though Nietzsche's views were reprehensible, he deserved commendation for his *life*, for the ✕ wholehearted manner he devoted himself to intellectual concerns. Nietzsche himself had said something similar about Schopenhauer. The real point is not that Nietzsche gave those preoccupations all his time and psychic energy, but that he pursued them with total *integrity*, and that this reflects on the standing of those conclusions. Given the intellectual background situation in which in fact we live, the paradox is that those who teach naturalistic, and hence non-universal, relativistic doctrines, may be impelled to do so by their commitment to the ideal of a single universal truth. It is unfortunate that the truth turns out to be naturalistic. But a loyal seeker after truth bows to logic and evidence, and does not censor the conclusions which honest inquiry imposes on him. Those, on the other hand, who *would* censor such doctrines, thereby display their lack of respect for truth. People may become subjectivists and relativists because respect for truth led them to such conclusions, and others may be absolutist out of opportunism and desire to embrace the comforting conclusion, whether or not it is logically warranted.

Naturalism is not the only point at which this paradox arises. There is also what might be called Hamlet's problem. A firm and resolute defence of those eternal values which, according to Benda, were being betrayed, requires firmness of character, *conviction*. But the cognitive ethic which inspired the modern explosion of knowledge contains at least two provisions incompatible with such firmness. It requires the investigator not to endow any idea with more certainty than the evidence warrants. Even more significantly, it also requires that even seeming certain, reliable convictions should be probed for weak spots. Descartes, who codified a cognitive practice embodying similar ideas, though he could nevertheless retain the required firmness in his personal life, by resolving to act in daily life as if the doubts he raised in his theoretical activity did not exist. But such a separation of the theoretical and practical life, which Descartes hoped would only be temporary, can hardly be sustained. Modern morality does in fact accord respect to honest doubt, rather than to ill-founded conviction. Here, once again, by a different route, respect for truth and for the sovereignty of evidence – and are these not eternal values? – at the same time also lead to the weakening of moral fibre and resolution.

Consider a related problem, arising out of the interdependence of all things, and, in particular, the interlocking nature of the modern world. This problem most commonly strikes the modern intellectual in the form – *To Sign or Not To Sign*? He is frequently presented with a protest against some iniquity in a part of the world not close to his own, and requested for his signature in support of the denunciation of the scandal in question. As no man can be fully informed of the merits of all the cases of this kind, to sign without question will inevitably mean occasional support for unworthy or questionable causes. (I understand that when the late Shah's principal police torturer fell out with his master, Bertrand Russell and Jean-Paul Sartre were induced to sign a protest on the man's behalf.) On the other hand, to refrain on principle from supporting any protest whatsoever, is to condone appalling injustices which, at least on some occasion, can be corrected by vigorous protest. It is virtually impossible to formulate any general rule for his kind of case. Our world is now so interdependent that it is impossible to specify the limits of one's responsibility. Who is really guilty of the treason of the clerics – he who never signs, or he who signs any appeal often phrased in plausible (and perhaps question-begging) terminology?

Consider the related problem of 'political realism'. Imagine an oppressive, unrepresentative regime which dominates a given society, but which can, with some justification, invoke the principle of the Lesser Evil. The regime can claim to be committed to averting a far worse evil which looms over the country, and to do it at the least possible cost – in terms of injustice and illiberalism – compatible with the given circumstances. But for us – the apologist of the regime claims – a national calamity would be upon us. We pay a certain price for averting it, but we do all we can to keep that price down to a minimum. A 'realist' will accept the case and co-operate with the regime; an 'irresponsible romantic' will refuse to do so. I am struck by the fact that in certain countries, there is a kind of spectrum of political positions such that, almost *wherever* a man happens to be located, he feels that the people on one side of him are irresponsible, unrealistic romantics, and those on the other, craven compromisers.

But *if* the irresponsible romantics can combine and form the overwhelming majority, their irresponsible romanticism may, suddenly, become a realistic option. The erstwhile realism will then appear as craven treason. But, in ambiguous and fluctuating circumstances, who can say with confidence which characterization is the correct one? You cannot tell which way the other individuals decide. A big majority of romantics becomes a majority of realists. But if they turn out to be a minority after all, they are irresponsible wreckers of the Least Evil compromise. But quite often, you do not know how the others have chosen when you are making your own decision.

The basic point I have been making is woefully negative and no doubt obvious. The background picture – sociologically, epistemologically, morally – in terms of which the intellectuals have on occasion been excoriated for committing treason is woefully inadequate. It is itself in conflict with those values. It is irresponsibly complacent, self-indulgent and prejudicial. It is not necessarily illegitimate to hold naturalistic theories of knowledge or morality. It is not necessarily wrong to display doubt rather than conviction. It is not necessarily wicked to be less than clear about the limits of one's responsibility. It is not always wrong to be realistic about the situation and to refrain from Quixotry. The recognition of these difficulties is itself a duty. The tacit deployment of a model which fails to do justice to the seriousness of these difficulties is itself a kind of intellectual treason. The strident denunciation of the treason of the clerics, which pretends that our situation is far clearer and unambiguous than in fact it is, is itself a form of betrayal of truth.

The model of the human situation in terms of which the treasonable conduct has been characterized is simply inadequate. The model may have been closer to reality once, but it is very distant from it now. The model assumes, for instance, that the moral agent knows the limits of the community to which he is accountable. This is not so for us: to claim to be concerned with all mankind equally is presumptuous and runs the risk of sacrificing concrete obligations close to home for hypothetical distant ones. But to circumscribe one's moral neighbourhood closely is just as questionable. The boundaries of one's community are not given, but nor is its structure: a man facing a moral dilemma in the context of a given institutional structure had an easier task than one who admits that formally, legally legitimate authorities may on occasion be reprehensible. Neither our moral nor our material environment is free of doubt and ambiguity. Naturalistic ethics, endeavouring to endow our values with an earthly rather than a transcendent basis, are not inherently reprehensible, and cannot be condemned out of hand. It is plausible to hold that our cognitive ethic is such that doubt is a more serious obligation than faith.

Those who have joyfully indulged in what has aptly been called epistemological hypochondria have often, covertly or openly, then made the transition to an unrestrained permissivism: because everything is in question, everything is allowed. A certain methodological antinomianism is rather fashionable. Nothing is further from my intentions. If I underscore the difficulties, it is not with the intention of giving anyone a cognitive or moral *carte blanche*. Quite particularly in the field of factual information about our social and natural environment, the famous under-determination of our vision of things by our data base has, like the death of Mark Twain, been grossly, self-indulgently and irresponsibly exaggerated. But the recognition of all this should not lead us to pretend that we live in an easier world, morally or cognitively, than in fact we do. This is the reproach I am addressing to facile versions of the 'treason of the intellectuals' sermon.

I am not saying that the treason of the clerics has never been committed. Deliberate disregard of truth in the interest of loyalty to doctrine is certainly an instance of it. When Jean-Paul Sartre refused to recognize or publicize certain facts about Stalinism, because he considered it more important to protect a French working-class district from despair, he was, unquestionably, committing *la trahison des clercs*. What I *am* saying is that the task of *not* committing is far, far more difficult than an appallingly simplified model of the intellectual's work situation would have us believe. We live in an interlocking world, in which no sphere and no area is insulated. To assess consequences is appallingly difficult. We cannot do everything at once, and must choose our priorities, and do it on the basis of inadequate evidence. To disregard consequences in the name of purity of principle can itself often be be a kind of indulgence and evasion. I do not know how this cluster of problems can be handled effectively. But that is no reason for pretending that the problem does not exist, that the path of virtue and loyalty to truth is clearly visible, and that only turpitude prevents us from following it.

3

The loss of responsibility

ELEMER HANKISS

The responsibility of their citizens is one of the most valuable assets of human communities and societies. In default of it, social interactions break down, societies develop pathological symptoms, human communities begin to dysfunction. It is not surprising then that societies, or their elites, will make huge efforts to develop in their citizens the sense of responsibility and will work hard on creating conditions which foster and help responsible behaviour.

Social responsibility is, however, a precarious and extremely frail and perishable social good. It depends on a whole range of economic, social, political and cultural factors; the breakdown of a single one of them, or an unfavourable set of relationships between them, may trigger off destructive chain reactions and may lead to a large-scale disintegration and corruption of the sense of social responsibility. This danger threatens every society, even those which have a good record of high civic responsibility. Instead of quoting well-known historical examples, we are going to analyse in this paper a recent case, that of post-Second World War Hungary. In this case, we may analyse the process of the almost total disintegration of social responsibility within a relatively short span of time. This will be a short survey, listing and briefly analysing how the main factors in the generation and maintenance of social responsibility have been destroyed, one after another, by socio-economic processes, and by conscious strategies of the ruling elite, in the decades following the Second World War.

We shall work with a simple, if not rudimentary, definition of the concept of responsibility, ignoring for the moment those analytical problems, pitfalls and subtleties that have been studied with such zeal and expertise by moral philosophers.

In our reading, responsibility presupposes the *motivation*, the *ability* and the *possibility* to choose between alternatives; it presupposes also a certain degree of *predictability* and *accountability*. We shall argue in this paper that none of these factors or conditions is given in present-day state socialist societies (or at least in Hungary). They have been destroyed by socio-economic processes, and various strategies of the ruling elite, in the last three or four decades.

MOTIVATION

By motivation we mean here the fact that people living in a certain socio-economic context are stimulated by various factors to act in a responsible way. Two of these factors, i.e. their absence, will be analysed here below.

Communities lost

The need to belong somewhere, to be accepted by the community, is probably the strongest factor motivating people to act in a responsible way. If one is the member of a community, and if this community is important for one's survival and/or well-being, then one will be prompted to act in such a way that the consequences of one's acts be not harmful to the community; then one will accept the fact of one's accountability to this community.

If this is the case, then the almost total destruction of all kinds of communities in Hungary must have destroyed one of the main sources of social responsibility. They were systematically destroyed after 1948 and their regeneration has been carefully obstructed ever since. Local communities were destroyed by the accelerated programme of industrialization and the forced mass emigration to the cities. Tamas Kolosi, who studied the restratification of Hungarian society, writes in this connection: 'In the period between the late 1940s and the mid-1960s, 70 per cent of the Hungarian population left its place of residence and moved to somewhere else. Labour migration of the same magnitude took 100 years in Great Britain and 80 years in Germany; in Hungary,

Table 3.1. *The liquidation of the multi-party system*

1. The harassment and final disintegration of the Independent Farmers' Party (1945 elections: 57.03%). The campaign starts already in early 1946 and is completed by February 1949.

1946	March 12	Under the pressure of the Communist Party, the IFP excludes 20 of its 'right-wing' MPs
1947	January	In the aftermath of the discovery of an 'anti-republican' conspiracy, another 20 MPs excluded
	February 25	The Soviets arrest Béla Kovács, the general secretary of the party
	May 20	Ferenc Nagy, the Prime Minister, is forced into exile
	September 5	Elections: IFP: 15.4%
1948	October	The IFP accepts the communist platform
1949	February 1	The IFP disappears in the 'Popular Front'
	May 15	Elections: Popular Front; 96.27%

2. The liquidation of the other parties.

1947	July	The Hungarian Freedom Party ends its activities
	November 19	The Hungarian Independence Party is dissolved (1947 elections: 13.4%)
	November 2	Centre and right-wing social democrats seek refuge abroad
1948	June 12–14	The fusion of the Communist Party and the Social Democratic Party
	September	The National Peasant Party accepts the communist platform
1949	January	Dissolution of the National Committees, which had been the organs of local coalition politics and self-government
	February	The Hungarian Independent Popular Front founded
	February 4	The Democratic People's Party joins the Popular Front and ceases to exist (1947 elections: 16.4%)
	March 3	The last minor parties merge into the Popular Front
	May	National elections: Popular Front: 96.27%

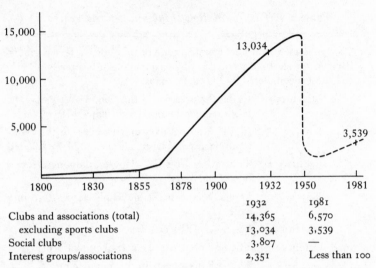

	1932	1981
Clubs and associations (total)	14,365	6,570
excluding sports clubs	13,034	3,539
Social clubs	3,807	—
Interest groups/associations	2,351	Less than 100

Figure 3.1   Clubs and associations in Hungary, 1800–1981 (excluding sports clubs)

they were condensed into 15 years.'[1] In the 1970s, there came a new wave of destruction with the new regional policy, which condemned about one third of the villages to 'de-development', syphoning away all their resources and depriving them of all their communal institutions and facilities (including the village councils, the resident doctors, the schools, etc.).

Social and political communities were liquidated, too. Political parties, with the exception of the Communist Party, were banned in 1948 and 1949. (See table 3.1) Trade unions were etaticized and transformed into the 'transmission belts' of the Communist Party in 1948. A frontal attack against all kinds of clubs and associations was launched in the same year. To show the extent of destruction in this field, we have charted in figure 3.1 the changing number of clubs and associations in this country from 1800 to 1981. As can be seen, the number of clubs and associations kept rising throughout the nineteenth century, began to rise more steeply in the second half of the century, hit a high watermark in the late 1930s and early

[1] Tamas Kolosi, 'Stratification and Inequality in Hungary', in Antal Bohm and Tamas Kolosi (eds.), Structure and Stratification in Hungary, Budapest: Tarsadalomtudomanyi Intezet, 1982, p. 25.

1940s, when there were between 13,000 and 14,000 clubs and associations in the country (if we exclude sport clubs). After the communist takeover, their number probably dropped to less than 1,000, and a very slow regeneration began only in the mid-1960s. According to a national survey conducted by the Central Bureau of Statistics, in 1981 there were 3,539 clubs and associations (sports clubs excluded). In spite of this slow regeneration, present-day Hungarian society is far less articulated, at least as far as spontaneous social networks are concerned, than it was in the 1930s.

This state of disintegration and atomization has radically reduced people's motivation, and ability, to behave as responsible citizens. Their communities, i.e. their spheres of responsibility, had been destroyed; they were left alone, as faceless units in a faceless crowd; they were forbidden to generate new communities; they were not allowed to feel responsible for their villages, their cities, their country. They had to withdraw within the walls of their homes and within the boundaries of their families, which became the last resorts of responsibility in an irresponsible society.

The extent of this social disintegration, of this individuation and loss of communal spirit is clearly shown by the results of the European Value Systems Study, which was conducted in 1982 in eleven European countries, including Hungary, and the United States. Table 3.2 gives the average values of responses to questions concerning attitudes of individualism versus altruism and sociability. As it can be seen, Hungarians turned out to be surprisingly more individualistic than their European counterparts. To the question, for instance, 'Is there anything you would sacrifice yourself for, outside your family?', 38 to 64 per cent of Englishmen, Frenchmen, Germans, Spaniards, or Italians answered: 'No'. In Hungary, the corresponding figure was 85 per cent. To the question 'Would you raise your children in respect for other people?', the European average of positive answers was between 40 and 60 per cent, while the corresponding Hungarian figure was 31 per cent. 'Loyalty and faithfulness' scored between 19 and 43 per cent in Western societies; it barely reached 10 per cent in Hungary. And the same differences between the average European and the Hungarian data can be observed in the other items, too.

Table 3.2. *Individualism and privatism in ten European countries*

	England	Ireland	France	Belgium	Germany	Holland	Spain	Denmark	Italy	Hungary
						%				
You may trust people	43	40	22	25	26	38	32	46	25	32
Is there anything you would sacrifice yourself for, outside your family! NO!	60	55	64	61	53	54	38	49	45	85
Parents have their own lives; they should not sacrifice themselves for their children	18	15	17	21	28	15	13	39	27	44
Child-rearing principles: respect for other people	62	56	59	45	52	53	44	58	43	31
loyalty, faithfulness	36	19	36	23	22	24	29	24	43	10
With whom do you prefer to spend your leisure time! alone	11	12	10	9	8	12	7	8	20	10
with your family	48	39	47	51	52	49	53	53	36	72
with friends	27	27	22	18	27	15	23	12	29	10
going out, seeing people	11	12	8	7	5	12	4	4	8	3

Source: European Value Systems Study, 1982.

The sense of ownership lost

It is not cynical to state that ownership, or the sense of ownership, is another important source of responsible behaviour. Owners usually take better care of their houses than renters. Public goods

Table 3.3. *Changing ownership of factories and mines*

Form of ownership	1938	1946	1948	1949	1950
Public (state, municipal and foreign)	238	346	453	1,661	1,950
Co-operative	52	300	366	94	–
Private	3,785	4,049	3,859	2,182	37

Source: Pető and Szakács, *A hazai gazdasag negy evtizedenek tortenete*, p. 114.

and facilities, towards which people generally feel much less of anything resembling a sense of ownership, are usually handled in a more careless and irresponsible way than one's own private property (except, maybe, in a few societies with very high civic responsibility). The large scale liquidation of private and group ownership in Hungary, in the late 1940s and early 1950s, led in this way to the wide-ranging destruction of social responsibility, too. Let us recall some of the landmarks of this destructive process.

1 The nationalization of industrial and commercial companies
 19 April 1948, Statute 1948: XXXVII: Nationalization of industrial companies with over 100 employees.
 28 December 1949, Presidential Council Decree 1949:20: Nationalization of companies with over 10 employees. (See table 3.3).
 18 January 1950: Nationalization of wholesale trade.
 7 May 1949, Government Decree 5380 and 72110/1948: Nationalized companies lose their legal independence. The new Constitution of 1949 (Statute 1949: XX) does not even mention companies as independent economic and legal units.[2]
2 The liquidation of the capital market and of the free capital flow
 22 September 1947: Nationalization of banks.
 21 March 1948: The Exchange stops its activities; it is legally

[2] Ivan Pető and Sandor Szakács, *A hazai gazdasag negy evitizedenek tortenete, 1945–1985* (The History of Four Decades of the Hungarian Economy, 1925–1985), vol. I, Budapest: Kozgazdasagi, 1985, pp. 104–5.

Table 3.4. *The collectivization of agriculture*

	Number of co-operatives	Number of members	Territory in 1,000 hectares
1949 June	584	13,000	55
1949 December	1,367	36,000	182
1950 December	2,185	120,000	444
1951 December	4,625	311,000	1,002
1952 December	5,110	369,000	1,501
1953 December	4,536	250,000	1,143
1954 December	4,381	230,000	1,082
1955 December	4,816	306,000	1,213
1956 December	2,089	119,000	597
1957 December	3,394	156,000	820
1958 December	3,507	169,000	958
1959 December	4,489	565,000	2,620
1960 December	4,576	960,000	3,941
1961 December	4,681	1,221,000	4,539 (June)
1975 December	1,833	1,006,000	4,738 (June)

Source: Bela Fazekas, *A mezogazdasagi termeloszovetkezeti mozgalom Magyarorszagon* (*The Movement of Agricultural Co-operatives in Hungary*), Budapest: Kossuth, 1976, p. 65, 76, 88, 94, 116, 129, 137, 293–4.

dissolved on 31 May 1949. (It resumed its activities, in a limited sphere, forty years later, on 19 January 1988).

3 The collectivization of agriculture
Creation of state farms, and forcing farmers into collective farms. After some experimentation immediately after the war, the process was accelerated in 1948 and, overcoming a serious setback between 1953 and 1956, it was completed between 1959 and 1962. (See table 3.4).

4 Liquidation of the independent artisanry and small business
The loss of economic independence by large sections of the

Table 3.5. *Proportion of independent economic existences and
their families in the population
(farmers, craftsmen, tradesmen, professional, clergymen, etc.)*

%

1930	41.7
1941	38.4
1949	51.3 [land reform]
1960	17.0
1970	2.6

Source: Petö and Szakács, *A hazai gazdasag negy evtizedenek tortenete*,
pp. 144–5, 713.

population was cataclysmic in the late 1950s and early 1960s as
shown in table 3.5.

Private ownership was replaced by state ownership, which was
thought to be a historically and morally higher form of ownership.
It did not fulfil, however, the elite's expectations. It did not
become an efficient basic motive force of the economy and did not
generate a higher level social consciousness and social responsibility. Just the contrary. It led to inefficiency, waste, negligence
and pathological irresponsibility. It dysfunctioned so heavily
already in the early 1950s that the ruling elite was forced to take
steps to boost the workers' sagging, or missing, motivation to work
in an efficient and responsible way.

Campaigns

First they used campaigns, with which they hoped to increase
productivity, and improve people's working morale and discipline.
They failed to achieve their aim. Each campaign focussed on, and
pushed, one single combat task and ignored all other objectives;
this strategy played havoc with the complexities of a modern
society and created an atmosphere of confusion and irresponsibility.

Rhetoric

After 1948, with slogans like 'Yours is the country, you work for yourself', the ruling elite strove to create the missing sense of social responsibility by convincing people that bureaucratic state ownership was in reality social ownership and so they had a stake in the system. But slogans like this must have lost their impact – if they had any after the first, feverish months of post-war reconstruction – soon after they had been invented.

Incentives

Personal and group incentives, even if they led to social differentiation and inequality, were introduced already in the 1950s by the Hungarian elite. In this way, they reintroduced, if not private property, at least private interest as a factor that would, or should, motivate people to work in a more efficient and responsible way.

Personal property and consumption

The creation and gradual extension of a market of personal and family consumption was a clever and more successful strategy than those mentioned above. People were allowed, however, only to consume what they earned and were not permitted to invest their money in the productive process (since this latter would have meant the direct reintroduction of the principle of private property into the system). This led to far-fetched consumerism and barred people from becoming responsible actors in the productive process.

The second economy

The emergence of the second economy, first obstructed, later cleverly tolerated by the elite, reintroduced private property as a motive force into the productive process. But while it increased responsible behaviour within this informal, private economy, it led to the further erosion of responsibility within the boundaries of the first economy.

Economic reforms: the 'simulation' of market and private property

After several years of expert work, discussion and political tug-of-war, the so-called New Economic Mechanism was introduced in 1968. This was a programme which, without ever openly stating it, aimed at establishing an economic system which would simulate the operation of a market based on the principle of private property and competition. Within the given bureaucratic system and power relationships, however, the New Economic Mechanism inevitably failed to achieve its goals. Directors have not become really cost- and price-sensitive, market- and profit-oriented, and they have not become responsible managers of their companies. They have been prompted ever since by their own, and their employees, interests not so much to maximize the medium- and long-term profits of their companies on the market as to improve their positions on the 'administrative market', that is, within a complex network of bargaining with state and party bureaucracies. In other words, this means that, from the point of view of the national economy and society as a whole, they have been motivated, or forced, ever since to act in an irresponsible and negligent way.

New forms of ownership

The latest wave of reforms (in 1987 and 1988) intends to create the necessary conditions for the free competition of a wide range of ownership forms (state property, co-operative property, corporate property, communal property, private property, etc.). If these reforms succeed, they may dramatically enhance the value of responsible economic behaviour. In the present, chaotic transitory stage, however, conditions still encourage irresponsible speculation much more than responsible calculation.

ABILITY

By ability we mean here the inner capacity of the individual to act in a responsible way; a capacity which is embedded in a strong personality, in attitudes, values, inclinations, will power, internalized routines, etc. Let us focus here on three factors.

Personality

A strong and mature personality is almost a *sine qua non* of human responsibility. Present-day Hungarian society, however, suffers from a chronic and extreme shortage of strong and mature personalities. For various reasons.

Anti-personality traditions

For long centuries, Hungary was colonized by foreign powers, by the Turks and the Habsburgs, and, in addition, people were subjected to the authoritarian rule of their own lords. Under these circumstances, it was a precondition of survival to disappear in the crowd, to withdraw into insignificance and social conformism. The relative weakness of democratic institutions, too, impeded the development of strong and autonomous personalities.

Anti-personality campaigns

The communist leadership, after they had come to power in 1948, began systematically to destroy human personality. By intimidating people; by depriving them of their rights and of their protective institutions; by depriving them of their economic autonomy and proletarianizing them; by an egalitarian and collectivistic rhetoric; by stigmatizing excellence and otherness; and so on. The system of dominance and the style of governance acted in the same direction. The artful paternalism of the Kadar regime infantilized people;[3] its strong authoritarianism fostered subject mentality; its clientelistic networks kept people in the status of subservient clients; the lack of democracy triggered off the 'if we have no rights, then we have no duties and responsibilities' chain reaction. And so on.

Social identities destroyed

If people are deprived of their social roles and identities, they will be lamed and paralysed; they will be less able to act in a conscious and responsible way. We do not contend that the ruling elite had premeditated and elaborate strategies for this purpose, but it

---

[3] Elemer Hankiss, *Diagnozisok (Diagnoses)* Budapest: Magveto, 1982.

remains a fact that they systematically destroyed social roles and identities. Let us refer here only to a few of these strategies.

The destruction of social groups, networks, associations
These were important sources of various social identities ('I am the member of the middle classes'; 'I am a member of this or that association'; 'I am a Catholic'; 'I am a social democrat'; etc.) We have already spoken of this destructive process.

Stigmatization of social identities
Class identities, for instance, which had been especially important sources of self-consciousness and autonomy, were replaced by feelings of guilt. If you were a blue-collar worker, for instance, then you were said to belong to the 'lumpen-proletariat' or to the 'workers' aristocracy'; if you were a farmer, you were labelled and persecuted as a 'kulak' or a 'hireling of the kulaks'; if you belonged to the intelligentsia, you were stigmatized as a 'lackey of the capitalists', and so on. And the same was done with national identity. Hungarians were called indiscriminately 'a nation of fascists', 'the last satellites of Hitler', 'a nation of chauvinists, who had cruelly oppressed their minorities for centuries', etc.

Substitution of pseudo-identities for real social identities
The idea behind providing these false identities may have been that these false identities would generate only vague and spurious feelings of togetherness and they would not organize or prompt people to any kind of social or political action. Slogans like 'We workers are the leading force in socialism', 'This is a country of workers and working peasants', 'This is the country of steel and iron', 'We are a nation of Nobel prize winners', 'We are the East European success story', or 'We are a sports big power' were among these pseudo-identities offered to people.

The substitution of diffuse generalities for well-articulated social identities
In the late 1970s and early 1980s, 'Social consensus' became the magic word in Hungarian politics. Beside other functions, it had also that of blurring important differences and conflicts between

various social groups and classes and suppressing distinct and militant social identities attached to these groups and classes.

It is needless to say that these diffuse and fake identities did not and could not generate any kind of social responsibility.

The crisis of social values

If people are deprived of their values, if they cannot rely on a relatively strong and consistent value system, they lose one of the most important organizing principles and regulatory forces in their lives. If their values are destroyed, it will be much more difficult for them to preserve their moral integrity and their sense of social responsibility. This is what happened in Hungary after 1948. The destruction was far-reaching or almost total. And due to this process, Hungarian society is still nowadays in a profound spiritual and moral disarray. The loss of the sense of responsibility is only a part – a result and a symptom – of this broader crisis. Let us briefly review some elements of this crisis.

Destruction of the traditional value system
The destruction was systematic and wide-ranging. Traditional value-generating institutions (churches, communities, associations, social movements) were dismantled or paralysed; families were disintegrated; traditional values were stigmatized, persecuted, driven underground; their followers were harassed, intimidated; they were indoctrinated against their own value beliefs and convictions; etc.

The dysfunctioning of the new, official value system
The new regime produced, or imported, only macro-social and political values and was unable to generate values indispensable in everyday life; in family life; in personal relationships; values relating to questions of life and death; to the metaphysical sphere;

The new regime was bound by its rigid ideology, which became, with the progress of time, more and more conservative; it was bound by a growing dogmatism; it became less and less capable of self-renewal and of adapting itself, and its values, to a changing world.

It was unable to construct a consistent value system; to resolve the inner contradictions of its value priorities; to bridge the gap between its principles (or rhetoric) and its everyday practice. It stuck to its revolutionary ideology and values in an age of conservativism and cautious reformism; it professed, simultaneously, egalitarian and meritocratic values; class struggle and social consensus; dictatorship and democracy. It preached human autonomy and dignity and enforced dependence and subject mentality. It propagated collectivism and forced people into individualism and privatism; and so on.

The social generation of new values obstructed
The communist leadership obstructed the spiritual and cultural renewal of society, which swept over the western world in the first years after the Second World War. By fiercely attacking everything and everybody (the churches, the parties, social classes, the nation as a whole) they forced them into self-defensive and, ultimately, into conservative pre-war positions. Later, they tried hermetically to isolate their society from the renewal of the 1960s.

Protecting their ideological monopoly and domination, they banned and persecuted all forms of non-conformism and did their best to impede the emergence of alternative world-views, which could have served as backgrounds for new values.

By monopolizing the public sphere they confined alternate values to an underground, twilight existence. They hindered people and communities from developing and maturing new values.

They tried to forestall the development of strong values and value beliefs by spreading cynicism and relativism. 'Where in the world is such a thing as complete freedom?' 'Who knows nowadays what is right and what is wrong?' But if differences between right and wrong fade away, responsible behaviour loses one of its most important anchoring points.

POSSIBILITY

By possibility, we mean in this context the presence of those outside conditions which enable the individual to act in a responsible way. Most of these conditions have been missing in this country.
Hungarian people could not act, they were not allowed to act, as

citizens responsible for their community or for their country. They were categorically excluded from public life; they were not allowed to participate in decision making either at the community or at the national level. All they were allowed to do was to obey the orders of those who were not responsible to anybody and to any elected body. This situation stifled the sense of civic responsibility in people and generated unbridled irresponsibility in the leaders.

Conditions were no better at the working place either. The productive system was dysfunctioning at all levels and in all its elements – to such an extent that it became a futile exercise to try to work efficiently and with a sense of responsibility because one could be certain that these efforts would be wasted at the subsequent stages of the productive process.

Workers and employees had no guaranteed rights. Their trade union officials were not responsible to them. Attempts at introducing some elements of responsibility into the system have failed so far. Let us illustrate this with a recent example. In 1985, Hungarian factories, with the exception of some big industrial complexes, became autonomous and have been run, since, by boards of directors, the members of which have partly been elected by the employees and workers of these companies., The idea was to involve them in the responsibility of managing their companies. But they have been caught, from the very beginning, in a trap of role inconsistency. Table 3.6 describes this state of inconsistency, in which conflicting responsibilities mutually extinguish one another. One could object, of course, that role inconsistencies and split responsibilities are ubiquitous in Western societies as well. This is true. But as far as managerial, labour and all-social interests and responsibilities are concerned, they are separated and relatively clearly articulated in those societies.

Irresponsibility and low-quality work led to a vicious chain reaction. You sold me stale vegetables; I will fit your gas stove in a skimped way; You came to me ten minutes late today; why should I not go to see you twenty minutes late tomorrow? Everybody is negligent and irresponsible around me; why should I be scrupulous and responsible? If they don't care, why should I care? And so on, ad infinitum. Only people with an exceptionally high degree of moral integrity can have the strength of mind to remain intact in this atmosphere of general social irresponsibility.

Table 3.6. *Conflicting responsibilities of factory boards' members*

First role:	Delegated by fellow workers and employees, they are responsible to their constituencies. They have to represent the interests of workers and employees. E.g. they have to fight for wage increases.
Second role:	Being a member of the board of directors, they are responsible for the profitable management and development of their companies; they have to vote, for instance, against wage hikes and for rationalizations, for more investment, etc.
Third role:	As a citizen in a socialist country, they have been indoctrinated for decades in the conviction that 'public interest' was the only legitimate interest and that particular interests are something devilish and anti-socialist. Consequently, they may feel it to be their duty to protect this vaguely defined and manipulated public interest against the particularistic interests of their own companies.
Fourth role:	As people who have lived in this country, subjected to an authoritarian and rigid bureaucracy, they will have a hard time to learn to forget their fears and to fight for the interests of their fellow workers or for those of their companies. They will feel themselves responsible for their families and may yield to bureaucratic pressures and interests..
Fifth role:	As clients in a client–patron network, their private interests and their reflexes, conditioned by many years of social praxis, would also induce them to act in line with their patrons', and not their fellow workers', interests.
Sixth role:	If they are party members, they are responsible to the party; they are compelled to obey the dictates of their superiors and, as a consequence, there would be cases in which they would be forced to represent the interests of the party against those of their fellow workers or their companies.

PREDICTABILITY

By predictability, we mean that people live in a socio-economic context in which they may calculate the consequences of their acts with a relatively high probability. In Hungary, this predictability has been almost entirely destroyed since 1948.

Lack of continuity

The economic and the socio-political system has been dysfunctioning from the very beginning. It had to be continuously adjusted, patched up; new and ever new regulations had to be introduced; the rules of the game had to be changed again and again. There has been, throughout these decades, a harassing lack of continuity. In this state of permanent uncertainty, it has been impossible to calculate the results of one's decisions and acts. In other words, it has been impossible to take decisions and act in a responsible way.

Overregulation

East European societies are notoriously and hopelessly overregulated. The number of legal and quasi-legal rules and regulations has been increasing ever since 1948. According to recent information, by the end of 1987 there were about 17,000 rules and regulations in Hungarian agriculture and there were at least as many in the field of industry. There may have been several causes of this self-amplifying process.

1 We have seen above that in the absence of a basic motive principle or force, state socialist societies have no auto-motion and auto-regulation. They have to be prompted and have to be regulated in their tiniest details, from outside, from the political sphere. This inevitably leads to a self-accelerating and uncontrollable process of overregulation.
2 Overregulation triggers off self-protecting mechanisms in society; people try to elude, and to escape from the grip of, regulations, which leads to more regulation and more extreme forms of overregulation.

3 Regulation, i.e. the process of imposing new regulations on society, is a demonstration of the existing, and a source of further, power. Elites have a natural penchant for the exploitation of this source as much as they can.

4 Overregulation creates a chaotic situation where there are already too many contradictory and self-contradictory regulations. This leads to the inflation and erosion of the whole regulatory system and to a state of chaos, unpredictability and ungovernability. Which, in its turn, triggers off further panics of overregulation.

Underregulation

The situation is further complicated by the fact that power can be derived as much from the *absence* of regulation as its existence. East European elites could not resist the temptation to try to exploit this source, too.

1 They created a dependent and loyal bureaucracy, which could be forced to interpret, or to break, the rules and regulations as they dictated them to do so.

2 They made the system of rules and norms *ab ovo* weak with loose and ambiguous legal formulations; they disintegrated and corrupted it even further by continuously changing the rules; by not enforcing the rules or enforcing them in an arbitrary and haphazard way; etc. All this enabled them to interfere with socio-economic processes whenever they wanted but, on the other hand, destroyed the chances of prediction and responsible action.

Discrepancies

In these countries, even the ruling elite is unable to plan processes ahead, to calculate the future results of its actions. The discrepancies between policy inputs and policy outputs are much greater in these countries than in their Western counterparts. Table 3.7 gives some examples of these discrepancies. In the right-hand column, a few of the basic and most cherished objectives of the communist parties in Eastern Europe are listed; in the left-hand

Table 3.7. *Discrepancies between policy inputs and outputs*

Inputs, goals	. Outposts, social outcomes
Central planning	Growing importance of (quasi-) market transactions
Rational planning	Growing irrationality of planning
Collectivized economy	Growing importance of private and group economy
Centralized bureaucracy	Oligarchy and clientelism
Growing prosperity	Decreasing prosperity, pauperization since 1975 (10–15% of population)
Equality	Growing inequality
The 'new socialist man'	Rampant individualism

column, the results they have achieved after decades of futile efforts are displayed.

Contradictions and incompatibilities

There is a rich literature on the fact that a whole range of alternative logics, forms of governance, basic organizational principles have developed in East European countries, in their post-totalitarian period. The principle of *etatist-bureaucratic* governance: 'bureaucratic authoritarianism' (Andrew C. Janos); 'participatory bureaucracy' (R. V. Daniels); bureaucratic 'state capitalism' (A. G. Meyer, M. Djilas). The principle of *corporatism* or neo-corporatism (Schmitter and Lehmbruch; S. P. Huntington; Viktor Zaslavsky; Feher, Heller, Markus; Valerie Bunce). The logic of *oligarchic* dominance (Kenneth Jowitt; T. H. Rigby; Dacrel Hammer). The logic of *clientelism* (Rigby and Harasymiw; Eisenstadt and Lemarchand). The logic of 'enlightened absolutism' (Wladimierz Brus; Feher, Heller, Markus). The logic of 'incipient', 'mirage', 'institutional' 'bureaucratic', 'centralized' or 'one-party' *pluralism* (Gordon H. Skilling; Eva Morawska, J. F. Hough; Hammer and Taubmann; Alec Nove). And so on.

The proliferation of these heterogeneous organizational principles or logics would not be, in itself, a liability. But in present-day Hungary, for instance, the ruling elite has not been able to co-ordinate their interaction; they have got entangled with one another; they are interfering with one another in a chaotic way. So much so that one can never tell which of these logics will prevail in a given interaction, how these various and often incompatible logics, and the various social interests behind them, will affect a given process. Under these circumstances, actions and behaviours are not predictable. How to predict, for instance, the behaviour of the manager of a company, who has various roles and who has to act in each of them according to a different logic. As the manager of the company, he has to compete on the market, and in this role of his, he has to work according to the logic of the market. But, at the same time, he is dependent on the state bureaucracy, and has to observe the rules of the game of the etatist-bureaucratic system. As a party member, he has to conform to the logic of the one-party system, which is not the same as that of etatism. As a member of the oligarchy, he has to act according to the oligarchic organizational principle. As the client of various patrons, and the patron of various clients, he has to play the game of clientelism, and so on, and so on. If we add to this, that everybody in this society is permanently compelled to switch to and fro between various incompatible logics, one can imagine the confusion in which predictability is almost nil and responsible action is hardly possible.

ACCOUNTABILITY

By accountability we mean that people act according to a certain set of norms and consider themselves accountable to a 'tribunal' representing these norms, i.e. to their conscience, to a group of people, to society, to the Almighty, or to any other real or symbolic tribunal. The absence of such tribunals, which is the case in Hungary, makes it even more difficult for people to act in a responsible way.

Missing authorities

The traditional sources of authority: social, cultural and political institutions and elites were destroyed after 1948. The new elite, and the new institutions, on the other hand, accumulated power but their legitimacy and social and moral authority has remained, throughout these decades, weak and questionable. They have been dysfunctioning; they have been corrupted by oligarchic, clientelistic and nepotistic influences; they have been regarded as nothing else and nothing more than instruments of dominance and political oppression.

The corruption of norms

If there are norms, then there are duties and there are rights. If there are no norms, then there is no gauge against which to measure one's actions and achievements; then one is not entitled, by a clearly defined right, to a certain reward or return service. East European ruling elites have been well aware of this possibility of depriving their subjects of their rights by obstructing the development of a clear-cut system of norms and have exploited this possibility. They disintegrated the traditional system of norms; they created only weak, ambiguous norms; they did not enforce too much of their own norms; they leniently and cunningly tolerated the corruption of these norms and that of the whole sphere of social interactions. The members of a corrupt society have no justification to claim their rights. But if there are no norms and no authority, there is no accountability and no responsibility. There are only a few people capable of preserving their moral integrity in a corrupt society.

THE HEAVEN AND HELL OF IRRESPONSIBILITY

It is fairly usual in moral philosophy, both in its realistic and nominalistic traditions, to speak of 'responsibility' as something given. As of an *a priori* concept denoting a more or less fixed ensemble of behavioural rules. We have argued in this paper that, seen from the point of view of sociology, responsibility is not something given, but is something that is being produced and reproduced by society. It is a social product, and a rather complex one at that. A great variety of social, political, cultural and economic factors contribute to its generation, and may contribute also to its degeneration and destruction.

We have shown that social responsibility has almost completely been destroyed in East European societies, or at least in Hungary. Almost all the conditions of its generation and maintenance have been missing in this society. With the disintegration of communities and the erosion of the sense of ownership, two factors that usually play an indispensable role in *motivating* people to act responsibly were destroyed. The destruction of social roles, identities, personalities and the disintegration of the value system have deprived them of the *ability* to act in a responsible way. They were deprived also of the outside conditions and the very *possibility* of acting as responsible citizens. They were categorically barred from taking part in public life and in the decision-making process, in general; how could they have felt responsible themselves for the myriads of (wrong) decisions which were taken without their participation or consent? Conditions were not better at the working place, either; the critical dysfunctioning of the productive system, in all its elements, disrupted the link between personal achievement and collective output, between responsible work and the final outcome of the productive process. The lack of continuity, the permanent changing of the rules of the game, overregulation combined with underregulation, the chaotic interaction of incompatible organizational principles made the *prediction* of the consequences of one's acts, and, hence, responsible action, impossible. In the absence of legitimate authorities and an authentic and valid system of norms, a further condition of the generation and the maintenance of social responsibility, i.e. the acceptance of *accountability*, was missing in this society.

It is easy to point out, and to prove, the fact of the erosion of social responsibility in contemporary Hungary. It would be extremely difficult, however, to specify how far this process has gone so far. Social responsibility is such a complex phenomenon that even a large arsenal of survey methods, laboratory experiments and systematic observations would not suffice adequately to describe its state and exactly measure the degree of its destruction. In the light of cross-national survey data and on the basis of everyday experience and observation, one can only state that social responsibility has got, after four decades of erosion, into an alarming state of disintegration and corruption (It had not been in a very good shape in the 1920s, 1930s, and especially in the 1940s, either; but it may have reached a high watermark in the years immediately after the Second World War.)

There are, however, a few signs of a coming, slow recovery. At least, some of the conditions of such a recovery are being created nowadays. The chart in figure 3.1 shows (see above) that the slow regeneration of communities began already in the mid-1960s; the economic crisis and the political opening has recently speeded up this process; it may gather further momentum if the new bill on associations is passed by the Parliament this autumn. Another new law will liberalize the economy by January 1989 and will create the conditions for the competition of a wide range of ownership forms; this, too, may increase people's motivation to act in a responsible way. The main objective of the latest wave of reforms is to create well-functioning economic mechanisms and new social and political institutions that would involve people, as responsible actors, in the economic and socio-political processes. And so on.

In this situation, the responsibility of East European intellectuals is broader than that of their counterparts in the West. They have to help, with all possible means, this process of recovery. They have to work on the regeneration of social responsibility in their societies. And last but not least, they have to work on their own regeneration. They, too, have to stand up and walk out of the heaven and hell of irresponsibility. For it is not only awful, but also delightful to live in irresponsibility. It is awful to live in a society where one has no rights; where one cannot calculate the outcomes of one's decisions and actions; where one is the victim of other people's irresponsibility; where one is lost in the hell of a normless world. But, at the same time, it is delightful and alluring to live in a world of childish irresponsibility, where one has no duties and where one is not called upon to account for one's deeds. It will not be easy to resist the temptation and the attraction of this heaven of irresponsibility.

4

Heritage and collective responsibility

JERZY JEDLICKI

In this paper I will discuss a highly peculiar kind of responsibility, namely, the reasons why various human communities and institutions – such as the family, nation, state, church, or a political organization – are burdened with responsibility for their historical past, that is, for the deeds of past generations.

Such a notion seems, on the face of it, strange to a liberal mind, accustomed to believe that responsibility is always personal, and that a man can only be held responsible for what he himself did or failed to do. The very idea that one can be held responsible for acts and events beyond one's influence, or even for those which happened before one was born, must appear to be either a delusion or a barbaric prejudice.

In fact, the demand to settle scores from the past of some nation is so often the object of political demagogy and so easily feeds poisonous prejudices that any suspicion is justified here.

Nevertheless, this notion of retroactive responsibility, responsibility for the past history of the family or society that falls on its living members, is deeply rooted in our civilization. The conviction that the heroic deeds and services as well as the transgressions and crimes of patriarchs are the heritage of their entire family is present in all European and many non-European cultures. It is the essence of the myth and doctrine of original sin, that transgression of the Law by the first parents which contaminated human nature and for which all mankind must do penance.

The Old Testament contains contradictory statements on the inheritance of the burden of guilt and sin. For on the one hand, just as the blessings of the Lord extend to the entire family of the righteous man, the anger of the Lord falls on the house and

53

descendants of the sinner: the God of Moses is 'a jealous God, inflicting punishment for their fathers' wickedness on the children ... down to the third and fourth generation' (Exod. 20.5; 34.7). And cursed for ever will be the descendants of him who does not hearken to the voice of the Lord and is not careful to observe all of His commandments (Deut. 28.15–18; 28.46; 28.58–9). But in the same book it is also said that 'fathers shall not be put to death for their children, nor children for their fathers; only for his own guilt shall a man be put to death' (Deut. 24.16). Amaziah, king of Judah, appeals to this principle when he spares the children of the murderers of his father (2 Kgs. 14.6; 2 Chr. 25.4), as does the Lord God Himself when through the mouth of the prophet Ezekiel He says that the one who lives by His statutes shall not die for the sins of his father (Ez. 18.19–20; and 29–30).

In the Greek myths a curse falls on the entire family of the person who has offended the gods. Parallel with the inheritance of the curse is the inheritance of the holy obligation to avenge the injuries and death of a parent. This duty became the theme of many myths and tragedies, to mention only Orestes and Hamlet. It became a custom in the knightly culture and in folk cultures and appears as 'the law of talion' in ancient legal codes. The inheritance of vengeance is therefore two-sided: the duty to carry it out falls on the children of the victim, while the act of vengeance can strike down the children of the murderer and even take on the form of permanent family vendetta.

With time the notions of 'family', 'heritage', 'ancestors' and 'descendants' expanded to tribal and estate ties. In them as well the idea of moral heritage, that is, the inheritance of the services, transgressions and obligations of ancestors, became no less strong and persistent than in blood ties.

Pride of one's ancestry, of a real or imaginary past and glory of one's tribe, nation, estate, class or church, is an omnipresent socio-psychological phenomenon and has always been an inseparable component of the feeling of collective identity. The nobles in all countries were apt to believe that they themselves became more grand if it could be proved that they were descended from ancient heroes – from Trojans, Athenians, Romans, Normans, etc. Genealogical myths of this sort were an integral part of the medieval and modern national consciousness.

With its strengthening the belief in common biological origin was no longer indispensable, though it would revive in the extreme form of racist nationalism. The metaphoric understanding of heritage, however, was broader: it also encompassed the adopted members of the national community. Thus the Polish peasant, the Polonized Jew, Ruthenian or German became the heirs of the Polish nobility and of the entire history of the Polish–Lithuanian Commonwealth.

The bourgeois pedagogy of the nineteenth century, which encouraged climbers to be proud of the fact that they had created themselves *ex nihilo*, was not a great success. To have a pedigree – real or imagined – seems to be an almost universal human need. The feeling of one's own worth depends on the quality of this pedigree: the search for 'roots' or heraldic snobbery are the best evidence of this. In all epochs, however, only a few could lay claim to an eminent pedigree. The majority had to content itself with the tradition of the community, which gives a feeling of collective power and sense of continuity to even its most inferior members. Starting from Edmund Burke, the romantic writers, who defined the nation as 'a union of dead, living, and still unborn generations', better than the rationalists understood this universal spiritual need; failure to satisfy it makes people homeless, uprooted, lacking the sense of affiliation.

People indeed feel that they have their personal share in the nation's past; and the more humble is our own actual lot, the more will we boast of the fact that our native land, however barren now, once gave birth to great warriors, prophets, statesmen, discoverers, philosophers or poets. Consequently, we often regard a criticism of our nation's past or an attempt at a destruction of our cherished historical legends as an assault on our own honour and property.

When the past becomes the collective possession of living generations, however, it has moral and psychological consequences which are not easy to face. For we inherit not only glory and the blessing of the Lord, but also wrongs and humiliations, sins and obligations. Can one accept the benediction and reject the curse? Can one accept the legacy and avoid the duty of paying its debts? Can one lay claim to the pride and reject the shame? Can one present oneself to the world with the services of ancestors and not accept responsibility for their sins?

All of this is possible, of course. All of this is commonly done under the slick motto of 'selection of tradition'. After all, we do not have the obligation to accept the entire heritage as an indivisible and integral whole. We have the right to take from it those models which are consistent with our position today. We are free: tradition is a choice and not a fatum. This is true. We should note, however, that under the motto of 'selection of tradition' are hidden two different and even entirely contradictory operations. One of them consists in a critical re-evaluation of the heritage and an honorific distinction of those of its components which symbolize the values we profess today. The other – which is more common – consists in an intentional or unconscious hidden selection, in ousting from the collective consciousness and often from the manipulator's own consciousness, those elements of the heritage which have become troublesome, inconvenient, ambiguous. It is symptomatic that this operation, though it takes place in social space – in literature, education, the mass media, in public ceremonies – is really identical with the ousting of shameful events and thoughts from individual consciousness and memory. This similarity can serve as an argument in favour of the possibility of using some methods of psychoanalysis to study the culture and mentality of social groups. More important for us at this moment is another conclusion: these defence and censorship mechanisms, these peevish reactions to criticism or belittling of the heritage show how strong our moral identification with the history of the community is. When we here, on the Vistula, see on the screen soldiers in uniforms of the Duchy of Warsaw raping Spanish nuns (A. Wajda's *Ashes*) or Polish peasants talking at length about 'kikes' (C. Lanzman's *Shoah*), it makes us feel just as offended and react just as nervously as though we ourselves were being shown. Consequently, we hush up and embellish matters in which we had no part and attitudes for which we are not personally to blame in the same way as the humiliating and shameful moments from our own life or that of our parents. These reactions generally elude conscious control.

Even educated people in some European countries would be very reluctant to admit that not a small number of their compatriots – not excepting artists and intellectuals – more or less willingly collaborated with Nazi occupants. No wonder that those who did have not been eager to confess. But psychological reality is more complex: when the days of settling the scores have passed; public opinion tends to forget the unpleasant, and the former resistance heroes may be the first to do so since they feel that it is they who are the true representatives of their country, while the others are unworthy of a place in national memory.

The Polish intelligentsia, historians included, for years seems to have been incapable of dealing with the problem of mass anti-Semitism in Poland in the nineteenth and twentieth centuries. I hardly have in mind its inheritors – they are not interesting. I mean those who despise anti-Semitism, who witnessed its outbursts with anguish and tried to fight it whenever they could. Even so, many of them are inclined to believe and argue that anti-Semitism in Poland was merely a product of extreme chauvinist demagogy or mob prejudice which never penetrated the healthy core of the nation. All evidence to the contrary is so easily passed over in silence, and, sometimes even worse, it is expurgated from published documentary sources. Why is this done by those who bear no guilt? By those who as individuals have no reason for shame and no need to conceal anything?

We do this because we are especially sensitive on this point which painfully offends our moral consciousness; and because we strongly feel collective national identity and know the great power of hasty generalizations and stereotypes. We know that shadows of the past fall equally on the guilty and the innocent. Our permanent dodge, avoiding the subject or misrepresenting it with phrases, the inability to investigate the truth objectively and present it as it is, seems not so much a political operation as a defence reaction which over the years has become established as a response to the generalized accusing stereotype.[1] For it seems to be a general law

---

[1] This paper had already been finished when in the Polish Catholic weekly *Tygodnik Powszechny* (11 Jan. 1987) appeared an article by Jan Błoński under the title 'Poor Poles Look at the Ghetto' (a paraphrase of the title of a poem written by Czesław Miłosz in Warsaw 1943: 'A Poor Christian Looks in the Ghetto'). Błoński investigates the Polish complex of guilt toward Jews, and the reluctance to admit it, deeper than any Polish author before him. His article provoked a storm of response: dozens of articles and readers' letters (most of them polemical) of which only a few were published. Błoński's analysis of the 'Principle of collective responsibility' is concurrent with the position I endeavour to defend here.

that an honest and unrelenting evaluation of one's past is most difficult to make when it is the object of accusation from outside. Similar measures and defensive attitudes cannot be explained without accepting the psychological assumption that people emotionally linked with a multigenerational community somehow feel responsible – and are regarded as such by others – for the evil which they have inherited, from which it still hardly follows that they want to and can bear the burden of this responsibility. After all, they can shirk it by reducing the dissonance between recognized historical knowledge and professed values: the victim of this operation is often common knowledge. So one has to agree with Jerzy Szacki's statement that the tradition of a social group is a kind of historical consciousness 'connected with the transformation of ambiguous *facts* of the past into unequivocal *values* of the present'.[2]

The same author characterizes 'atraditionalism' as an attitude 'whose element is complete indifferentism to all group values and also to the group heritage'.[3] It is obvious that this representation – when applied to the national community – describes the disappearance of patriotic feelings. It also seems obvious – by virtue of a tautology – that those to whom the national heritage and opinions about their nation are a matter of indifference cope most easily with the national heritage, those who therefore feel no obligations on account of their birth and education and do not intend to pay national debts. So they have the best reasons for rejecting all notions of responsibility separated from personal authorship and especially the idea of collective responsibility for the past.

This is a consistent attitude and certainly more widespread today than in the past, but rather in the West than in Central-Eastern Europe, where patriotic sentiments seem much stronger. These sentiments, however, cannot be reconciled with an indifferent attitude toward the heritage.

Hence the typical process for European civilization (or Western, if one wishes) of the individualization of moral subjects has come half-way, as it were, revealing the conflict of attitudes afflicting our

[2] J. Szacki, *Tradycja: Przeglad problematyki* (*Tradition: A Survey of Problems*), Warsaw: PWN, 1971, p. 275.
[3] *Ibid.*, p. 198.

culture. Here is how Peter L. Berger describes one of the spiritual experiences of the autonomous individual: 'I am responsible for my own actions; I am not responsible for the actions of others; no one else is responsible for my actions.' This conviction – Berger continues – whose roots are both Hellenic and Biblical – has caused a moral revolution: 'It liberates men from moral bondage both in the present (the collective responsibility of, say, one's tribe) and to the past (carrying along the moral accounts of one's ancestors).'[4]

In light of the above analysis, however, one may doubt whether this liberation can be complete; whether, in other words, a complete separation of the individual from his social background is possible and, following in its wake, complete autonomy of individual conscience. It is also a matter of axiological choice to decide to what limits such autonomy is desirable. Whatever contemporary philosophical anthropology thinks about this, our world hardly resembles a stage on which individual actors, free from social ties, play roles of their own choice and give account only of their performance.

The individualization of responsibility has been more complete in penal law in modern times, but not in civil or in international law.

In theology – if a layman may be permitted to say something about this – the matter seems somewhat more complicated. The Christian churches teach that every mortal individual will render an account before God of his deeds: we will be saved and condemned as individuals, and it is not known how those righteous persons will come through the Day of Judgement who once on Earth loved wrongdoers and the eternally condemned.[5] Nevertheless, in the history of Christian culture the collectivization of sin and responsibility was not a marginal phenomenon: the teaching of Christ was reconciled with the conviction that there is no salvation outside the Church (one or another) and that therefore entire large religious groups can be cursed by God. The religious

---

[4] Peter L. Berger, 'Western Individuality: Liberation and Loneliness', *Partisan Review*, 52, 4 (1985), p. 327.

[5] 'because as it turns out we will be saved as singles', writes Zbigniew Herbert in his poem 'U wrøt doliny' ('At the Gate of the Valley') which is an ironic picture of the day of the Last Judgement.

faith of our times has renounced these views, but nothing indicates that Christian personalism is heading toward the other extreme, that is, toward cutting the bonds of solidarity that link the human person with the community of his fellow men. On the contrary, the precept of solidarity is continually mentioned in the teaching of the present pope. Solidarity does not allow us to separate ourselves from the common historical fate or to repudiate the heritage of the past.

As long as we unite within ourselves an individual nature and a social nature, biography with the continuity of culture, as long as each of us perceives himself and the other person as autonomous individuals and at the same time as parts of some (usually not one) collective subject, contradictory ideas of individual and collective responsibility (including ancestral) will coexist in our perception of the world. The practical task, then, is not to chase the mirage of man's total liberation from 'moral bondage' but to mediate between the consequences of these two principles in such a way as to minimize the conflict between them. An essential condition for such mediation is to make more precise the meaning we attribute to collective responsibility. If it is to mean the inheritance of blame and a curse as well as the right – man's or God's – to punish children for the sins of their fathers, this understanding cannot be reconciled with the individualizing principle of justice. It is another matter if we understand responsibility of the community as the inheritance of obligations. For the principle that the debts and obligations of the testator fall on the heir to a legacy is not inconsistent with the principle of individual justice.

2

Deeply rooted in human hearts, in human nature, and coded in every historical culture is a sense of moral order.[6] A crime destroys the order and thus – like in Greek tragedy – the balance must be restored. This sense of order, this demand of redemption, rather than any pragmatical reasons, seems to be the very core of our notion of justice. The moral order of the world must be restored, but it may be done in many different ways. The guilty may be

[6] See Leszek Kolakowski, *Religion*, London: Fontana Paperbacks, 1982, p. 193.

punished, or he may repent and beg forgiveness, or may redress the wrong he has done in a way prescribed in this or that particular culture: e.g. by pilgrimage to the Holy Land, by charity or by paying indemnity to his victims' kin. All these are in fact only symbolic compensations, because the harm caused by a crime cannot be undone. Still, such a symbolic retaliation and reward, obtained through a judicial verdict or through the confession of guilt, is a condition for restoring the moral order. And if the culprit cannot be reached, the obligation of admitting the crime falls on his heirs, however innocent they may be. If, in their turn, they take no responsibility for acts done without their consent, then the ghosts of the unredeemed past will haunt the memory of the victims' kin or tribe and blind vengeance will remain the only means of restoring the balance.

This is what happened after the extermination of the Turkish Armenians in 1915–16, which in historical literature is regarded as the first classical example in modern times of planned and organized genocide.[7] A Polish historian writes: 'The shadow of this crime is all the darker because to this day neither Turkish historians nor politicians want to admit that genocide really took place.'[8] Despite the trial of the Young-Turkish leaders conducted *in absentia* in 1919, the Armenians never received even the symbolic compensation given to the Jews who survived the Holocaust in the form of the well-known trials of Nazi criminals after the defeat of the Third Reich and revealing to the world the complete truth about the *Endlösung*. So the Armenians took bloody vengeance into their own hands. The leading architects of the extermination were struck down by Armenian assassins after the First World War, and sixty years later Armenian terrorists take revenge on what can by now only be purely random Turkish victims for the mass crime that has never been redeemed. This is not the only chain of hatred and retaliation that has lasted for generations.

[7] See Leo Kuper, *Genocide*, Harmondsworth: Penguin Books, 1981, pp. 101–19. There are many monographs and source editions on this subject, available in English.

[8] Tomasz Wituch, *Tureckie przemiany: Dzieje Turcji, 1878–1923* (*Turkish Transformations: A History of Turkey, 1878–1923*), Warsaw: PWN, 1980, pp. 238, 244.

Unlike Turkey, successive governments of the Federal Republic of Germany have stated on many occasions that they accept responsibility for the crimes of the Third Reich. They established special relations with Israel and paid compensation to at least part of the survivors of Nazi terror.[9] It is obvious that such an open admission of German guilt became possible only thanks to the complete military defeat of the Reich and a severing of the historical continuity of the state. For it is significant and also very important for our argument that the collective responsibility of their nation was primarily, if not exclusively, admitted by those who were not burdened with participation in the crime either personally or through party affiliation and even more often by those who themselves were victims of oppression or fought actively against the criminal regime.

When the Federal chancellor knelt down in front of the Warsaw Ghetto's Heroes monument, nobody could interpret his gesture as an individual expiation. In his person it was the new Germany paying tribute to the victims of the Holocaust. And the fact that Willy Brandt himself fought Hitler gave him in the eyes of the world more right to perform this public act of repentance.

The painful and involved problem of German 'collective guilt' tormented Karl Jaspers immediately after the war. He was aware of the fact that 'people's opinions and feelings all over the world are largely governed by collective ideas' and tried to find out whether there was some truth in thinking in such categories. This was a time when Germans from all sides were charged with national responsibility in the literal sense, that is, either in the sense of complicity or at least tacit consent to Nazi genocide. In accordance with the already mentioned psychological law, these accusations mobilized defence mechanisms: hence it became common to protect oneself by appealing to the liberal principle of strict individualization of guilt and also to present to the victorious allies a list of the German's own sufferings and wrongs.

Jaspers emphatically rejected generalizing the crimes of the Nazis to the entire nation, but not in order to relieve his countrymen from carrying the burden of history.

---

[9] Until now, however, the claims of those survivors of Nazi concentration and forced-labour camps who live in Poland or in other communist countries have not been acknowledged.

We feel [he wrote] almost as though we share the blame for the deeds of our family. This feeling cannot be objectively described. We would reject every kind of common liability. But we are none the less inclined to feel implicated whenever a member of our family commits an injustice, and therefore also inclined . . . to atone for it, even if we have no moral or legal liability . . . Furthermore, we feel ourselves to be party not only to what presently is being done, that is, as sharing in the guilt for the deeds of contemporaries, but also to the tradition to which we are connected. It is incumbent upon us to take on the guilt of our fathers. We all bear a share in the burden of guilt for the fact that the spiritual conditions of German life made possible such a regime.[10]

This entire argument of Jaspers – who in the Third Reich was a lonely 'internal emigrant' – is filled with a strong feeling of the national bond understood as a special duty that results from 'participation in German spiritual and emotional life'. I can – he said – spiritually identify with many other communities:

But the fact of being German (that is, of living and having one's being in the mother tongue) is so lasting that I feel myself, in a way which rationally is neither intelligible nor even defensible, to be implicated in the present and past deeds of Germans. I feel myself to be closer to those Germans who feel as I do, and to have less in common with those who spiritually deny this connection.[11]

There were never very many who felt the same way and expressed this openly: a handful of writers, historians, humanists, some leaders of the Church, especially the Protestant, young idealists from Aktion Sühnezeichen working as volunteers in Auschwitz and Majdanek as a sign of penance for the sins of their fathers and the desire to establish reconciliation with the victims of Nazi aggression. Such attitudes create a model that is worthy of respect, but they are not possible on a mass scale. In the GDR the official ideology dealt more easily with the legacy of Hitlerism, repudiating it as though it were a foreign occupation of the country. In the Federal Republic, on the other hand, the change in the moral and political climate seems to be not so much a result of a critical re-evaluation of the past as of little interest in it, which has been fostered by prosperity and the cosmopolitan education of

[10] Karl Jaspers, *Die Schuldfrage*, Heidelberg: Lambert Schneider, 1946, pp. 70–1.

[11] *Ibid.*, pp. 71–2.

young people, who today – on a mass scale – are free from both nationalism and from the national complex of guilt, who are simply normal, in other words. For them Hitlerism now is only an incomprehensible and ridiculous madness of psychopaths, an episode that is just as exotic as the butcheries of Tamerlane. It might seem that this is the most healthy and natural way of overcoming the nightmarish past.

It is not certain, however, whether the problem of inheritance has thereby been neutralized once and for all. Recently, from both German states there are signs of a certain revival of German patriotism (Prussian in the GDR), which once again puts on the agenda the need to reconstruct the national tradition. In May 1986 a meeting of intellectuals was held in Aschaffenburg (FRG) on the subject 'Patriotismus nach Auschwitz?'. Can one be a German patriot after Auschwitz? Various answers were given to this question, though from the press reports one can infer that most participants hold the view that attachment to one's country implies not only pride in its historical and cultural accomplishments but also shame for its crimes.[12] 'No one will free us from this shame' – these words were uttered by the first president of the Federal Republic, Theodor Heuss in 1952 at the unveiling of a monument to the victims of the Bergen-Belsen concentration camp.[13]

The fortieth anniversary of the capitulation of Germany aroused a new wave of already dormant emotions in the FRG, revealing once again the ambivalence of attitudes. Such different politicians as Helmut Schmidt and Franz-Joseph Strauss, while admitting that the stigma of ignominy has not been erased, warned at the same time that the continual thrusting of the Germans into the prison cells of history can ultimately lead to a moral paralysis and even a new catastrophe. No nation – Strauss said – can live forever with 'a criminal past'.[14] At the same time, all public opinion polls show that interest in the sources and crimes of Hitlerism is clearly greater in the post-war age-groups than among

---

[12] *Frankfurter Rundschau*, 6 May 1986.
[13] *Reden der Deutschen Bundespräsidenten*, ed. D. Sternberger, Munich: Carl Hanser Verlag, 1979, p. 21.
[14] Quoted from the Polish Press Agency (PAP) bulletin 'RFN – Berlin Zachodni', nos. 18 and 20, 1985.

those who remember the Third Reich,[15] which would confirm the thesis that the complex of guilt blocks an honest appraisal of the past.

President Richard von Weizsäcker, in a carefully weighed and well-received speech at the joint session of the Bundestag and Bundesrat on 8 May 1985, attempted to reconcile contradictory feelings and attitudes. There is no collective guilt – he said – just as there is no collective innocence.

The vast majority of our society today were children at that time or still had not been born. These people cannot admit to deeds which they did not commit. No sensitive person will expect them to wear robes of penance only because they are Germans. Their ancestors have left them a painful legacy, however. All of us, guilty or not, young or old, have to *accept the past* [my emphasis]. Its consequences embrace all of us, fall on all of us ... There can be no reconciliation without remembering.

And further: 'Young people are not responsible for what will result from this in history. We, the older generation, owe young people not only the fulfilment of their dreams but also honesty.'[16]

As we can see from this superficial review, embarrassment over the dark pages of one's country's history is inseparable from the feeling of collective identity.[17] This uneasiness – whether we call it shame or the feeling of disgrace, responsibility or the obligation to remember and pass judgement – can be suppressed, but this very suppression testifies to its presence. This notwithstanding, the idea of responsibility for the national past remains ambiguous and not clear enough. One's native country, even though one can abandon it, is not after all a voluntary organization with a common doctrine and declaration of faith. The history of every nation contains contradictory political ideals, ethoses and patterns of

---

[15] Data from *Allensbacher Berichte*, nos. 12 and 13, 1985, quoted after the same bulletin.

[16] Quoted from the same bulletin, no. 20, 1985.

[17] Instructive in this respect are surveys of post-war interpretations of the contemporary history of Germany; see, e.g., Theodore S. Hamerow, 'Guilt, Redemption, and Writing German History', *American Historical Review*, 88, 1 (February 1983), pp. 53–72; or Gordon A. Craig, 'The War of the German Historians', *New York Review of Books*, 33, 21–2 (15 January, 1987), pp. 16–19.

behaviour, among which one can freely choose, admitting to only part of the heritage.

The matter seems otherwise with formal institutions such as political parties or churches.

3

Every institution which exists long enough faces the intricate problem of continuity and change. Its ways, if not its declared ends, may have changed several times; it may have acquired a new ethos, a new world outlook, new rules for bringing up its members. And yet it remains the same, with the same allegedly sacred purposes and mission, with the same prophets and martyrs, with the same holy books. Its origins and its later tradition serve its legitimization, but at some point it may turn out that some of the tradition contradicts the present-day values or even is a cause for shame. What then? Tradition cannot be repudiated, and strongly integrated organizations generally do not give up the official interpretation of their own history. This interpretation can change over time, but it is a delicate operation. An uncompromising reassessment of the past record carries a danger of disruption of continuity, of rising scepticism, perhaps of a schism. A most common solution is to rearrange the heritage in such a way that the historical discord of values will be played down. Bad periods will be, so to say, placed in brackets or elliptically circumvented as casual episodes, temporal vitiations which did not affect the secular mission. Some historical personalities will all but disappear or their portraits will be retouched.

Such operations notwithstanding, the question of the responsibility of an institution such as it is today for its past crops up time and time again and can cause troubles. Communist Parties which have lost their earlier radicalism of goals and means and have become more pragmatic, more conventional, even conservative, today have serious problems with their tradition, starting from the revolutionary origins. For here the aforementioned disharmony of symbolized values is revealed: the ethos of radical non-conformism of the old fighting revolutionaries is difficult to reconcile with today's emphasis on tranquillity, order, respect for the government and obedience to the laws. The passing over in almost complete silence in Poland of the eightieth anniversary of the revolution of 1905, that storm of strikes, demonstrations and street fights, economic demands and the struggle for freedom, is a typical example of confusion concerning the canon of one's own tradition. Similarly, the 'Bolshevik' legacy becomes troublesome whenever one party or another tries to stress national values.

A more serious problem is connected with the period of Stalin's regime on account of the compromising legacy of the methods used at that time. Two attitudes are possible here, both of which have some arguments in favour of them. On the one hand, one can say that if a man can be held responsible for all his crimes until they are redeemed, why cannot an institution which claims its unbroken continuity? But on the other hand, an institution is people. New leaders, new members are not guilty of the old persecutions: some of them, in fact, were even their victims. They are pursuing new goals using more moderate means. Why should they bear the burden of somebody else's sins on their conscience? And why should they answer inquisitive questions concerning a closed chapter of the past?

Since they themselves do not have to fear indictment, one might assume that it would be easier for them to reveal the truth, the more so as distance in time cools emotions and favours re-evaluation. In practice, however, the matter is not simple. After every shock and change of the ruling group, a 'settlement of accounts' for the previous period is permitted: a few critical publications, obstructed films and novels appear, commissions are formed to investigate the illegalities committed, sometimes monuments are erected to the victims. But as soon as the emotions liberated by the change die down and the new order of things stablizes, everything is hushed up, the reports of the commissions are censored or hidden in the archives, and the incomplete settlement of accounts comes to an end.

What causes this blockade? In part, certainly the fact that the change of personnel was never complete, and so bringing to light revelations from the previous period must encounter the opposition of those who remain in the field of danger. Stronger than this, however, seems the fear of institutional danger: bringing to light the entire truth about the past would cast a shadow on the party as such and thus would also undermine the authority of the new leadership. So far there has been no opportunity to test whether this fear is justified: we know that it is paralysing.

What is most interesting is that as a rule actual *disclosure* is not the issue. The important facts are known to people either from their own experience or from foreign and illegal publications. The matter concerns *admission* or the act of accepting responsibility. Through such an act the psychological and political function of information changes rapidly, even if its content remains unchanged.

The ruling Communist Parties are shackled by a neurotic complex of historical guilt, which comes out most strongly in recollection of the ever more remote Stalinist period, still a mined area of silence or guarded euphemisms. Here and there allusions are permitted, sometimes – in films or novels – a bolder picture of the atmosphere of terror, but no party so far has dared to admit openly and fully what has already been known for a long time.[18] That is why the spectre of the past still haunts us and will continue to do so until symbolic redemption restores the moral order of the world.

4

Neither can the Christian churches, among them especially the Roman Catholic Church, liberate themselves from the difficult problems of coexisting with their own past. During the past two decades, the Catholic Church has changed past all recognition, leaving behind its long and rich tradition of authoritarianism and intolerance.

To be sure, there is a tendency to present this change as evolutionary and organic, but this does not alter the essence of the matter. In times of profound axiological changes we always find people who try to salvage the continuity of tradition as well as

---

18 This is the case, among others, of the murder of several thousand Polish army officers in Katyn, near Smolensk. Everybody in Poland, if not outside, knows who did it and when, but the official version still keeps to the story of the Nazi authorship of that crime. Consequently, this is still a matter of excitement for Poles. Hopes were raised recently that a joint Soviet–Polish declaration may be issued concerning this and other long-established historical facts. This still remains to be seen.

those who sharpen the conflict of new principles with old ones: these interpretations are complementary and not contradictory. We are interested here in conflict, since it generates the problem of responsibility. The burden of the past increases rather than diminishes with the departure from its institutions and practices. It is just because the attitude of the Church toward other faiths – Christian and non-Christian – has changed so radically, and because no less seriously has changed its attitude toward secular science and various movements of social and national liberation, that axiological contradictions between the teaching and behaviour of the Church today and in the past are becoming more and more dramatic, giving rise to the ever more pressing need for a reconsideration of the entire historical legacy, explaining it and separating the wheat from the chaff.

It cannot be denied, after all, that many of the former decrees of the Holy Office, canons of oecumenical councils or papal bulls, full of invectives and hatred, slandering and excommunicating dissidents, pietists, Jews, alleged witches, genuine scientists, philosophers, writers, freedom fighters or radical social reformers, are hardly reconcilable with the position of the Church today. The ideology of the crusades and the extermination of the Albigenses, the doctrine and practice of the Holy Inquisition, witch trials, *Index* and *Syllabus*, anti-Semitism, the support of tyrants and the might of this world cannot be reconciled with it.

The revision of tradition, however, is a psychologically more difficult task than the change in positive teaching that has already taken place, for it touches a deeper emotional level. Neither can the scope or possible effects of such a revision be foreseen. In any case, even among those raised to sainthood centuries ago we find fanatic persecutors and instigators of religious pogroms such as John of Capestrano and Vincenti Ferrero. What should one do with this? Should we recommend a revision of canonization proceedings in every case which looks doubtful from today's point of view?

In the face of such dilemmas the historical thought of the Church clearly lags behind theological and moral thought. It betrays anxiety and uncertainty, lack of courage; it takes refuge in a cloud of euphemisms and half-truths, especially when it has to deal with the problem of religious violence and persecutions.

Some authors react with impatience and suspicion to all

reminders of this sort. A Polish Catholic writer wrote two years ago: 'As far as the stakes are concerned, they burned when people were firmly convinced that error must come from bad will, which is not true. When they became aware of this untruth – they admitted that they had done wrong. What else were they supposed to do? Lie prostrate to the Day of Last Judgement?'[19]

Others attempt to present the history of hatred and fear as a side stream, almost incidental, as 'errors and perversions' which here and there muddied the pure stream of Christian love; or they remind us that the persecutions, tortures and stakes belong to the legacy of European culture as a whole and not just to the institutional history of the Church[20] – which is absolutely true, except that the secular philosophy and historiography have been dealing with this since the eighteenth century and the feeling of European identity has been no obstacle to this.

Sometimes it is emphasized that evaluations of the past should be made by considering the specific features of a given mentality, e.g. medieval, which seems more consistent with axiological relativism and rather inconsistent with the Christian moral doctrine. John Paul II referred to this position in a speech given in a Roman synagogue: 'Consideration of age-old cultural determinants cannot be obstacles to judgement of acts of discrimination, unjustified limitation of religious freedom, and also oppression in civil liberties with respect to Jews as phenomena *objectively* deserving the most profound regret.'[21]

The Committee of French Bishops on relations with Judaism stated in 1973: 'Obviously, a revision of all the statements made by the Church over the centuries and of all of the historical attitudes is not possible in one day.'[22] This is certainly impossible. What is important is that despite all of the quite understandable sensitivities and defence mechanisms, the process of the critical re-evaluation of the heritage has begun, showing the acceptance of responsibility for it.

[19] Tadeusz Żychiewicz, 'Rozmowa z czytelnikiem' ('A Talk with a Reader'), *Tygodnik Powszechny*, no. 6 (1984).
[20] See, e.g., Father Jacek Salij's commentaries in *Legendy Dominikańskie* (*Dominican Legends*), Poznan: Wdrodze, 1985, pp. 113, 157.
[21] Quoted from *Tygodnik Powszechny*, no. 17 (1986).
[22] *Znak*, no. 339–40 (1983), pp. 199–200.

Significant from this point of view are such facts as the official 'wiping out from memory' of the mutual excommunications of the Eastern and Western Church; taking up again, with the approval of the pope, investigation of the case of Galileo; or the recent article of Professor Stefan Świeżawski in *Tygodnik Powszechny* calling for a revision of the trial of John Hus. Świeżawski's article, written by a scholar who enjoys great authority in the Church, is – especially in view of its uncompromising appraisal of the atmosphere of the Council of Constance – evidence of the existence in Catholicism of a trend of historical thought that is overcoming previous inhibitions. For as the author says, the consequence of an open orientation consciously chosen by the Vatican II Council and constituting 'the very essence of the famous *aggiornamento* of the Council' is 'the pressing need to revise today many church condemnations and prohibitions'.[23] There is little doubt that this painful revision and revalorization now facing the Church, if it is to be consistent, must be carried out on a hitherto unheard of scale. This can be ventured only by an institution which need not fear for its prestige.

5

'We had no government, and that is the only reason for our fall' – wrote a Polish historian a century ago. 'During 123 years we experienced six uprisings' – writes a Polish historian today.[24] A strange 'we' which does not contain a speaking subject! And it need not contain any physical subject at all: for no one lived through six uprisings. The historical 'we' is an admission – conscious or unconscious – of solidary participation in the life and values, in the glories and declines of a multigenerational community. We Poles, we Germans, we Christians, we socialists … we Europeans, we Whites: was it not *us* whom Sartre enjoined to feel responsible for the excesses of colonialism?[25] We people – sometimes thinking

---

[23] *Tygodnik Powszechny*, no. 6 (1986).

[24] M. Bobrzyński, *Dzieje Polski w zarysie* (*An Outline History of Poland*), 1st edn, 1879; Warsaw, 1974, p. 400; and S. Kieniewicz, *Historyk a świadomość narodowa* (*Historian and National Consciousness*), Warsaw, 1982, p. 333.

[25] See the preface by Jean-Paul Sartre to the first edition of Frantz Fanon, *Les Damnés de la terre*, Paris: F. Maspero, 1961.

with horror about what *we* are capable of. Responsibility thereby expands to the dimensions of 'metaphysical guilt'. It is difficult to cope with this.

I am aware of the methodological difficulties and the sometimes dangerous practical consequences which can result from admitting that we cannot avoid responsibility for the past we inherit. I believe, however, that whether we consciously recognize it or not, this principle is present in social life and in our moral sense. It becomes especially strong when we repudiate it by consigning troublesome events of the past into oblivion. History cannot be buried, however, because someone will always be found to unbury it and hold it up to us as we to him. The heritage is given to us, and on us only depends what we do with it.

Collective responsibility – I wish to repeat with emphasis – I understand here as the obligation of symbolic compensation for wrongs once committed and not as anyone's right to retaliation. Symbolic compensation in human society has purifying properties, properties of catharsis: it prevents the breeding of hateful emotions and extinguishes the right to retaliation.

Probably the most effective form of symbolic compensation is revealing and teaching the fullest possible, most comprehensive and objective truth. Yet no one better than us, professional historians from Central Europe, knows how many fears and constraints in oneself have to be overcome – fears of the guardians of the word, but also fears of the public – how many clever evasions and complexes of one's own have to be surmounted, how many interests violated in order not to avoid such an obligation by selecting easier and safer paths.

What is worse, however, if historical truth is to serve as catharsis, is that it is not a matter of indifference who reveals and who teaches it. It is not the same whether evidence of the extermination of the Armenians in Anatolia is presented by Armenian or Turkish historians or, finally, by scholars from a country not involved in the conflict. It is not indifferent whose *imprimatur* stands behind this or that history textbook, 'short course' or edition of documents. It is entirely indifferent from the point of view of scholarship but not in social life, where no knowledge itself of the facts is the issue but collective feelings, fanned or extinguished by facts, by fabrications and concealments, by justifications and verdicts.

Finally, dealing with the burden of the heritage is not necessary only for the sake of others: those to whom we owe truth and compensation. No one today will speak up in the name of the Albigenses exterminated root and branch. It is easy to say: let the dead bury their dead, we are faced with tasks for today and tomorrow. Unfortunately, the memory of unburied skeletons shackles our steps, does not permit us to be honest with ourselves, diminishes the boldness of reforms and the formation of new, open attitudes. Up to a certain time apologetics can be useful for integration and the collective morale of the community, but not for its development. For development – individual as well as collective – is not possible without the overcoming of suppressed fear. That is why knowledge of history and its courageous acceptance has therapeutic properties.

January 1986 – January 1987.

POSTSCRIPT (APRIL 1988)

When I wrote this essay, the now famous debate of West German historians (Historikerstreit), focussing on the reassessment of the Nazi period and on its place in the continuity of German history, was only developing and I did not yet know its full record. In this heated controversy a connection between academic history and the shaping of national identity and moral consciousness of the new generations seems to have been an important issue. Whatever positions were taken by the participants in the debate, and whatever ambiguous terms were used – like 'burden of history', 'historical responsibility', 'inheritance', 'obsession with guilt', 'collective memory' and its 'repression', etc. – the basic dilemma was very much the same as I tried to outline in the above article.

One year later, in 1987, the 'glasnost'' proclaimed by Gorbachev encouraged some Soviet historians, writers, film-makers and columnists to inquire into mass crimes and atrocities committed in Stalin's times. This work is gaining momentum. In spite of many obstacles one taboo falls down after another, evidence is step by step unearthed, while the impact of this dramatic re-examination of the recent past and of its official version upon the consciousness of Soviet citizens remains as yet unclear. They also must learn to live with their true and cruel history of which their fathers, if not themselves, were either co-authors, or victims, or both.

At the same time the Armenian communities in the West were still striving in vain to get a recognition by Turkey of the mass murder perpetrated in 1915. However, taking advantage of the fact that Turkey was anxious to join the European Community, the Armenians started lobbying the European Parliament in Strasburg. Finally, in June 1987, they scored a symbolic victory when the Parliament passed a resolution recognizing, without euphemisms, the historical fact of Turkish genocide. 'Such a vote [commented a Paris newspaper] constitutes the principal act of international recognition of the moral and historical claims of the Armenian diaspora'.

The Barbie trial in Lyons refreshed the memory of the Vichy regime and its willing collaboration with Nazi Germany in the destruction of French Jews. The trial inspired bitter controversies in the French press, proving once more how painful or shameful some wartime recollections and evidence are, even for many of those who were born later.

All these and other similar developments have strengthened my conviction that the problem dealt with in my paper is by no means an academic one. The way people see and interpret their collective (i.e. national, confessional, or partisan) history influences their present attitudes and, vice versa, is strongly influenced by them. Historical controversies, accusations and revisions, heat the audience, since they deeply concern people's sense of belonging to and solidarity with a large multigenerational community, and touch their common feelings of righteousness. It is worthwhile to ask why it is so.

My paper, before its publication, was discussed in several circles, in Vienna (the Institut für die Wissenschaften vom Menschen) and in Warsaw. Its theoretical assumptions were attacked from many sides. As I had expected, the very notion of collective and inherited responsibility without personal guilt was most often criticized. A collective subject, argued some critics, is only a hypostasis and one should beware of treating it like an acting entity: no nation can be as a whole blamed for wrongs done by its ruling powers; consequently cannot be obliged to account for them. Only he is responsible who is free to choose and who participates in a criminal action of his own accord.

One critic aptly remarked that the concept of historical responsibility has no temporal and social limits, since there is no reason why one should feel responsible for the faults of the previous generation and not for those of earlier ancestors. Or why not for all sins and crimes of mankind? But then all people would be equally responsible for everything that happened in history which means that in fact nobody could be held responsible for anything.

It was also argued that there is no logical connection between solidarity and responsibility. One can sympathize or solidarize with present aspirations of a group of one's choice without being obliged to carry the burden of its historical tradition. I was advised, then, to do away with the concept of 'heritage and collective responsiblity' or to leave it to God alone, together with the idea of original sin.

My stress on the importance of symbolic compensation in inter-group relations was also challenged. The main argument was that there is no general law according to which an expiation should satisfy and disarm a victim of violence, or a community that had suffered a wrong. Indeed such a recognition of past wrongs may even serve to provoke the making of hitherto unmade claims, whether they be justified or not.

In sum, it seemed as if I might be able to deal with these objections by simply agreeing to changes of vocabulary rather than to changes of substance. This might be done easily enough. For instance, instead of speaking of 'collective responsibility', I could speak of personal obligations generated by one's belonging to a social group. I doubt, however, whether any such mere change of terms would really solve the problem. I chose the concepts and categories not in order to permeate the analysis with my own moral philosophy, but better to describe some aspects of 'social construction of reality'. Therefore I am not so much seeking a rational or metaphysical justification of a moral norm, as trying to investigate its social and psychological functions.

I may readily agree that the nation, church and social institutions are nothing but hypostatized non-entities, and that it is only human beings who act, think and feel. The trouble is that not all human beings are nominalists and many of them do regard nations and other communities as very real, to the extent that collective identification and a sense of belonging may be no less important for them than individual identity or self-awareness. Thus people usually feel deeply hurt by accusations, stereotypes, slanders or jokes levelled not at them personally, but at their group as a whole. Similarly, a historical debt of this group, or memory of misdeeds committed in its name, may weigh heavy on its members' conscience, the grace of their late birth notwithstanding. As all debates mentioned above seem to prove, one can accept this burden of the past, or can try to get rid of it in various ways, but there is no denying the feeling of its existence, whether we consider this rational or not.

I am not attached to any particular use of terms and categories. It may be that some of those I have used are confusing. Still, any conceptual framework which would replace them must contain and explain the socio-psychological phenomena of which evidence is abundant.

At the same time, I should have stressed more strongly than I did the moral and political responsiblility of the historian. This profession has never been innocent: today it is even less so. The German debate showed very clearly that in the era of mass media the voice of the historian sounds louder than ever before and his words are listened to by a big audience. Certainly, the gap between critical history and common knowledge is still huge, in quality no less than in quantity. And yet, our professional, academic constructions of the past may nowadays exert a stronger impact upon people's minds – and, consequently, upon political life – than we are ready to admit. The historian's words may inspire or extinguish hatred, may contribute to shape an open, or a closed, xenophobic society. The historian's conscious and subconcious choices of topics and interpretations may make people remember what ought to be remembered, or may help them to forget the events they do not like to think about.

5

Power and wisdom: the expert as mediating figure in contemporary Polish history

JACEK KURCZEWSKI

Experts, advisers, counsellors – how many of them I have seen in my life here – mostly nice, intelligent people caught in an inherently frustrating role. And when, already as a student, I was involved for the first time in applied social research, I suddenly found myself in that role as well, since – however much this may surprise foreigners – communist Poland was quite eager to offer such roles to its educated sons and daughters. However, the intelligentsia has not been converted into an unreservedly supportive force. Although, since 1944, intellectuals and professors are amongst the incumbents of the top official positions in the country, it would be hard to describe the intelligentsia as contributors to, or benefactors of, the stability of the system, apart from the patriotic motivation, generally acknowledged, of those who enter political life in this or any other way. As this may run contrary to the experience of some other Eastern European countries I prefer to concentrate here simply on the Polish experience. Idiosyncratic though this may be, it is nevertheless a really remarkable experience that deserves to be first expounded and then given a more general analysis. Here I can attempt only the first of these tasks. I will do this by way of citing some instances of expert advice as a type of interaction through which we may study the nature of the relationship between the worlds of power and of learning.

The tradition of Polish professors involving themselves in the government's running of worldly affairs was initiated by 'Stanczycy', the influential conservative faction in Austrian-dominated Galicia.[1] In the old independent Rzeczospolita men of wisdom and

[1] Marcin Król, 'Konserwatyści karakowscy 1831–1865', *Archiwum historii filozofii i mysli spolecznej*, 19 (1973).

education were often found among the noble politicians, whether clergy or laymen, but there was no link between the city and, on the one hand, the royal court or, on the other hand, the castles of the nobility or manors of the gentry such as could lead to the appearance of the scholar on the stage of public affairs. The figure of the scientist emerges only slowly in the nineteenth century and his social role, as displayed in the press and in books, reflected the frustrations of Polish society under alien rule. According to the social pattern then prevailing the eminent scientist was a social leader, with social authority based on his knowledge and genius, but independent in his political, moral and religious views; a hero and a martyr devoting his life to the accumulation of knowledge; an individual engaged in disseminating scientific knowledge among the wider population, but a good citizen and patriot too.[2]

A citizen scientist was above all expected at that time to care for the needs of the lowest and poorest classes. Those who educated the countryfolk, established schools and banks for peasants, prevented begging in the cities through the development of proper jobs and hospitals were greatly applauded; and the hero of Positivism, John Stuart Mill was worshipped for vindicating human rights, universal suffrage and women's liberation. It was not just the scientist who pursued his research with the good of his nation in mind who was the good patriot, but also any scientist whose achievements brought credit to the nation. Direct involvement in politics, however, was valued positively only in so far as it was related to the management of education and culture, since national enlightenment was the only good that ranked higher than the direct improvement of the fate of the country's lower classes. Direct assumption of power by men of knowledge was approved by Polish public opinion for such reasons, but under the condition that it was done in the context of an at least autonomous political life. What was approved in the Kingdom of Poland until 1831, when Polish autonomy was abolished by the Russians, or in Galicia, after some measure of local autonomy was granted to Poles by the Austrians, was impossible in other places and at other moments of the tragic, turbulent nineteenth century.

2 Joanna Kurczewska, 'Społeczny wzór uczonego na podstawie warszawskiej prasy pozytywistycznej', in R. Czepulis-Rastenis (ed.), *Inteligencja polska XIX i XX w.*, Warsaw: PAN Instytut Historii, PWN, 1985, pp. 136–59.

Poland, though relatively lagging behind its Western neigh-
bours in economic development, is one of those happy societies
that prize education and allow those whose education has reached a
certain stage to climb the social ladder. In the course of the
nineteenth century an intelligentsia was formed to which belonged
not only the educated and uprooted gentry, but to which too
Polish-speaking Jews, burghers of various ethnic origins and
peasants had access through university education which had been
progressively democratized towards the end of the century.
Although in social terms the aristocracy had taken a leading part in
diminishing the influence of a large mass of the nobility and in
establishing links with Polish–Jewish–German capital, still it
remained a basic fact of social structure that this society was
commanded from outside. The Old Republic became a colony of
three partitioning powers until 11 November 1918. Towards the
end of this period it was only in the Austrian-dominated part of
Poland called Galicia that Polish society was given both extensive
home rule and access to the relatively democratic parliamentary
institutions of the Empire. Only there was experience in the forms
of political life of a sort that was normal in Western Europe won
before the regaining of independence. As the only Polish legal,
scientific and academic institutions were located in this area too, it
was possible for men of learning to enter the world of official,
public and legal politics. The conservative 'Stanczycy' and their
neo-conservative followers, though rooted in the wealthy gentry,
had as their political representatives professors of the Jagiellonian
University in Cracow and the University of Lwów. This political
camp sent Polish professors to the local Parliament in Lwów and
the national Parliament in Vienna as well as to government posts in
Galicia and to the cabinet in Vienna.

In her study of 1,092 full professors in independent Poland
between the two world wars Dorota Mycielska established that,
following Galician tradition, at least 10 per cent took an active part
in the political life of the new Polish Republic, serving as presidents, prime ministers, ministers, members of parliament or
senators.[3] This decidedly direct political involvement in national
affairs was continued after the coup d'état effected in May 1927 by

---

[3] Dorota Mycielska, 'Postawy polityczne profesorów wyzszych uczelni w
dwudziestoleciu między wojennym', in *ibid.*, pp. 293–335.

Marshal Józef Piłsudski, himself a doctor *honoris causa* of the
University of Warsaw, a good writer and the brother of the
thoroughbred scientist Bronisław; it ceased only after the death of
this charismatic leader in 1934, when totalitarian tendencies
became apparent in the moods both of the opposition and of the
governing camp. After 1935 elections were boycotted by the
opposition while the government indulged itself by reforming the
universities with the aim of limiting their autonomy. The political
activity of the intellectuals, which had in the meantime assumed
all the colours of the political spectrum, more and more took the
form of the intellectual opposition which had first been expressed
much earlier in the protests against the internment of the opposition politicians in 1930. In seeking an explanation of the protests
of intellectuals against the authorities in post-Stalinist Poland
since the 1960s, one needs to take account of this first protest of
1930 as constituting a precedent for subsequent generations
acting under a different, but evidently no more democratic,
regime.

In 1966 an elegant book was published in Poland by Adam
Podgórecki, who had already established himself as the founding
father of the sociology of law in Poland.[4] This book, called *Principles of Sociotechnics* – the word 'socjotechnika' was deliberately
used rather than 'social engineering' – referred to a much earlier
work by the same author. In that work he had developed Leon
Petrazycki's idea of a scientific legal policy, *Rechtspolitik*, and
Tadeusz Kotarbinski's praxiology, or theory of efficient action,
into a new type of social science, 'sociotechnics', dealing with the
rational changing of social reality. The author had studied
Machiavelli, the Jesuits, Clausewitz, Lenin, small group theory,
and psychological warfare in order to distil from these scraps of
practical skill and knowledge some more systematic and general
principles of social action, aimed at altering both collective and
individual conduct.

Professor Podgórecki was at first rather optimistic about the
chances for this new discipline's development in the political conditions of Poland. In 1968, discussing the role of sociotechnics in
a socialist country, he wrote:

---

[4] Adam Podgórecki, *Zasady socjotechniki*, Warsaw: WP, 1966.

In socialism, more than anywhere else, the opportunity is offered of breaking the magic circle: sponsor-expert [...] For certain fundamental reasons socialism provides conditions for intense sociotechnical action. Socialism is distinguished amongst other things by the great emphasis laid on planning social and economic life; by treating law as an instrument of social change; by a systematic and uniform use of the mass media and, finally, by particular stress on the education system as the main instrument of the creative and socially involved personality. Such actions need as a foundation not charlatanry but conscious scientific premises. It is precisely the task of sociotechnics to provide such information. Socialism therefore gives scientists an opportunity to initiate research not initiated by practical men, the immediate utility of which is invisible. This makes it possible to launch research in the social sciences that is dictated by the general good, as represented not by a particular sponsor but by scientists as mandataries.[5]

He kept his optimism till the mid-1970s:

The pathology of social life, as expressed in the categories of thought of the bourgeois system, purposely confined socially negative events to social and individual problems. Purposely too it neglected social, and particularly institutional, determinants. It is otherwise with science in systems based on principles of socialist coexistence. Such a science has no duty to respect the taboo imposed by the various formations. On the contrary: it even has a duty to reject such a taboo.[6]

And in ending this fourth or fifth on the list of volumes on sociotechnics in 1974, he added:

Some express reservations about sociotechnics and say that it may help to promote socially negative values. One may easily answer that, just as a dentist is not only a dentist, so a sociotechnician is not only a sociotechnician, but also a citizen, a human being, an individual conscious of the rights of others and of obligations.[7]

[5] Adam Podgórecki, 'Miejsce socjotechniki w ustroju soccjalistycznym', in A. Podgórecki (ed.), *Socjotechnika. Praktyczne zastosowania socjologii*, Warsaw: KiW, 1968, p. 53.
[6] A. P[odgórecki]., Preface to A. Podgórecki (ed.), *Socjotechnika Funkcjonalność i dysfunkcjonalność instytucji*, Warsaw: KiW, 1974, p. 5.
[7] A. Podgórecki, 'Rola nauk humanistycznych w sterowaniu procesami społecznymi (strategia społecznej zmiany)', in *ibid.*, pp. 568–9.

The reason for this remark is clear. Though never tired of repeating that his beloved sociotechnics is axiologically neutral, as neutral as a knife that can be used for good or evil purposes, Podgórecki felt it necessary to psychologize the solution of the moral dilemma raised in the debate on sociotechnics, to psychologize it in the good old manner of the Positivist tradition. Our doubts concerning sociotechnics are answered by referring to the moral quality of the social engineer himself or herself. Socialism is welcomed as a form of social organization in which there is much more room for free sociotechnical activity directed at others. When asked what the guidelines are that, apart from expediency, restrict our freedom of action directed at others, the author refers us to our inner goodness, if not to locally held patterns of customs and values.

The book on the principles of sociotechnics – and these principles are the very sociotechnical rules of efficient social action – did not so much start a specific discipline in the social sciences as a certain peculiar socio-political movement which, though on a small scale, had some influence in Poland in the late 1960s and early 1970s, and traces of which may still be found in Poland. The conferences organized by Podgórecki, as well as the books he edited, have provided a point of contact for fairly heterogeneous groups of people: communists and non-communists, members of academic as well as political establishments. The curious name of the new discipline, suggesting an opportunity for the social scientist for direct influence on social reality, and for direct scientific and expert advice to be translated into a programme of practical action by politicians, was at least an occasion for probing the potential resources and opportunities that the worlds of science and of power have to offer each other. In this respect it is of the utmost interest to look into the contents of the successive volumes on sociotechnics as well as into the lists of contributors.[8]

[8] One finds there such diverse personalities and topics as, e.g., the late Colonel Dr J. Graczyk writing on 'The Influence of the Army on the Group and the Individual', ex-Ambassador Kazimierz Sidor on 'Styles of Policy of the Arab States', the ex-officer and writer Jan Gerhard on 'The Style of Charles de Gaulle's Policy', ex-deputy director of the National Bank Dr Leopold Gluck writing on expertise and experts, Prof. Jan Szczepański on access to university education, Prof. Klemens Szaniawski on decision-making, Prof. Kazimierz Doktór on the applied sociology of work, frequent

But, despite the pronounced optimism, the story ended badly. This was not due to any lack of discipline in the movement – as is sometimes suggested – but simply because the whole idea of an axiologically neutral sociotechnics was not endowed with the axiological appeal that movements in the political sphere need to have in order to attract the loyalty of followers. On the other hand the movement offering expert advice did not find its political sponsor. In such a social void the first report on the state of the country, unsolicited by the authorities, led to repression and to personal tragedy for Podgórecki, whose chair was abolished in 1977.

One of the most intriguing cases of futile expert advice has been described by one of those responsible.[9] I am referring to the scientific-political star of the late 1970s, Professor Paweł Bożyk, who in 1977 became the chief of the team of experts advising the then First Secretary of the PZPR (Communist Party), Mr Edward Gierek. After the pathetic fall of the advisee himself, Professor Bożyk described in vivid, though not detailed, prose the good intentions of the team and the faults of its sponsor in a book published in Poland in 1983. He then went to universities in America probably to teach them about his innocent experience and to support his future claims to offer further economic wisdom back home to help the millions of victims temporarily left behind.

According to Bożyk everything was fine as to the substance of the reports and memoranda prepared by the team. Ten general reports were prepared, not to mention several memoranda and hours and hours of collective and individual conversations with Mr Gierek. All this written and oral expert advice was never made public until the summer of 1980. Afterwards much of the information was published by members of the team who – with the notable exception of Professor Beksiak – duly served their term on the team. Reports made by the team after prolonged debates, including knowledgeable people from outside, were – as Professor Bożyk proudly contends – 'officially and unofficially transferred to

contributions by ex-security officer Prof. Adam Krukowski on criminal policy and by Prof. Magdalena Sokołowska on the health service. The author contributed twice as well.

9 Paweł Bożyk, *Marzenia i rzeczywistość czyli anatomia polskiego kryzysu*, Warsaw: PIW, 1983.

many people from the establishment or from outside', though such leakages cannot be equated with publication or dissemination in the usual meaning of those terms.

The reports, besides being the main way in which the team performed its supposed function,

[were] also the foundation for debates with Edward Gierek lasting for several hours. There was no unnecessary decorum during these meetings. Members of the team at large criticized social and economic policy and advocated dozens of necessary changes in it. Edward Gierek rarely opposed the opinions expressed by team members, though he sometimes pointed out that he had a different view about a given matter. He never, however, questioned a critical assessment of the state of the economy.[10]

This puzzling information, so crucial to any evaluation of the work of the whole team as well as of the advisee himself, was confirmed by other members of the team too, sociologists, economists, lawyers, engineers, all of them professors and members of the Communist Party. Wladyslaw Markiewicz writes:

Expert advice and statements prepared by the team of advisers were absolutely open, drastically realistic and many-sided in approach.

Bohdan Glinski:

The first expert advice that we presented to E. Gierek was unequivocal in its content – the government is conducting a mistaken policy that will result in catastrophe.

Antoni Rajkiewicz:

Everybody could write whatever he thought. And the talks with the First Secretary too were absolutely free [. . .] There were no suggestions of control over the substance. At the first meeting when one of the members started to express his gratitude to E. Gierek for being appointed to the team of advisers, the First Secretary said he expected to be told only the truth, as he had had enough of the temples being built to him and as the documents he received from various sources all contained the same evaluations – he, however, wanted to know the truth about the situation, though he reserved to himself the right of discussion and reaching a conclusion.

[10] *Ibid.*, pp. 197–8.

Augustyn Wós:

Our team was a team of scientific advisers. Members [...] never participated in the decision-making process.

Alojzy Melich:

We came to the conclusion that our main task was to change the boss's mentality (!), to make him comprehend the seriousness of the economic and social situation, and the consequent need for prompt action.[11]

Józef Pajestka:

Were these data known to the decision makers? There is no doubt of it. Did they understand it and how? – That is another question.[12]

Once published, the team's experience was fairly unanimously evaluated in a negative way, though this does not mean that such an evaluation was made of all the participants. Perhaps Professor Andrzej Tymowski came to the best conclusion in his review of the book:

In conclusion I would like to emphasize that the experiment at giving scientific advice described in the book ought to be considered a failure, though an instructive one. A failure, because none of the scientific knowledge was implemented in the improperly conducted social and economic policy, in the system of power that was inadequate to the contemporary country. Instructive, because events proved that the method of enlightening decision makers behind closed doors is inefficient, if it is not accompanied by proper social pressures, which need, however, different sociotechnics.[13]

Tymowski is one of the few social scientists entitled to pass such harsh judgements. He himself all his life followed two rules in giving expert advice: first, always say what you think on the subject and, second, say what you think on the subject whenever there is occasion to do so. No wonder he struggled with the authorities for years to get the very notion of a social minimum accepted in the official language. He started with his book published in an

[11] After Bożyk, *ibid.*, pp. 221–2.
[12] Józef Pajestka, *Polski kryzys lat 1980–1981. Jak do niego doszlo i co rokuje*, Warsaw: KiW, 1981, p. 53.
[13] Andrzej Tymowski, 'Patologia doradzania', *Nowe Książki*, 11 (1983), p. 101.

edition of fifty copies; in 1980–1 he tried to convince Solidarność of his views about rational social policy; now he tries to do the same with the government. According to him the main criterion is the ability to publicize one's own point of view. If one is right – he seems to think – then in the longer run success will come.

If we were to represent the history of scientific expert advising in Poland graphically, it is beyond all doubt that the relevant curve would reach its climax in the years of massive rebellion between 1980 and 1981. The real need for enlightened advice from informed people led the strikers on the Baltic coast to seek help from those who arrived with a letter supporting the strikes. The letter itself originated during the long strikes of August 1980, when the silence of First Secretary Gierek and the hostility of the mass media made people afraid of an imminent bloody pacification, on the model of Poznan 1956, Gdańsk and Szczecin 1970 or, at least, Radom and Ursus 1976. It was initiated by Tadeusz Mazowiecki of the Warsaw Club for the Catholic Intelligentsia, the editor of the Catholic *Więź* monthly, a former independent Catholic parliamentary representative. The letter was worded so as to express the opinion of intellectuals not directly involved in the conflict, supporting the just demands which the authorities should take into consideration and, above all, appealing to the authorities to refrain from using violence. The letter was signed overnight by dozens of eminent intellectuals: both scientists and artists, members and non-members of the Communist Party. Bronisław Geremek, a historian from the Polish Academy of Sciences, in this way became a messenger, transmitting the support (at least moral and verbal) of the nation's intelligentsia for the strikers who had already won some local support from intellectuals on an individual basis. The leaders of the strike in the Gdańsk area were eager to get help from people who had not, in a politically inconvenient way, been labelled as members of the KOR (a Committee for the Defence of Workers established after the pacification of strikers in 1976); and they asked for assistance in negotiating with the authorities' representatives. Both sides, therefore, used their own 'experts'. The role was institutionalized by means of the lists of names exchanged between the different sides in the negotiations and special permits providing legitimation both then and subsequently. The whole issue of the role of experts was, of course, very complex from the start. The mediatory tone of the intellectuals' letter might suggest a mediatory role to be played by them in the negotiations between the strikers and the authorities, but it became clear to Mazowiecki and Geremek and their group from the first moment that such a role could not be sustained if their advice were to be accepted. What was sought, moreover, was not mediation but help in strengthening a partisan position. Except for a professor of law, an otherwise bright and sympathetic man, everybody in the group acting on behalf of the signatories of the intellectuals' letter agreed to join the strikers and form their intellectual division, to put it in the most appropriate terms. On the other hand, when the experts arrived, they felt their own power, as behind the line in Warsaw, permanent arrangements were made for co-ordinating the activities and resources of signatories to the letter, so that problems sent in from Gdańsk for solution were settled, the legal and other work requested was dealt with, the new team of experts was sent to another striking centre in Szczecin, and alternate experts were recruited and briefed.

For the experienced the word 'Solidarność' evokes the word 'expert'. Out of the small leading group of experts in the Inter-Factory Strike Committee, which won applause during the aftermath of the victory of August 1980, the institution of experts developed farther and more widely. Here it is enough to mention that, besides the 'original' experts, the larger body of members of the Consultative Programming Council and of the Centre for Socio-Professional work at the KKP (the National Co-ordinating Commission of Solidarność) were given the official title: 'experts of the KKP'. Furthermore, there were attempts from time to time to create competitive expert teams at the KKP apart from this list, and this resulted in practice in recognizing as an 'expert' the sociologist Jadwiga Staniszkis, who was not affiliated with the aforementioned groups and bodies; and all the regional branches of the new trade union had their permanent or *ad hoc* experts who, in such larger centres as Warsaw, Łódź, Cracow or Poznan, were well organized and very influential. Throughout 1981 other social organizations also organized teams of experts to work on their behalf and to assist them in their negotiations with the authorities as well as in other activities. In a sense the typical figure of those days was the fiery social activist who moved between the platform

and his experts: advisers who wrote speeches, prepared statements, planned action, exchanged views with government advisers
and briefed the foreign and Polish press.

Not surprisingly, the role of the experts was hotly debated from
the very beginning. The strike leaders, following the advice of the
experts, accepted, with slightly different wording, the clause
recognizing the leading role of the Communist Party in the
country which was already in the amended Constitution despite
the protests made in 1971. As this clause was quickly invoked by
the government and party against any claims that went beyond the
limits of the Gdańsk and other agreements, the experts were soon
burdened with responsibility for a clause afterwards felt to be an
unnecessary, and at the very least inconvenient, concession to the
authorities. It is a crude fact of mass psychology that what is one
day seen as an almost unexpected victory achieved against chilling
risks, is experienced the day after as an incomprehensible sign of
weakness – a weakness no longer experienced. Lech Wałęsa,
therefore, as the strike leader, was criticized for this as well as the
experts. It may be added that such criticisms help greatly in
putting the one criticized on the defensive, or at least they seek
such a result.

When, in the first months of 1981, Solidarność suffered from
the widespread discontent of members and activists as the new
union's activities were blocked by the government, Jadwiga
Staniszkis dramatically voiced the resentments that were growing
amongst the union's middle-level militants. She thought that
fulfilment of the demands and interests of the members of
Solidarność needed continued pressure from the movement as
such. The regional, middle-level, activists felt frustrated because
they needed to sustain an aura of radicalism even if they were not
in fact as radical as they seemed. However, Staniszkis did not
explain the apparent contradiction in this picture. After criticizing
the way meetings of the KKP were conducted, she also stressed
that:

All this results in disenchantment and some resignation amongst
KKP members who, when they arrive back in the regions, are often
criticized for misrepresenting the rank and file members of the union
and for being insufficiently radical, for not voting the right way. Thus
they pay with their authority for the way in which KKP functions.

There are more and more doubts amongst the workers about the role of experts and an anti-intellectual mood is appearing.[14]

Among other remedies she advocated the decentralizing of decision making, so that regional union branches could vote by telex through their representatives, bound by the regional vote; absolutely prohibiting secret dealings with the government; ordering structures and ranking priorities, etc. It is interesting, and symptomatic of the climate of internal debates in the union, how often she advocated suppressing the role of experts:

> The right to make compromises ought to lie with KKP as a whole after consultation with (regional) MKZs, and not with narrow working groups which are often more than half composed of non-elected persons (experts) [...] KKP needs to create a permanent group to contact Parliament (so that contact will not be confined to secret 'diplomacy' by experts) [...] The manner of working with experts should be changed, creating a bank of names of specialists from various fields at KKP and MKZs, asking different experts on any given matter so that their opinions can be compared.[15]

According to the assessment I made at the time, Staniszkis was, more or less consciously, accepting one of the competing viewpoints in particular: that of the union's regional activist.[16] In fact, as I was able to confirm personally, problems about compliance with the rules and related matters were similar at all levels of the union's organizational ladder, from the KKP at the top to the local chapters at the bottom. The dissatisfaction felt by middle-level union activists was a quite healthy phenomenon when considered in relation to other facts. Really active movements which are on the move, as she expected this one to be, are fuelled by such dissatisfactions felt at all levels of internal organization. What I did not say at the time was that, in expressing distrust for the experts, the author accepted the complaints as true and, contrary to normal sociological practice, did not ask *Cui bono?* And the daily life of Solidarność provided enough evidence that, in

---

14 Jadwiga Staniszkis, 'O niedemokratycznych tendencjach w Solidarności', *Robotnik*, 74 (20 March 1981).
15 *Ibid.*
16 Jacek Kurczewski, 'O niedemokratycznych tendencjach w Solidarności', *Robotnik*, 74 (20 March 1981).

addition to their overt function of providing expert professional advice, the experts served a very important, and by no means secondary, function as well: that of channelling the dissatisfactions and doubts of trade union politicians about their own decision making. Though it was not usual for a leader, when asked to explain some disputed decision, to point the finger at experts as the scapegoats, this result was brought about in a more subtle way. It seems to me that criticism was aimed at the experts instead of directly at fellow union militants and activists; but Lech Wałęsa at least, who most often came under fire from his ambitious colleagues, never defended himself by blaming his experts.

I will return to this point later. But let me note here that the charge made against the experts that they had too much influence on decisions made by the union and its various agencies had a counterpart in one of the criticisms made by intellectuals: this time that the experts too often yielded to the masses and to the wishes of their leaders. For instance Jerzy Jedlicki, an historian, observed in May 1981 in a discussion of the role of independent trade unionism in the Polish socio-political system:

An important question was raised during this debate: is it possible to have, in any measure, some 'intellectual direction' of the movement, which would shape the opinions of its members and activists? I think that the Centre for Socio-Professional Work was formed, *inter alia* in the conviction that such a shaping of opinion is possible and that it ought to be attempted. I believe in this connection that it is bad that up to now the numerous army of intellectuals, sensible people who willingly participated in the union's work, only played the role of experts within it. Their professional economic, sociological or legal knowledge serves the union's interests. The relatively ephemeral orders issued by Solidarność are furthered. But I think the role of intellectuals should not be confined to that. They should also have the function of creating early warning systems. As has often been confirmed, we do of course have many built-in mechanisms of fear, we are less well equipped for direct action, we do not have the courage for initiating new and great things. But perhaps we have in us subtler antennae for detecting dangerous areas. And perhaps we are better able to formulate the longer term aims which the movement needs to discover as it develops. This task, which is one that can be performed by men of letters and of science, has not yet been fulfilled. What has happened has been self-abnegation before the spontaneous power of the movement of which we also are members. We decide only how to serve its interests and we do not – no, for God's sake not! – sometimes oppose such of its demands as seem to us irrational, or even dangerous. This is a dangerous self-abnegation.[17]

It is striking how opposed to each other are the views taken by the two intellectuals, Staniszkis and Jedlicki, about the same social role: that of the expert. While the former wishes to explain this role in terms of perfect servitude to the interests of the members and the movement itself, the latter sees the role of the expert as an already over-simplified disguise assumed by the intellectual, whose real task goes far beyond anything imagined by his supposed technical social knowledge. Staniszkis devotes her energy to devising ways in which the expert's very individuality can be neglected. Experts are to be organized in an office or bank, their assignments to the organization are to be only temporary and *ad hoc* when and only when their services are called for, their services are to be asked for only in respect of specialized and compartmentalized knowledge, and even in this case constant checking of the experts' reliability and skill is to be guaranteed by means of involving the competitive services of others. The logical development of this model is to register all members according to their skills and to call on their services only when, and for so long as, they are needed. We do not know the extent of the bank of expert advisers working on a voluntary or a paid basis. We need to remember that the expert advice was offered to Solidarność *gratis*, except for those few front-rank experts who were employed by the union, and for some of the technical costs like travel and accommodation; this is in contrast with union officials who, following the wishes of the members, were relatively well paid. Jedlicki thinks in terms of an intellectual who must not degrade himself or herself by becoming the blind follower of decisions and orders originating from others. Staniszkis thinks in terms of the masses, the activists, the organization, and Jedlicki in terms of the intelligentsia as a social category with a special vocation deriving from their intellectual potential. According to Staniszkis an intellectual, once he or she has entered the service of the union, is under an obligation

17 Jerzy Jedlicki, '"Solidarność" w polskimsystemie społeczno-politycznym', *Ruche Związkowy, Zeszyty OPSZ*, vol. 1, Warsaw: IWZZ, 1981, pp. 15–18.

to follow its orders; whereas according to Jedlicki an intellectual, even when serving the union, has a duty to transform it according to his or her conscience. This apparent opposition ceases to be symmetrical, however, when we realize that Staniszkis herself has in fact simply followed Jedlicki's idea, by serving the union through suggesting such necessary changes as her conscience dictates; though there would be no freedom for other intellectuals to do the same if her advice were followed to its conclusion.

But what was the real situation in Solidarność? A fragment from the transcripts of a meeting of the KKP during the same period may serve as a good example of the real interaction in the union between men of power and men of learning.[18]

Z. Bujak: I request statements from the experts on the proposed strike deadlines. Short ones. Thank you.
[...]
A. Celiński (Chairman): There is a counter-proposal.
P. Kosmowski: Yes, a counter-proposal. Let those who led the strike speak on the strike deadlines and the ways of leading them. Those who have led strikes can say most about them, not the experts. Experts are not experts on strikes.
[...]
B. Geremek (expert on the KKP): It seems to me it would run counter to the role of the experts if you were to listen to their opinions about the timetable now. If you want to listen to the advisers it could be done during the debate when arguments are considered for the alternative solutions that you will later decide on.
[...]
L. Wałęsa: Ladies and gentlemen, I'm sorry, I have a different opinion. Why do we have expert, outside people? To elicit what a general strike is in principle? I don't know if half of you know what a general strike is. [...] Even so, the very proposal for a general strike is, I also think ... I think it is bizarre. Bizarre! It can't be passed. And the experts ought to make statements even on this topic, since they know a bit about it. And it's not true that someone has been leading the strike. You have led a strike but not throughout the whole country and not a general strike.

---

[18] Citations taken from transcripts edited as *Posiedzenie Krajowej Komisji Porozumiewawczej NSZZ 'Solidarność' 23–24 marca 1981 r.*, Warsaw: Nowa, 1986, pp. 64–76.

That's why I again ask for a discussion and for the experts, for us to listen to the experts, so they can explain this issue for us. [...]

W. *Siła-Nowicki (expert of the KKP):* Ladies and gentlemen, I am taking the floor as one of the experts on the formal issue. We did not get to know each other just today. I am willing to serve in all sorts of offices and functions from the lowest to the highest. But I am never going to be a sham. So if all decisions are going to be made by the union after listening to the experts, and the essential decision is going to be made without our voice, then I am extremely sorry, but I will bow to the Commission and take my leave! Me, a clown – never! That is why, ladies and gentlemen, if we are to be taken seriously, please listen to my colleagues Mazowiecki, Geremek, Olszewski and me. (Applause) [...]

K. *Modzelewski:* [...] I make a formal motion: to open a debate in which both members of the National Co-ordinating Committee and the experts will be entitled to participate. I appeal to the members of the KKP to believe that they themselves have the power to decide, whatever the experts will say [...] [...]

M. *Domińczyk:* Ladies and gentlemen, to start with I'd like to remind you, especially the members of the KKP, of the earlier meetings. Why are we recoiling against this ... against this group from the team of experts? We need to recognize that all these decisions and meetings do not originate with us, but that it's done by the team of experts. I will give you an example ... Please don't interrupt, this is serious. Well, we work like this: first we hear the views and decisions of particular MKZs, don't we? Then debate follows and statements by the experts, and what the experts say simply changes everything at once ... our, these, another decision emerges. It was always like this – remember.

Voice from the floor: [unreadable] [...]

L. *Wałęsa:* [...] I want to say that it has never yet happened that an expert has spoken out against anybody from one of the regions. Let us behave in the same way. That is why they are here, in many cases we couldn't manage without them. I propose ... It was probably right, don't let the experts speak at the end, but let them be treated normally, just as we are; hands up please. If we do it like this, the possibility of distortion right at the end won't come about [...]

[...]

T. Mazowiecki (expert of the KKP): First I'd like to say that there are no experts on the matter we're discussing here. There simply are no experts on the matters that are being decided here. Nobody in the world ever faced the task [. . .] of giving expert advice in the face of decisions like this. That is why I speak with this title, but I speak above all as a member of Solidarność and as a citizen of this country faced with the serious decisions you have to take [. . .]
[. . .]
J. Olszewski (expert of the KKP): [. . .] If I take the floor it is because I have been asked to reply. And I want to warn you at the outset that I have two requests to make. First, please take into account the fact that my voice is not just the voice of an expert, since the matter on which I am going to speak transcends my professional competence [. . .] Just before I came to the microphone, one of my colleagues on the National Commission, this young colleague came up to me and said he wanted to ask me not to take offence at the words that had been addressed to the experts since – as he put it – 'we youths are hotheads'. Ladies and gentlemen I have no grievance, but I do ask for reciprocity. Please don't feel offended at what I shall say in a moment. We are not here to say pleasant things, but important things.

This is perhaps an unforgivably long quotation from a document that is both political and sociological. One needs to take into account what is the question at issue. The young union had been humiliated by a physical assault by the security forces on one of its regional leaders. Faced with what was known as the 'Bydgoszcz affair', the representatives of the union pressed for open defiance of the ruling apparatus in the country at large with the help of a general strike. Wałęsa had been in secret talks in which he had also been warned of the possibility of foreign intervention. Activists who were sincerely expressing the [renewed revolutionary mood of the mass membership started to discuss the timetable for a strike after it had become clear that a strike was a must. In such dramatic circumstances as these Wałęsa and four experts entered into a long struggle which resulted finally in acceptance of Wałęsa's moderate proposal to have a four-hour warning strike followed by renewed negotiations with the government before deciding on a general strike.

The stormy exchange, only small fragments of which have been cited, was not concerned with what particular technical issue was to be assigned to one specialization or another in the division of knowledge, but a political decision: 'political' in the common sense that far-reaching consequences, the lives of millions of people, could depend on it; and 'complex' in the sense that making such a decision involved millions of small consequences in all sorts of domains. It looks as though there was no exaggeration in what the experts said: that they appeared not merely as experts, or, rather, that being 'experts' only gave them a right to speak on the same level as Commission members, a formal right to speak, that is to persuade, that is to influence, but not a substantive right to say anything that was authoritative *per se*. They expressed this by referring to the common denominator joining them with their listeners, membership of the union; though this could not be the case made for the lawyers Siła-Nowicki and Olszewski, for whom common citizenship was the foundation on which the authority of their statements rested.

There was also an interesting sociological context by means of which the experts recovered the ground they had lost through the aggressive attitude of 'youth'. Two lawyers had spent years acting for the defence in political trials, and saw former clients amongst the audience. Difference in age could be played for as a positive factor only in so far as the years dividing them were not lost years. The gains made by the experts derived from widespread knowledge that they had spent years and decades of their lives in a proper way, working on the same side as that on which 'youth' was now working. Of course this 'youth' included some who also had their own independent political records but they were in a minority on the KKP. The latter was a much more heterogeneous group including people with a much lower level of education, prestige and experience. The experts considered as a group were, therefore, on a higher level than the average of the members of the KKP. This may also explain some of the attacks made on the experts.

On the other hand, one needs to realize how often the lines dividing expertise and power were blurred. In fact, the KKP as well as the regional MZKs included a much higher percentage of people with higher education that did the union as a whole, and this over-representation of the better educated increased, first, with each level of the union's hierarchy and, second, with successive elections. This strange situation is best illustrated by two who were opposition activists from the late 1960s and who worked together; in 1980–1 one of them, Jacek Kuron, best known for his involvement in the KOR, served Solidarność as an expert, the second Karol Modzelewski, an historian of international renown, successfully went through the routine trade union elections to become a member of KKP. In time the number of professors, lawyers, research workers, university teachers, mass media people, increased, unbalancing the relationship between them and the body of experts. Yet the institution survived and, verbally abused until the last days of the union's official existence, experts continued to fight for what they conceived to be good both for the union and for the country. Ironically, the last moments of the final meeting of the National Commission on 12 December 1981 were devoted to the presentation of a list of members of the proposed Council of National Salvation, a list consisting solely of professors, some of whom were to reappear years later in the Consultative Council of General Wojciech Jaruzelski.

This being the best way to stop our excursion into history, let us attempt a step by step recapitulation of the whole story. In the case of Solidarność the divergence of views concerning the role of experts has been noted: some wanted to turn them into narrow specialists who must be suspiciously cross-checked, while others expected them to exert pressure and influence to lead those they were advising in the direction they thought proper. Even the fragmentary evidence I have quoted seems to show how naive was the first, technical, view of the experts. Its naivety springs from the falsity of the very assumption on which it is based: that the issues that have to be tackled in a political process are to be fragmented into pieces that can be assigned to this or that scientific specialism. What may be possible in engineering seems impossible in the social engineering of reality. There are no specialists on strikes except those who have organized them while, at the same time, to have organized a strike does not mean that you will know what to do next time. Changeability of context, contextuality of situation, situational character of decision making – all this speaks against the assumption. Perhaps in this respect Podgórecki's strange notion of 'sociotechnics' as a new branch of social science gains in value, in the sense that from the point of view of social

praxis the distinctions that are important may be different from
those taken into account in the development of theoretical sciences
like sociology, psychology or economics. Moreover, 'sociotechnics' was developed in relation to concrete practical matters –
leaving aside methodologically futile general discussions – such as
warfare, the army, the provision of health services, success on the
market or in negotiations. This may also explain away part of the
failure of Gierek's experts and other similar efforts in Poland and
elsewhere. The point is that you fail at the very start if you think in
inductive terms, beginning with the field of expertise compartmentalized into various fragments to be analysed and then
summed up or, worse, summed up by the sponsor or recipient of
the expert advice himself or herself. What is usually needed from
experts and advisers is an educated guess at the general decision to
be made in the concrete circumstances, involving a general
opinion which, yes, needs to be elaborated in terms of details but
which is not a simple sum total of these. When Gierek's former
experts complain that he probably never grasped what a catastro-
phic picture emerged from what they wrote and said to him, we
cannot rule out *a priori* the possibility that they never actually
expressed the catastrophe they had in mind and that, rather than
trying to convince through details, they needed to start with their
main revelation in a brutal form.

But now we come to the nature of the relationship. I have
deliberately chosen my examples to show how diverse in fact this
may be. On one hand real conversation and interaction, on the
other purported dialogue that is in fact a soliloquy. Political
involvement through protests, open letters, unsolicited reports
and memoranda, corresponds closely to the sociotechnical movement which is full of discussions on how others are to influence
social reality. The correspondence consists in the fact that all such
actions are no more than a doorway which the second party need
not enter. Repression is often the only visible reaction and all that
remains to one is to console oneself with the pleasures of a clean
conscience. But all this looks different considered from the point
of view of the actor's intention – whether or not he or she is willing
to co-operate with power. The co-operation may sometimes be
well concealed as when by the strong wording of one's protest one
deliberately provides the authority with a pretext for doing

something. But if there is no such intention, there is also no need to check the futility or efficacy of one's action. This may be clear, but it is less clear whether one's action is to be judged in moral terms. Again, from the actor's own point of view, yes! – but since no interaction was intended, there is no reason to make any judgement about its unwanted existence or non-existence.

How different are cases where a relationship really does develop, no matter on whose initiative! And how these cases can differ amongst themselves! We have seen both Gierek's and Solidarność's experts alarming their respective sponsors. In the first case, we are told, there was no opposition. Gierek listens, nods, asks for details, and does nothing. The positive assumption is that Bożyk and the other experts hope to succeed next time and so continue their work, however futile it may look from the outside. Only one of the team leaves because he does not see any results. The Solidarność experts fight with a 'sponsor' who denigrates them, does not seem to listen, forgets to ask their opinion; but they win. They threaten to resign if not listened to. The end awaiting both stories is catastrophe, but there is a difference in the judgements to be pronounced on the two cases. How is one to explicate this difference?

There are always two kinds of judgement to be made on experts. The first relates to the content of their advice, whether it was good or bad according to our standards: 'content' here includes context, the addressee of the advice, its intended and achieved results. This is the most natural approach to involvement in political life. But there is another kind of judgement too, that has more to do with the relationship to power than to the substance of advice. Once he has given his opinion the expert always starts afresh in his role. One can be expert only through holding an opinion. One of Gombrowicz's heroes says he is not so mad as either to have or not to have an opinion in our present times. But one has to in order to be an expert and this is why one is sought after. But the relationship has to be interactive. One is an expert only in so far as one's advice is taken into account or, at least partially, followed. Nobody is expert just in and for himself or herself. In this sense Gierek's advisers ceased to be experts after their first report was not implemented in economic and social practice. It may be that in some cases we totally reject the relationship as offending our moral sense, while still appreciating the quality of the bond itself. Advice that is otherwise stupid must be pressed on the advisee if the adviser is to hold a proper status in our eyes. If the experts are stupid, the authority that has selected them is responsible, but if the authority is stupid, responsibility falls on the experts.

But there is something about the distinction that worries me and makes me think that the idea behind the title of this paper has not been dealt with. The 'expert' is a figure of interest in so far as he or she mediates between two forces and two worlds. This means in fact that the expert combines both elements. Even Gierek's failed experts were surrounded by an aura of power for those outside the arena, though they themselves explained their failure in terms of lack of power. One may think that it was the illusion of possible power that kept them in office. The Solidarność experts speak as though they had power, and in fact they did. It consisted in the will to represent the deep interests of those same millions whom the union activists also wished to represent. This common will was behind the power both of the experts and of those whom they advised. I think this is the deepest lesson to be learned, even if it is not new. Reference to the common stock of values to be served by both men of learning and men of power provides an opportunity for an exchange in which the experts serve as mediators in an ultimate fulfilment of their vocation. This is something the sociotechnical approach neglects by focussing its attention on the relationship between the two.

6

Textual responsibility

J.-J. LECERCLE

ETYMOLOGY AND PARADOX

My starting point is a simple question: how can you ascribe responsibility for his text to an author? I shall attempt to capture the straightforward and commonsensical, but at the same time slightly odd, flavour of this question. For in an obvious way it is right that an author should be held responsible for his text. Authorship is a kind of agency: the text is a result of a series of speech-acts, or, synecdochically, of a single inclusive one. And as the law of libel shows *speech*-acts involve the same kind of responsibility as common-or-garden ones. Yet – and this is where the slightest uneasiness creeps in – like certain (but not all) acts, they seem to be defeasible (to use this old legal term which has recently found a new lease of life in pragmatics[1]). We all know the warning which appears at the beginning of so many films: this is a purely fictitious story, and any resemblance between the characters and actual persons can only be the result of coincidence. From which it appears that fiction may involve the same responsibility as straightforward public insult, but that the charge can be defeated because the author is allowed to plead coincidence, i.e. irresponsibility. 'This obnoxious character may have looked strangely like you, only it is not, for *I did not mean it so*.' This particular type of defeasibility (a more straightforward type would be: I seem to have acted wrongly, but I did it for the sake of a more general good, which overrides the local evil) is the cause of my

[1] See H. L. A. Hart, 'The Ascription of Responsibility and Rights', in *Proceedings of the Aristotelian Society*, 49 (1948–9), pp. 171–94; see also S. C. Levinson, *Pragmatics*, Cambridge: Cambridge University Press, 1983.

uneasiness. For it shows that the ascription of responsibility to an author, and the possible plea of irresponsibility, presuppose a theory of meaning as intention (*vouloir-dire*) – for instance, Grice's theory of non-natural meaning.[2] The trouble with that theory is that it is highly dubious. What happens, then, to the author's responsibility, if we hold a conception where meaning does not reside in the speaker's intention to communicate a message to the hearer, but is rather an effect of the workings of the linguistic system, partly, and sometimes totally, independent from the speaker's intention? Can an author be responsible for his text if, to use the Heideggerian phrase, 'it is language that speaks'?

We might be tempted to dismiss the problem by saying that in the case of a text, or of a speech-act, 'responsibility' is metaphorical. But apart from the fact that such a move would be counter-intuitive, it would be deeply misguided, for authorial responsibility, far from being an indirect or peripheral kind of responsibility, is on the contrary central to the concept. In a nutshell, etymology or usage suggest that (a) authorship is a relation of responsibility and (b) responsibility is a textual, or linguistic, relation. I have in fact already supported claim (a) by assimilating authorship to a form of agency: an act, like a text, typically involves an author. If we read Michel Foucault's famous essay, 'What Is an Author?', we shall discover that what we know as 'the author of the text', a fairly recent historical development, is contemporary with the appearance of the law of libel, i.e. with the practice of ascribing penal responsibility for a text. ('Historically, this type of ownership [i.e. authorship] has always been subsequent to what one might call penal appropriation.'[3]) An author is an author to the extent that he can be punished. The argument for (b) is etymological ('responsibility', like 'answerability', its Saxon doublet, implies response, i.e. dialogue) and grammatical. The basic grammar of a 'responsibility sentence' is: x is responsible for y to z. But this has the same form as the classic schema of communication: x says y to z. To be responsible is to be prepared to answer questions about what one is responsible for. Responsi-

[2] H. P. Grice, 'Meaning', in D. D. Steinberg and L. A. Jakobovits (eds.), *Semantics*, Cambridge: Cambridge University Press, 1971.
[3] M. Foucault, 'What Is an Author?', in P. Rabinow (ed.), *The Foucault Reader*, New York: Pantheon Books, 1984, p. 108.

bility is profoundly dialogic, even if, following Canetti on the use of questions,[4] we consider that the language games which involve questions are biassed, more adequate for the establishment of relations of power (*we* are asking the questions here' as the interrogator says in the B-type thriller) than for the free flow of communication. Has it not been remarked that one is responsible not for felicitous events, but for events that go wrong or are likely to (this is even clearer in the case of 'answerable')? So my provisional conclusions are that (a) authorial responsibility *is* responsibility; (b) conversely, responsibility is a textual or linguistic relation, presupposing a theory of meaning whose historical and theoretical limitations are only too apparent.

It is because I hold that the theory of meaning-as-intention is inadequate that I perceive a problem in the notion of 'authorship responsibility'. Since this is a conference on the 'political responsibility of intellectuals', I shall start my discussion by evoking an historical and political question: the punishment meted out at the end of the war to those well-known intellectuals who had supported the Nazis and fascists or had collaborated with them. As we all know, Robert Brasillach was shot, Ezra Pound was interned in a psychiatric institution for a number of years, Céline had to lie low for a while, and Heidegger found himself under a cloud. To be perfectly clear about the matter, I must state that I do not intend to deal with the *historical* problem. I have no quarrel with the punishment imposed on these people – this is not one of these attempts at rehabilitation which are at present fashionable in France. If the question were asked bluntly, my answer would be that, yes, in the circumstances I can understand why they sentenced Brasillach to death, although I am not a supporter of the death penalty. Nor do I claim to have made a special study of the facts of the cases. My point has more limited scope: why did they shoot Brasillach, and declare Pound mad? Why this difference in treatment, whereby one was held responsible for his obnoxious texts, and the other irresponsible for broadcasts which I am told (for it is difficult to get hold of the texts even now) were equally disastrous? Of course, an immediate answer might be that the details of the cases are different, the amount of guilt not equal, the

[4] See E. Canetti, *Crowds and Power*, 'Question and Answer', London: Gollancz, 1962.

circumstances of the arrests not the same, which accounts for the difference in treatment. But does it, even if we grant this? Probably not, for the difference is not quantitative, in the amount of punishment (the death penalty v. ten years), but qualitative: one was judged responsible, and tried; the other irresponsible, and interned, after a token trial (in order to be treated, not punished). With the consequent paradox, which is at the heart of my problem, that this reputed madman had, in the immediately preceding month, written some of the best-known poems in the English language, the *Pisan Cantos*. As a professional student of literature, I must confess that I am glad they did not shoot Pound, as they thought for a time they would, or as the British hanged Lord Haw Haw. But, not being a follower of Lombroso, i.e. not equating genius with a form of madness, I cannot help being struck by the paradox. All the more so as I have a lurking suspicion that if Lord Haw Haw was hanged, it is because he was *William* Joyce, not James, i.e. a nonentity, and that if Brasillach was expendable, it was also because he was a second-rate writer, whereas the literary recognition granted to Céline and Pound made them untouchable. Again, I have no quarrel with this state of affairs – indeed, my whole point is to give more precise meaning to this trivial statement – but, stated in this form, it does not solve my problem. Authorial responsibility and irresponsibility remain mysteries. But perhaps we have now an idea of where to look for an answer: if one's place in the literary canon determines the extent of one's responsibility, we ought to look at the ways literary criticism makes up this canon, and ascribes responsibility for a text to its author.

EXTENDED RESPONSIBILITY VERSUS EXTENDED IRRESPONSIBILITY

Traditionally, literary criticism, or its ancestor, textual criticism, has conceived the relation between author and text in two different ways. I propose to call them extended responsibility and extended irresponsibility. Either the author is totally responsible for his text, down to the slightest detail, and corrupt lines or words must be carefully weeded out, or the author – I should say the scriptor, for the very term 'author' belongs to the first conception – is only someone's mouthpiece: the god that speaks through the oracle, the dream that dictates his words to the poet. The first conception could also be called theological, the second Romantic.

To evoke the theological conception, we can look at three types of critical practice. The first was rife among the Alexandrian grammarians who sought to restore the purity of Homer's text by tracking down interpolations. The criteria they use to decide which lines are interpolated sketch a theory of the 'natural' narrative – a natural narrative being one in which the author says what he means, and the text is made up of only what the author actually meant. Todorov, who studies the practice,[5] has isolated six main 'laws' for the natural, or 'primitive' narrative. These are:

1. The law of verisimilitude, whereby the actions and speeches of the characters must abide by the rules of psychological verisimilitude – a speech made out of character by, say, Achilles, cannot have been composed by Homer.
2. The law of the unity of style – stylistic uncertainty, or the appearance, within the same passage, of various levels of style, can only be due to corruption.
3. The law of the priority of the serious, whereby the comic cannot precede the serious version of an anecdote (Marx's theory of historical repetition as farce is a distant offspring).
4. The law of non-contradiction, which, every Shakespearian critic knows, applies to Lady Macbeth and her children.
5. The law of non-repetition, which states that repetition can only be the outcome of corruption – a responsible author does not repeat himself.
6. The law of non-digression, which states that any digression from the main action is a late addition to the text.

Behind this, of course, there lurks the figure of the responsible author, Homer without the nodding: a conventional psychologist, perfectly mastering a constant style, a serious author who rarely indulges in comedy, and only as an afterthought, and whose high sense of responsibility forbids him to have recourse to contradiction, repetition and digression. The most striking point about those refreshing 'laws' is that they are meant to create an author, Homer, who may not have existed as a single person, and therefore

5 T. Todorov, 'Le Récit primitif', in *Poétique de la prose*, Paris: Seuil, 1971, pp. 66–77.

that they construct a text which, as such, never was. They can therefore be seen as a means of imposing authorship, after the event, on a naturally irresponsible text, a matter of conjuring up a ghost rather than describing a reality. Not to mention the fact that most modern texts, even if *they* can be ascribed to an individual author, are beyond the pale of this natural aesthetics: Pound *must* have been completely mad to write the *Pisan Cantos* as he did (indeed, one of the symptoms mentioned by the psychiatrists who certified him was his tendency to rambling, i.e. to systematic digression).

The second practice is that of Biblical criticism: how to sort out the apocryphal from the genuine. Foucault[6] cites Saint Jerome on how to find out whether several works have been written by the same author. The learned father proposes four criteria: first, if one of the books is inferior to the others, it must be struck off the list; secondly, if one book contradicts the doctrine of the others (poor old Wittgenstein!), it is apocryphal (it is now obvious that the second critical practice is largely a repetition of the first); thirdly, the same applies if the work is written in a different style from the others; fourthly, if the work mentions events that occurred after the author's death, these passages at least must be considered as interpolated. I must say I like the down-to-earth aspect of the last criterion. But it does contribute to the building up of a picture of the author as (in Foucault's terms) first, a constant level of value; secondly, a field of theoretical coherence; thirdly, a stylistic unity; fourthly, a historical figure at the crossroads of a number of events. As Foucault shows, this figure is an historical one: texts have not always needed an author; it is not obvious that they so do any longer. But we must remember that the science of 'discourse analysis' first appeared during the war in the United States, where techniques similar to these (although more sophisticated) were devised to trace concealed Nazi propaganda in texts, i.e. to ascribe political responsibility to shifty authors. Indeed, the criteria seem to be close to those used in trials: we must make sure that the defendant is the right person (he can hardly be held responsible for events that occurred before his birth), that he is coherent in his acts (i.e. that he did not act in a state of temporary insanity). And if

---

[6] Foucault, 'What Is an Author?', pp. 110–11.

the facts have not been established beyond doubt, defence lawyers will certainly make much of the fact that the crime their client is alleged to have committed does not tally with his usual behaviour, that it defies the law of psychological verisimilitude. There are indeed strange parallels between authorial and penal responsibility.

My last instance describes the emergence of the criticism of attribution, as opposed to the criticism of evaluation, in the field of art history, and its insertion within the developing paradigm of criticism as detective work. I am referring here to a well-known essay by the Italian historian Carlo Ginzburg,[7] on the paradigm of traces, where truth is reconstructed from signs, hints and tokens, rather than experienced at once in a crucial experiment. The primeval hunter and Sherlock Holmes are both guided, in their respective activities, by this conception of truth. In the field of art of texts, the paradigm presupposes the total responsibility of the author for what he writes or paints: the practice of close commentary of literary texts, which the French enjoy so much, is based on this (he must have meant even the semi-colons in his text), as well as the method for the attribution of authorship to paintings (admittedly more useful to the valuer than to the art historian) devised in the second half of the nineteenth century by the Italian art critic Giovanni Morelli. According to him, you can tell that a painting is by Leonardo not by looking for the obvious elements, composition, colour, etc., which any competent forger can imitate, but for the minute ones, which are so many unconscious signatures, like the delineation of an ear, the shape of a hand, etc. True responsibility, for Morelli, lies in the detail, not the global design – another way of saying that responsibility extends *down to* the details.

There is no doubt that this tradition of extended responsibility has long been dominant. It has followed the evolution of persona to person which Mauss describes:[8] textual responsibility is a concomitant of the appearance of the author as person. But it has

---

[7] C. Ginzburg, 'Spie. Radici di un paradigma indiziario', in U. Eco and T. A. Sebeok (eds.), *Il segno dei tre*, Milan: Bompiani, 1983, pp. 95–136.

[8] M. Mauss, 'Une catégorie de l'esprit humain: la notion de personne, celle de "moi"', in *Sociologie et Anthropologie*, Paris: Presses Universitaires de France, 1968, pp. 333–64.

always been opposed by another tradition, which I have called Romantic, although it is in a way as theological as the first. Here irresponsibility is extended, to obliterate the figure of the author: he is either possessed, a *vates*, the inspired mouthpiece of a god or of imagination, or absent, lost in the convolutions of *écriture* or in the collective arrangements of utterance. Romantic poets, from Coleridge, who claimed that *Kubla Khan* had come to him in a dream, and Hölderlin, to the Surrealists, who sought to theorize this irresponsibility, are obvious examples. This tradition insists on the lack of mastery of the subject and on the proliferation of meaning. A recent illustration can be found in the *Anti-Oedipus* of Deleuze and Guattari, where their technical concepts of schizophrenia and paranoia embody the opposition of the two traditions. On the one hand paranoid texts are constrained, rule-governed, a locus for suture which imposes the coherence that goes with responsibility – in other words they have an author; on the other hand, schizophrenic texts are unconstrained, subverting rules and systems, productive rather than restrained in their attitude to meaning; and they cannot be assigned to a single authorial source. The shift of emphasis from the interpretation to the production of texts, which is at the root of their critique of psychoanalysis (with its well-known tendency to proffer the old Oedipal answers even before the new symptomatic questions have been asked) is typical of this attitude. The dominated character of the tradition, however, is apparent in the contradiction that dogs the Romantic conception of the text: on the one hand, there is ultimate irresponsibility, as the author is inspired; on the other hand, the genius of the author, i.e. the most individualized form of authorship, makes the relationship between author and text one of ultimate responsibility.

I do not offer this as a definitive account of the two traditions of textual criticism. It would take a book to chart their history and assess the balance of power between them within a given conjuncture. They seem to have cohabited, and subverted each other, from the very beginning. In the present conjuncture, the domination of extended responsibility over irresponsibility accounts for the straightforward matter-of-factness and the secret unease of my initial statement. Perhaps this secret unease is the mark of a contradiction. On the one hand, in our culture, a text is treated as an act, and its author is not only ascribed responsibility but also granted authority: an author is an authority (on his text) and has authority (over his readers). And an authority he is indeed, if we believe the natural aesthetics of the text: serious-minded (no farce for him), coherent, going straight to the point, completely in control of his style, and therefore of his meaning. But on the other hand, the text is also produced by another, non-authorial, entity, be it the gods, the unconscious or the discourse of class. There, the scriptor loses authority: he is little more than some kind of a copyist, or at best he who unleashes the forces of production of meaning, which he never controls – the increment (the author is he who adds) is never really his. The contradiction lies in the fact that modern texts seem to hesitate between author and scriptor, responsibility and irresponsibility. We celebrate 'le texte enfin libre' – free of authorial or individual guidance – in the works of Joyce and Pound, but we still insist on having proper names on the covers of our books. In other words, we need the concept of an author (and therefore of his responsibility for his text) even to read a text: authorless ones are much sooner confined to indifference or oblivion. But what we seek in those texts is, at the same time, the multiplicity of speaking voices, the irresponsibility of the narrator, the absence of the author.

As we can see, it is well nigh impossible to escape the dilemma of authorial responsibility and irresponsibility. Perhaps it is this very fact which accounts for the difference in treatment between Brasillach and Pound: the first was granted responsibility, he was considered liable for his text because he was sufficiently authoritative; the second was not punished in so far as *he* was not speaking, but spoken by his demon, like Son of Sam, the American mass-murderer, or his voices. An author is made to feel the authority of the law in proportion to his own authority. But this surely will not do, for it suggests that Pound's *penal* irresponsibility is the same as his *poetic* irresponsibility, in which case the *Pisan Cantos* are nothing but instances of these *textes bruts* destined to rot in the archives of lunatic asylums until some charitable psychiatrist publishes extracts from them as illustrations of a case history.[9] The distinction then turns out to be one

---

[9] See, for instance, M. Thevoz, *Ecrits bruts*, Paris: Presses Universitaires de France, 1979.

between various language games and textual genres: Pound was irresponsible because he was a poet, Brasillach responsible because he was a novelist. The serious and the mimetic involve responsibility, the comic and the poetic do not. Or again, essays and various types of non-fiction ascribe authority, fiction does not. (For where is the author's true mouthpiece?) We are close here to the old Puritan ideas about the irresponsibility of fiction (a moral irresponsibility in this case, which does not escape condemnation, for fiction is assimilated to lying). This is somehow unsatisfactory, a symptom of the paradox, not a solution. We cannot be content with just shooting the writer of essays and interning the poet. And what would be our reaction if faced with a piece of blatantly anti-Semitic fiction, or a play which would put forward the notorious 'revisionist' theories of M. Faurisson? The contradiction (between responsibility and irresponsibility, between two traditions or authorship) must be explored further.

THE CONTRADICTION IN LANGUAGE

If the contradiction remains with us, it is because every user of a language faces it. For every speaker is the author of his speech and at the same time no author. The trouble with Grice's theory of meaning is that it is one-sided: it fails to take into account the other aspect, which Heidegger's formula states. The contradiction, therefore, is between 'I speak language' and 'language speaks' (henceforward ISL and LS). I speak language: I use it as an instrument to communicate my meaning, I say what I mean and mean what I say. In other words, I am an author, the author which the Alexandrian grammarians construct with their natural aesthetics. This pole of the contradiction dominates, as the authorial theory of textual interpretation dominates over the scriptural one. But the other pole, language speaks, subsists, and insists: it will make itself heard, like a slip of the tongue in the middle of an official speech, which causes unexpected and unwelcome laughter. And indeed slips of the tongue are just one of the ways in which language, not the subject, speaks. The frailty of the dominant pole will appear if we just recite the litany of the incarnations of the other pole: the possessed, who speak in tongues; the delirious, who let their language dominate them – for these are not the

schizo's words, but those of his mother, of his language; the
garrulous, who cannot stop talking, compulsively, endlessly, and
yet who say next to nothing – although some of the most violent
affects can be conveyed by this 'nothing', as any reader of Pinter
knows; the stupid, who, like Bouvard and Pécuchet, only talk in
quotations, clichés and proverbs; the literalists, like this patient of
Bateson's,[10] who could not go past the door of the psychiatrist's
office, on which was affixed a 'please knock' sign, without knocking
– Bateson interprets this, quite rightly, as some sort of Brave
Soldier Schveik tactics, where the literal interpretation of the
injunction is a means of ironically subverting the symbol of the
doctor's arbitrary authority (irresponsibility here is tactical); and
finally, the linguist whose love for language impels him to take
risks with it (Saussure's anagrams are a case in point, as is the
invention of Esperanto) and the poet, who is the only one capable
of going to and fro, from one pole of the contradiction to the other.

It is not by accident that I end on the poet: for the Heideggerian
analysis of poetry provides ready-made terms for what I am trying
to say. The nexus of language (as the privileged vehicle for the
disclosure of Being that truth is) and art (the Poem as the essence
of language, taking risks but also opening up towards Being) could
be read as the grounding for the statement that 'language speaks'.
Although I confess that the origin of my formula is in Heidegger, I
am not entirely happy with this – even if I intend to go back to
Heideggerian formulations towards the end of this paper: the main
reason is that by 'language' I mean 'language', that is, not some
idiosyncratic type of *Sprache*, but what common sense, as well as
the linguist, mean by this. this reference to linguistics is what
distinguishes my statement from the master's most sharply. And
my point here is that although every self-respecting grammar
accounts for the ISL aspect of language (there are even such things
as 'communicative grammars' of English), it always leaves a
residue, or remainder,[11] in the form of exceptions, stylistic, social

---

[10] G. Bateson, *Steps to an Ecology of Mind*, St Albans: Paladin, 1973, p. 197.
[11] This residue is both syntactic (i.e. what a Chomskyan modular grammar
      necessarily leaves out in actual language) and pragmatic: whatever prag-
      matic rule – for instance Grice's rules of conversation – is constructed, it
      will leave out a remainder of perfectly respectable speech-acts that never-
      theless break it. Take, for instance, Patrick Nowell-Smith's first 'rule of

or dialectal variations, or linguistic change. And this remainder embodies the other aspect of language, LS: in the midst of my most grammatical sentence there may always appear a solecism, an anacoluthon, a conscious or unconscious pun, which seriously questions the laws of the system – and a system with laws, be they of grammar or of communication, there must be if I have to use my language as an instrument not only of expression, but of communication: my instrument must be the same as my neighbour's.

With LS, therefore, irresponsibility is firmly entrenched in the very core of language – in the remainder necessarily left unaccounted for by any system of rules. The danger is in the medium, not in a temporary aberration in its use. But by saying this, I am giving a new formulation to the opposition between authorial responsibility and irresponsibility: I am equating them to the opposition, within the speaker between ISL and LS. This sounds straightforward enough (LS delivers me from any responsibility in what I say, ISL commits me to it), but the situation is perhaps a little more complex.

For there are two ways for language to speak through the subject, or for the subject to use language as a tool. One is private, the other public. We may oppose the privacy of delirium – which comes closest to that celebrated impossibility, a private language – to the public character of *cliché*: in both cases, nevertheless, it is language, not the subject, which speaks. Or we can oppose the privacy of expression (I am using language in an attempt to make public my private thoughts and the infinite nuances of my individual meaning) to the publicity of communication, where I speak from a position in the language game of dialogue and use words fitting with or to that position. In other words, I am

contextual implication' (in his *Ethics*, Harmondsworth: Penguin Books, 1954, p. 81): 'When a speaker uses a sentence to make a statement, it is contextually implied that he believes it to be true.' This is how Nowell-Smith begins his next paragraph: 'This rule is often in fact broken. Lying, play-acting, story telling, and irony are all cases in which we break it either overtly of covertly.' His three rules of contextual implication (no. 2, the speaker implies he has good reason for his statement; no. 3 what he says is relevant to the interests of his audience) chart a map of textual responsibility. The exceptions which he himself mentions show that another map, of textual irresponsibility exists in the interstices of the first, and can never be totally ignored.

drawing attention to the potential contradiction within the hack-
neyed phrase 'language as a means of communication and expression'. Poetry is often about the opposition between the public
character of communication and the privacy of expression. So that
instead of having a straightforward opposition between ISL and
LS, I have now four terms, or three, if we consider that the middle
terms overlap:

		2b		
		(irresponsibility)		(responsibility)
		(*cliché 2*)		(*expression*)
1		ISL public	v.	ISL private
LS private	v.	LS public		3
(*delirium*)		(*cliché 1*)		
(irresponsibility)		(responsibility)		
		2a		

Positions 1 and 2a are opposed because one is private (delirium),
the other public (cliché). The first is clearly a position of authorial
irresponsibility: a disorder is there, devastating and deep-seated,
for everyone to see. The scriptor is *non compos mentis* and could
never incur penal responsibility. But compared to this, the second
is a position of (at least potential) authorial responsibility: for the
schizophrenic patient who manages to survive by clinging to other
people's language in the guise of clichés, although he is not
expressing any private contents, produces an appearance of
mastery, at least limits the risks by sticking to well-ploughed,
public, ground. This is the position of the wary literalist, who has
learned to avoid clashing with others by echoing their tritest
phrases. It is only when the patient goes over the pale, when crisis
destroys these precarious verbal defences, that the reality of the
subject's lack of mastery appears. In other words, the surface
productions that emerge from this position are not different from
those of position 2b, as the repetition of the word cliché shows. But
in the latter case, cliché conceals something else: not a lack of
mastery, but a refusal to show one's hand, to assume full responsibility for one's speech. This is the position of the shifty customer
who finds it more expedient, or easier, not to express his private
thoughts. We are in the realm of the white lie, of the phatic use of
language, of the innocuous discussion about the weather or the

state of one's garden, of the agreement, too rapid and too empha-
tic, with the consensual views on politics or religion. This is in fact
the position where the speaker abandons his responsibility: the
difference with 2a is now clear. In 2a, the schizophrenic patient
feigns responsibility to conceal his deep lack of it (this is the
utmost point he can reach on the road to authorial mastery); in 2b
the conformist temporarily abandons his authorship to make life
easier for himself (this is the lowest point he is prepared to reach in
this controlled descent towards delirium). The common point is
that both positions are instances of public language (the contradiction within public language being the responsible and at the
same time irresponsible character of conventional communication). The last position, 3, is both responsible and private: it is
the position of expression. For these are my thoughts, and this is
my language. I may be hermetic, and it is the reader's task to see
through the fog. My words may have the appearance of delirium,
but they are fully meant, for I am a poet, or a philosopher; the
sheer difficulty will give rise to commentary and a wealth of
conflicting interpretations.

What I have outlined could be called the dialectic of enunci-
ation. Not only is my speech torn between ISL and LS, it is also,
and often at the same time, private and public, responsible and
irresponsible. The question which remains is: to what extent does
this cast light on my political/historical problem? For, at first
sight, it merely seems to make it undecidable. How can I hold
Brasillach and Pound responsible for their texts, if I cannot decide
to what extent the ordinary speaker is responsible for this most
banal assertions?

TEXTUAL RESPONSIBILITY

I could first try to apply my diagram to the cases of Brasillach and
Pound. They would both be present in the positions of cliché,
their anti-Semitic broadcasts and articles being rife with those.
The language of racism is in fact heavily dependent on clichés. For
cliché provides the best formulation for an irrational statement: it
does not have to be justified: the 'responsibility' I assigned to
position 2a (the mental patient's clichés) is only metaphorical, the
frail disguise for lack of authorship. Cliché is the natural vehicle

for racist discourse, which relies on *ingrained* prejudice. The 'theoretical' versions of racism are always short-lived, its clichéic formulations always reborn Phoenix-like from the ashes of their conjunctural destruction. The difference between Pound and Brasillach would be that Pound's position moved towards 1, Brasillach's towards 3. But is this not merely saying that Pound was mad, Brasillach fully conscious, in which case my argument is circular? I might wish to show that there is a quality of obsessional rage in Pound's diatribes which made them close to delirium (the same has been argued about Céline), and a cold-blooded sense of control in Brasillach's public denunciations which sent people to concentration camps, which makes him fully responsible for the consequences of his texts. But this is deeply unsatisfactory for several reasons. First, I do not know at this stage how to argue from a text to the consequences that may have sprung from it (the only case where this is clear is a performative utterance or the text of a law). Secondly, it will involve me in expressing a preference for Pound's broadcasts over Brasillach's article, whereas clearly they are equally odious (Pound's utopian view of fascism was in no way the mere result of obsessional delusions). There are certain things – certain texts – which can neither forgive nor forget. Thirdly, it takes me back to my paradox: the Americans did not shoot Pound, simply because he was mad – whereas I have a strong feeling that the decision was a matter of convenience, that the only plausible answer is 'because he was a well-known, or a great, poet'. What I really wish to show, therefore, is that Pound, far from occupying position 1 (the madman), occupies position 3 (the poet), even if in his broadcasts he was in 2, like Brasillach (and it can be argued that this is where Brasillach remained). In other words, I wish to distinguish between *authorial liability* and *textual responsibility*, and argue for a revised version of my diagram:

1	2	3
irresponsibility	authorial responsibility/liability	textual responsibility
LS	ISL(LS)	ISL/LS
(delirium)	(cliché and communication)	(the poet)

I must go back to the grammar of responsibility. 'Responsible', as we saw, is a predicate which takes three arguments – in terms of case a nominative, an objective ('for') and a dative ('to'). I wish to distinguish between the last two arguments, i.e. between two kinds of responsibility. An author is responsible *to* his readers, a public relation which makes him liable for his text; a scriptor is responsible *for* his text, a relation both public (he has a reader) and private (it by-passes that reader). I am not defending here an idealistic conception of a scriptor's genius (he is so involved in his art that he creates for himself, not for an audience). I am distinguishing between two types of responsibility which whoever writes a text incurs. Exactly as a baker is responsible *for* his bread *to* his clients. What does the distinction imply? Most notably that liability, i.e. the possibility of incurring legal sanctions, should be limited to the first type of responsibility. In other words, I am introducing a new type of defeasibility: I, as the author of this text, cannot incur liability if I can show that my textual responsibility *for* my text, which overrides my authorial responsibility *to* my readers, justifies what I have written. I believe that this type of argument lies at the bottom of the textual equivalent of freedom of speech: the author, or rather the scriptor, is not accountable, first and foremost, *to* the laws and conventions of the society in which he lives, but *for* his use of language.[12] There is such a thing as a duty of textual disobedience, even if most texts result in a rightful compromise between author and scriptor, between the expectations of the potential reader and the needs of a developing language. But here I have to define 'textual responsibility', otherwise anything – including Brasillach's anti-Semitic texts – will be justified.

What is the specific responsibility of the intellectual, which Brasillach and Pound betrayed, but which Pound also fulfilled? I would like to suggest two aspects of what makes a 'good' intellectual – I am using 'good' here as an attributive adjective in the sense of Geach[13] (you can be a good intellectual and a thorough bounder). The first is that his task is to save language, as the philosopher seeks to save truth, except that his position is also that of the baker – a good baker's task is to make good bread and ensure that it remains that way. So the poet's task – for now I can abandon

[12] On this, see the paper by Ian Maclean in this collection.
[13] P. T. Geach, 'Good and Evil', in P. Foot (ed.), *Theories of Ethics*, Oxford: Oxford University Press, 1967.

the ugly word 'scriptor', coined to account for the subject of that authorial irresponsibility which has turned up to be textual responsibility – is to preserve and develop language, to work it, as one works the soil, which is also to let it work, for the French expression 'le travail de la langue', which most aptly describes what I mean, is ambiguous between an objective and a subjective genitive. The poet's responsibility is to let language speak, which involves the greatest self-control and the greatest purposefulness, but also the greatest abandon (the symbol ISL/LS in my revised diagram means that the two aspects of the contradiction are on an equal footing, the symbol ISL(LS) that the first one is dominant). Language speaks, the poet responds and answers: there lies his textual responsbility. But, and this is the second aspect, this implies taking risks, renouncing the comforts of cliché, but also the trusted paths of communal language – expression at the expense of communication. And it involves a certain excess, a refusal of compromise, which position 3 in my diagram shares with position 1 – this is the rationale behind the decision to intern Pound. I might call my position an existentialist view of language, for it means that, to pastiche a famous Sartrian formula: 'every poet, without any support or help whatever, is condemned at every instant to invent language'.[14]

Textual responsibility is therefore primarily linguistic: keeping the language alive is the specific duty of the poet – a duty which may have political and historical consequences. If we go back to the grammar of responsibility sentences, we may distinguish between the position of the hack (he is liable, i.e. responsible for the consequences of his texts to the victims of these consequences);[15] and the responsibility of the poet: he is responsible for his text to language. But his linguistic responsibility soon turns out to be ontological. For language as it is conceived here is not an

---

[14] See J.-P. Sartre, *L'Existentialisme est un humanisme*, Paris: Nagel, 1946.

[15] This is the answer to my question about how to reason from a text to the consequences it may have had in a given conjunction. Tradition in moral philosophy distinguishes between two meanings of the word 'responsibility': first, merely causal responsibility, where the consequences were not intended, and secondly, premeditated, or full, responsibility. Textual responsibility does not imply premediatition because it does not imply a conception of meaning as intention. See F. Vivian, *Human Freedom and Responsibility*, London: Chatto & Windus, 1964, pp. 132–6.

instrument, a mere tool, but a place to dwell in, and a way of access to truth. I said that I would have to go back at the end to Heidegger's conception of language. My description of textual responsibility indeed corresponds to the role he assigns to the *Dichter*, not any poet, but the one who, in his relation to language, discloses Being – Hölderlin, Trakl or Rilke. Being responsible for language and to language is indeed the highest form of responsibility. And it may well turn out to be moral and political-historical as well: 'Each language is the advent of the Word, in which, for a people, its world historically opens.'[16] I would like to comment on this sentence by developing an intuition of George Steiner, in his *Antigones*,[17] for the quotation does ascribe to the *Dichter* an historical and therefore political responsibility (in another passage, Heidegger assimilates the grounding of a language to the founding of a state). Steiner wonders why the Greek myths are endlessly repeated, and why they are the only ones to be: every year a fresh Antigone is born, not a new Hamlet or Lear. His answer is that their 'eternal charm' is due to their embodying the fundamental grammatical oppositions which structure our Indo-European languages – distinctions of tense, mood or gender. The eternal stories that spell out our deepest moral quandaries are in fact based on the structure of our language. This is giving a new and unexpected turn to Anglo-Saxon moral philosophy: the main concern is no longer the language of morals but the morals of language.

From this point of view, we can easily distinguish between Pound the racist and Pound the poet. It is not only that racist discourse, relying heavily on clichés, betrays language because it refuses to invent it, but that it betrays the morality of language by proposing a myth which grows outside the structural oppositions which found language – basically, the racist myth denies human status (or semantic 'human' subcategorization) to the third person pronoun, he who is absent from the dialogue but is the subject of it: the child, the madman, the alien. But most languages (and English made me use 'who' and not 'which' at the head of the last relative clause) distinguish between 'he/she' and 'it'. A myth which

---

[16] Martin Heidegger, *Holzwege*, Frankfurt am Main: Vittorio Klostermann, 1949, p. 83.

[17] G. Steiner, *Antigones*, Oxford: Oxford University Press, 1984.

deliberately sets out to ignore this threatens language. The poet's task is to defend it against this threat. The passage in Pound from the broadcasts to the cantos is a passage from betrayal to renewed fidelity. In other words, the Americans were right not to shoot him because he was a poet. All I have tried to do, by examining the grammar of responsibility, sentences, distinguishing first between authorial responsibility and irresponsibility, and then between authorial liability and textual responsibility, is to found this trivial truth.

POSTSCRIPT: OBJECTIONS AND RESPONSES

My argument can be accused of being idealistic on three counts.[18] First, I read too much into my historical example and take for moral or political necessity what was the result of mere historical accident. Had Brasillach been tried six months later, he would probably not have been executed; had Pound fallen into the hands of the Italian partisans, he might well have been shot. I try to persuade myself that the real is rational. But it is not. Secondly, I implicitly claim that the Good is also the Beautiful and True. But it is not. There is no necessary reason why a professed anti-Semite should not be a great writer. Pound perhaps (and Céline certainly) was just that. Indeed I am told that there is no difference in Céline's style between the infamous pamphlets and the famous novels. Thirdly, my view of language is ahistorical. I have failed to take into account the historical, cultural and institutional determinants which contribute to the responsibility of authorship. No doubt Pound's marginal position with regard to the fascist state apparatus, and Brasillach's closeness to the centres of power in occupied France, would justify the difference in treatment (were it not, of course, the result of historical accident).

I acknowledge the force and factual correctness of these objections. They will compel me to 'mettre de l'eau dans mon vin'. But even if I have to defend a watered-down version of my position, I wish to preserve what I consider to be its core, the notion of textual responsibility.

The conception of language which I have – loosely – borrowed

---

18 I wish to thank Ernest Gellner, Jerzy Jedlicki, Grahame Lock and Ian Maclean for their objections and comments.

from Heidegger need not be ahistorical. The language that opens up to truth is firmly grounded in a culture and is sedimented in an historical tradition: it is the heritage the present generation owes to its predecessors, and it embodies the complex and often violent story of the people that speak it. This is why it may have been possible for great writers, from Shakespeare to Céline, to be anti-Semitic – and why it is no longer possible. After the Holocaust, lyrical poetry is still possible, but not of an anti-Semitic type: the Célines of today are mere Faurissons. Not that anti-Semitism has been eradicated: it would appear it has not. But the words for it are no longer available – only evasion (M. Le Pen's celebrated 'detail' of the gas-chambers), cliché (cf. the revival by the Saudi-Arabians, a few years ago, of the forgery of the Protocols of Zion) or silence. Not so much the silence of shame as the silence of wordlessness: if we believe that Heidegger was anti-Semitic, and there is good reason to believe it, this is probably the explanation of his famous silence about what happened during the war.

This, I believe, answers objection number three, but concedes number two. I would like, however, to maintain that even if Céline and Pound were anti-Semitic, their anti-Semitism can only be a marginal part, and potentially a paradoxical part, of their writing. In other words, a great poet can be a thoroughly nasty person (the Beautiful is sometimes the Unsavoury), but *qua* poet he is not accountable for this. His moral or political authorial liability is cancelled by his textual responsibility. There is an element of *abyme* in this. Since the publication of Victor Farias' book,[19] we know that some of Heidegger's texts on poetry and language, which I have used in this essay, were published during the Nazi period in collections of Nazi propaganda of the worst kind. This does not affect their philosophical value. I am comforted in this by the fact that the most explicitly Heideggerian poet was Celan, who, George Steiner has decisively demonstrated, is *the* poet of the Holocaust. Textual responsibility is a position of excess. It is a dangerous and exposed place, and makes one liable to fall into the greatest errors, the errors of irresponsibility, of delirium. It is difficult not to see a symptom in the anti-Semitism of Pound's broadcasts. From the excess of Sade's fantasies to the banal

[19] V. Farias, *Heidegger et le nazisme*, Paris: Verdier, 1987.

horrors of rape or child-molesting, there is only a thin line. Nevertheless, it is a line that must be carefully maintained and, as Bataille has shown, eroticism is not pornography.

The only objection which I find unanswerable is the first. But need I answer it? My point is not historical: I only attempt a fictitious *a posteriori* justification for what was never justified (and did not have to be). For I find the historical situation more satisfactory than if, for instance, Pound had been shot and Brasillach saved. And there *is* food for thought in this.

I wrote this essay before the publication of Farias' book and the subsequent development of the 'Heidegger affair', which caused havoc in Parisian intellectual circles. I find the recurrent ritual murder of the intellectual father slightly distasteful (Marx was subjected to a similar treatment a few years ago when it transpired that not only did he go to bed with his wife's maid, but he was the moral instigator of the Gulag). In any case my essay dispenses me from having to add my voice to the outcry. I regret that the True is not also the Good and the Beautiful, but I maintain that textual responsibility is responsibility *for* inventing language before it is responsibility *for* speech-acts, *to* the community of speakers as speakers rather than *to* the moral law, universal though it may be. When Heidegger took his now historically documented turn from political involvement to involvement in/with the poetry of Hölderlin, he made it clear that he had realized that the moral task of the author was to conform to the morality of language, which the Nazis (as Karl Kraus was one of the first to demonstrate), and therefore he himself, had emphatically betrayed. The Rectorate speech makes sorry reading. Not so the texts on Hölderlin. And unfortunately, awareness of the morality of language in no way guarantees rectitude in morality *tout court*. We have to live with this contradiction: our great philosopher was and remained a nasty individual, such as no one should have bought a used speech from. And our most insightful literary critic has since turned out to have been a detestable young man. There is a positive aspect in all this: perhaps it will rid us for good of the drift from critique to hagiography, from philosophical to moral discipleship to which French intellectuals of the 1960s and 1970s were so prone.

7

Politics, technology and the responsibility of intellectuals

DAVID J. LEVY

This paper aims to explore certain fundamental issues relevant to the political responsibility of the contemporary intellectual from the perspective of an historically oriented philosophical anthropology. By this I mean a philosophically explicit conception of man's nature and place in the world, which is sensitive, at once, to the unchanging conditions of man's specifically given form of life – to the range of what Arnold Gehlen calls 'anthropological constants' – and to the historical novelties which this underdetermined and ecologically unstable life-form renders possible. In this perspective, which owes much to the seminal work of Max Scheler and his more or less faithful followers in the development of philosophical anthropology, the specific differences of man's contemporary existence, which we shall group together under the heading of 'modernity', are to be understood as *existential* novelties developed within and dependent upon a continuing and constant *ontological* framework, whose persistence alone renders human life possible.[1]

Seen thus, modernity is to be understood as the historically unprecedented realization and continuing development of certain existential possibilities which were, for all the novelty of their outcome, implicit from the beginning in man's mode of being. These possibilities, realized through history as a result of human action, tend over time to enlarge the extent to which, and regardless of his intentions, as a matter of fact rather than of right, man becomes responsible for the maintenance of the conditions which alone render possible the continuation of life itself.

[1] David J. Levy, *Political Order: Philosophical Anthropology, Modernity and the Challenge of Ideology*, Louisiana: Louisiana State University Press, 1987.

Following, in particular, the theses developed by Hans Jonas in *The Imperative of Responsibility*,[2] I want to explore the problem of the contemporary nature and range of human responsibility in general, and of the responsibility of intellectuals in particular, against the background of the extension of man's power – above all through the development of technology – to change the condition of the world on whose existence his own depends. While it is the development of modern technology itself, or, to be more precise, the extension of the range of technologically induced effects into the very structure of the supporting world, that must be regarded as the primary cause of the enlargement of the scope of human responsibility, the problem of what principles are to guide us in the exercise of that responsibility is nothing new. These principles are coeval with mankind: not in the sense that they are always known or that men are always capable of stating what they may be, but because they are rooted in the survival imperatives of the human being as such, as emergent life form which is, from the beginning, uniquely responsible for its own fate. To put it at its simplest, while other animals are attuned to survival in a given ecological niche human beings are responsible for the creation and maintenance of an equivalent space in nature in which their continued existence becomes possible.

In relation to the articulation of the principles governing the exercise of responsibility, the particular problems we face today are not simply to be regarded, in deterministic fashion, as direct and necessary results of the development of technology as such. Rather that development, which is always governed by its own immanent imperatives based on the single principle of increased practical effectiveness – the sole principle of a purely technological rationality – tends, by reason of the magnitude of its achievements, to cloud the issue of whether there may be considerations other than that of practical effectiveness which must be taken into account in determining the proper course of action now and for the future. The development of technology itself contributes directly to the novelty of the contemporary problems of responsibility only in the sense that it extends the sphere of being for which man is *de facto* responsible. Beyond this the problem of responsibility is not

[2] Hans Jonas, *The Imperative of Responsibility: Towards an Ethics for the Technological Age*, Chicago: University of Chicago Press, 1984.

caused, in any unequivocal sense, by the extension of technology but, rather, by the human psychological tendency, in the face of that development, to extend the model of a purely technological rationality to all areas of life. And this, as I shall argue, at a time when, as a result of the extended range of purely technical competence, the *logos* proper to technology – that of a technological rationality which takes account only of practical effectiveness – is no longer, alone and of itself, sufficient to order the conduct even of the most strictly technological activity.

There are, no doubt, many ways to approach the problem of the political responsibilities of intellectuals in the contemporary world. The approach adopted here abstracts from the significant differences which derive from the variety of present cultural, political and economic circumstances in order to focus on the problem of this responsibility in its most universal aspect. I adopt this approach not because I underestimate the significance of the differences between free and totalitarian regimes, nor those that divide the economically advanced from the less developed portions of the world, but because there is, it seems to me, a universal problem of responsibility which has devolved upon mankind – one which, for the first time, involves the question of whether or not the species is to have a future at all.

The particular responsibilities of intellectuals within this state of affairs are to be understood against the background of the general responsibility of man for his own future. The political character of this responsibility derives, in turn, from the fact that, in the course of becoming subject to human control, nature – the perennial object of technological activity – whose continuing existence could once be taken for granted, has acquired the status formerly and rightly attributed exclusively to social and political institutions. That is, nature has become what institutions always were – a reality objectively necessary to human survival but whose own future endurance is now manifestly dependent upon human ingenuity, cultivation and care. In the words of Hans Jonas:

The boundary between 'city' and 'nature' has been obliterated; the city of men, once an enclave in the nonhuman world, spreads over the whole of terrestrial nature and usurps its place. The difference between the artificial and the natural has vanished, the natural is swallowed up in the sphere of the artificial and at the same time the total artifact (the works of man that have become 'the world' and as such envelop their makers) generates a 'nature' of its own, that is, a necessity with which human freedom has to cope in an entirely new sense.[3]

I shall return to Jonas later. For the moment what needs to be brought out of his words is the implication that the scope of political responsibility now extends over a level of reality, the stratum of physical, inorganic as well as organic, nature, to which it could formerly remain relatively indifferent. Many writers, Marxists in particular, have drawn attention to the way in which the works of man, realized in the institutional forms of society or culture, tend to form a 'second nature' – 'a reified' realm of objectively existing constraints upon the human subject from whose activities they nonetheless derive. What fewer have noticed, at least until recently, is the other side of the coin: that just as the stabilization of cultural practices in institutional form creates a new, quasi-natural, because objectively given, framework within which human life is necessarily conducted, so, primarily as a result of technological activity, nature acquires over time some of the ontological features of culture. The continuation of nature *tout court*, the ontologically given basis which renders human life possible, becomes as dependent on human activity as the 'second nature' of culture.

The sphere of political responsibility, which is broadly coextensive with the range of human life-conditions alterable by human decision, is radically enlarged by the reduction of nature to this quasi-institutional status. While the origins of nature, in distinction from those of culture, are not attributable to human activity, its continuing integrity has become so. Within this process, whereby the results of action oriented by knowledge of its assumed consequences enter ever more deeply into the structure of the human environment, two elements stand out as especially relevant to consideration of what, if any, are the particular responsibilities of those we call intellectuals.

The first relates to the status of the intellectual as possessor of a specialized range of practically effective knowledge – the intellectual in his role as a 'professional' or 'expert' to be consulted in

[3] *Ibid.*, p. 10.

relation to projects directly relevant to his own field of knowledge. The second relates to the less 'technical', more generally 'philosophical' role often attributed to or claimed by intellectuals. That is the role of determining, on the basis of the analytical, discursive skills developed in intellectual activities as well as on possession of a particular profession perspective and stock of knowledge, the likely overall consequences of particular courses of action and, hence, the desirability of pursuing them.

In the first case the intellectual speaks from a position authorized by his possession of specialized knowledge. In the second, possession of such knowledge is almost incidental and what counts is a presumed ability, supposedly born out of engagement in intellectual activity, in estimating the long-term results of a multitude of originally distinct actions – 'multifactorial' analysis which may, at the limit, amount to the synthetic 'science' which its practitioners call 'futurology'.

The real value of the latter activity is, of its nature, difficult to assess; and, given the variety of speculative conclusions to which it gives rise, it may be tempting to attribute its undoubted influence to rhetorical factors alone. The intellectual, it may be said, is a specialist in the use of words, but his forays outside his own specialized field of knowledge are of no more cognitive value than anyone else's. When it comes to matters of practical philosophy, judgements of value and speculations about the future course of events, we are all more or less percipient amateurs. Though there is a certain truth in this, the temptation to dismiss the wider 'philosophical' role of the contemporary intellectual, and hence the attribution of particular, political responsibilities attaching to it, ought to be resisted.

The reason for this is that though intellectual activities do not, of themselves, make those engaged in them either any wiser or more obviously practically or politically responsible – the reverse indeed has often seemed to be the case – the nature of our technological civilization is such that both specialized knowledge and the ability to determine, even speculatively, the likely long-term risks and consequences of present, knowledge-guided action assume today an importance they have never previously possessed. The distinction between theoretical and practical knowledge, which underlies the Aristotelian view of politics as an activity requiring no more knowledge than that we may reasonably expect of the mature citizen, is undercut by developments which make specialist, preeminently theoretical, knowledge an unprecedentedly significant aspect of our knowledge of the political environment. This is an essential part of what we mean when we think of ourselves as living in a uniquely 'technological age'.

The phrase 'technological age' is used by so many people in so many different contexts that we have come to take it for granted that we know what it means. And, at a certain level, we do. We inhabit a world where the effects of human technology are everywhere to be seen, and not only seen but used and relied on. As once men conceived the limits of their lives to be defined by the presence and pressures of implacable nature – a realm not made by man and ultimately beyond his control – so their descendants have come to see technology itself as representing the new and intrinsically unlimited horizon for the individual and the human race alike. This expansion of possibilities is obviously a human achievement, the result of human efforts and thus, in principle, it falls within the range of human responsibility. And yet the technologically defined world of modernity is, as much as the natural world, experienced as subject to dynamics of its own; tending to move in a fixed direction toward an unknown and uncertain end. The careful calculation of appropriate means to chosen ends, which is characteristic of each individual technological project, seems to play little or no part in the process of technology as a whole, which advances ever outwards, expanding human powers without regard to what the consequences may be.

Thus people today tend to think of the sphere of technology with the same ambivalence with which they once regarded nature. Technology is the object of both their hopes and their terrors. It promises the material for a life of happiness and ease and is, at the same time, sensed to be pregnant with apocalyptic possibilities. It is simultaneously worshipped, cultivated and feared as an inescapable and dominant reality in the life of the species. Those who claim to know its secrets are, like the magicians of old, consulted without ever really being trusted; and this not because they are thought to be any less intrinsically trustworthy than the rest of mankind, but because they are suspected of meddling with forces ultimately beyond their control in ways whose consequences cannot be foreseen.

This ambivalent attitude to the power of technology is characteristic of the mood of the present day. It is an essential part of what we mean when we say that we live in a technological age; for an age tends to characterize itself, above all, by what defines its hopes and fears. And yet the term is in some respects thoroughly misleading, suggesting as it does that technology is a new factor on the scene setting us apart from our human predecessors.

The classification of distinctive epochs in terms of some specific difference that separates the mode of life of their inhabitants from what went before is one of the ways we make sense of the past. As a classificatory scheme it enables us to extend our comprehension of the human story into the shadowy realms of prehistory. When we speak of the bronze age or the iron age we are referring to epochs in man's history in which the horizon of human possibilities was extended by the discovery of the use of a new material. When we think of the development of agriculture as marking a new epoch in human existence, the start of the agrarian age, we are thinking of the ways in which man transformed his way of life by bringing under his control and guidance processes that were already present in nature. The term 'technological age' is not like that, if only because the development of agriculture, like the working of metals and of stone before them, was already an essentially technological achievement, the result of the development of techniques which involved not merely the manipulation but the modification to human ends of materials and processes originally found in nature. The essence of technology is not to be found in the use of such materials and forces, a capacity we share to a limited extent with tool-using animals, but precisely in their modification to serve human purposes. In that sense, though, every stage in human history has been an age of technology; and if we want to understand the real specific difference of our 'technological age' we would do well to remind ourselves of this.

To put it another way; the use of technology and even our dependence upon it, far from setting us apart from our human ancestors, represents one of the most striking elements of continuity in man's story. Such dependence is not a mark of the uniqueness of the modern age, but a feature that primordially separates the human mode of being from the life-form of the other animals. From the beginning the capacity for technological achievement introduces a unique dynamism into the relationship between man and the world he is fated to inhabit; for the modification of naturally given elements by technique does more than extend the possibilities of individual and group survival. The application of technology to the problems of organic survival tends cumulatively to transform the world in which we live. This in turn creates the opportunity and even the necessity for the development of new technologies, and hence transforms the world still further. The dynamism of technology is intrinsically an ecologically destabilizing factor; and this makes it qualitatively different from what may seem, at first sight, to be the equivalent, though organically given, 'techniques' that ensure the survival of other species.

There are many species of animals which have proved extraordinarily well able to cope with the changes that human activity has brought about in their environments. Others have been less fortunate. But whether or not an animal species survives always depends upon its capacity to adapt itself to an environment over which it has no control. The human case is different; for though man is, no less than the animal, ecologically dependent upon a supporting world, the only world that can afford him the support he requires is one whose elements have, to a greater or lesser extent, been modified by human technology. The effects of such modifications are, as I have suggested, cumulative, and tend, over the long term but with increasing rapidity, to alter the 'balance of power' between man and nature.

If today we feel ourselves to be in a unique position it is not because we have entered an unprecedented stage of dependence on technology, but because the perennial development of world-transforming technique has reached a stage at which our possibilities seem to be limited by technology alone. This has been part of the human prospect from the beginning, even if it is only in retrospect that it can be understood as such. It is entailed in a form of life that is unique to man: a life-form that ensures its survival, not by adaptation to a given environment, but by modifying the environment to suit its own ends. Such a project must end either in a failure which would mean extinction or, as I have suggested, in a success whose mark is the reduction of nature to the status of a quasi-institution – that is a level of reality necessary to survival but no longer capable of endurance without constant human care.

It is, I think, awareness that we have now reached this position, rather than any widespread appreciation of what, if anything, may be qualitatively different about modern technology, that gives rise to the feeling that our's is an unprecedentedly technological age. For while it is very difficult to pin down any qualitative as opposed to quantitative difference setting modern technologies apart from those we have inherited, it is impossible to ignore the extent to which the development of technique, in the widest sense, has made us responsible for the future of man and world together in a way that is indeed qualitatively different. In other words, it is a sense of increased *de facto* responsibility more than anything inherent in the nature of today's technology that tends to make our contemporaries uneasy. The characteristic anxiety of the technological age is based less on mistrust of technology than on man's increasingly conscious mistrust of himself. This is not a function of any change in human nature but of a new and disturbing awareness of the disproportion between the powers at man's disposal and his capacity to judge rightly how they are to be used. The alteration in what I have called the balance of power between man and nature gives rise to a situation in which, ever more clearly, problems of technology are bound up with ethical and political problems with which we seem ill-prepared to deal.

Some thirty years ago Arnold Gehlen identified a crucial feature in this situation when he wrote:

What men fear are not the monstrous destructive energies of the atomic nucleus, but their own; not the H-bomb but themselves. They sense, rightly, that they cannot count on an internal constraint upon the use of a power one holds in one's hands to emerge suddenly in the final stage of a development, whose main tendency for two hundred years has been exactly to remove such constraints, to further and enhance a purely objective, rational and technical concern with effectiveness.[4]

Underlying Gehlen's words is the recognition that the increasingly rapid development of man's technical powers over the last two centuries has been accompanied by a decline in the effectiveness of any spiritual or moral factor that might constrain their use. The

[4] Arnold Gehlen, *Man in the Age of Technology*, New York: Columbia University Press, 1980, p. 101.

very success of technological achievement has tended to destroy man's sense of dependence on any power, natural or supernatural, greater than himself. And so at a time when we seem urgently to require some form of authoritative guidance to cope with the ethical and political issues opened up by the advance of technology, we lack both the ethics and the institutions that might provide it.

Gehlen's own approach to these problems is based in a distinctive theory of man and the human condition that understands the political and technological dynamic of human achievement as a many-faceted response to an initial state of organic and instinctual deficiency which has no parallel in the animal world. 'Ultimately,' he writes, 'all attainments of the human mind remain enigmatic; but the enigma would be all the more impenetrable if not seen in connection with man's organic and instinctual deficiencies; for his intellect relieves him of the necessity to undergo organic adaptations to which animals are subject, and conversely allows him to alter his original circumstances to suit himself.'[5] How or why such a form of being arose is beyond the scope of our present considerations. In a sense, it is even irrelevant whether or not we accept its historical accuracy as a picture of man's primordial state. In heuristic terms alone, Gehlen's model of man as an organically and instinctually deficient being would retain its value as a way of making intelligible the diverse dimensions of human activity as well as by helping us to understand something about the problems we now face. For the need to respond creatively – that is through forms of activity guided by conscious reflection – while providing sufficient reason for the development of forms of political organization and of technology, also gives us a clue as to why the states of being we attain remain for ever fragile and problematic.[6]

The source of this fragility, which underlies the problem of responsibility in its broadest sense, emerges clearly when, like Gehlen, we set the life-forms of man and animal alongside each other in order to discover what seems to make them distinct from one another. Man and animal alike face the problem of ensuring their survival in a potentially threatening world; but while the solutions available to the animal are entailed in its genetic inheritance,

---

[5] *Ibid.*, p. 4.   [6] See also on this the writings of Helmut Plessner.

those of man must be formed and transmitted through intellectual processes entailing conscious reflection, cultural creation and the appropriation of tradition. No organism is or can be responsible for its genetic inheritance, but responsibility, the Janus-faced concomitant of man's reflective consciousness, is inseparable from the burden and benefit of culture.

The problem of man's responsibility for the maintenance of a humanly possible state of being is thus, like technology, a primordial feature of human life. It becomes, however, more pronounced the further man goes in modifying and all but transforming his environment. In the course of history the world he comes to inhabit is one in which the marks of human artifice are increasingly deeply inscribed. At least since the agricultural revolution the art of man has entered into the very structures of nature and, as a result of this, the boundary between the ontologically given and the humanly chosen loses its original clarity; shifting without vanishing to the point where it ceases to have any correspondence with the common and apparently related distinction between the natural and the artificial. Thus, almost imperceptibly at first, man's responsibility for his own survival tends to become a matter of responsibility for the world as a whole.

This development must lead us to question the general validity of the dictionary definition of the word 'artificial', according to which it means 'produced by art and not by nature' or 'produced by art and not existing in nature'. In the area that concerns us here this mutually exclusive distinction is unhelpful. Adopted uncritically it may even be dangerous; encouraging, in the face of present anxieties, the development of ecological thought in the direction of a romantic primitivism as impossible as it is inhuman. For, less than ever, is it possible to make a clear distinction between the works of man and the resources of nature which support him. The earth bears the inexpungeable marks of human efforts and the very fruits of the field are cultivated for consumption in forms created by centuries of selective breeding. Only the existence of such 'artificial' forms of life – sub-species created by man and incapable of independent survival – allows the human race to exist in anything like its present numbers.

This is anything but an unmixed blessing; and it may well be that even the present size of the world's population produces tensions that will prevent us from solving the problem, at once political and technological, of how our species is to survive in a world for whose own survival it has made itself factually responsible. At the same time any efforts we make to cope with this situation are and must be further steps along the path of artifice – measures to be politically decided and instituted by whatever means may seem technically appropriate and ethically acceptable. The point I wish to emphasise here is that there is no self-regulating balance of nature on which we, as a species, could fall back. At this level at least, history is irreversible and with it the burden of responsibility we have assumed.

Starting from assumptions closely related to those of Gehlen's philosophical anthropology. Hans Blumenberg interprets the course of human history in terms of the unceasing effort to overcome an initial situation in which man is subject to what Blumenberg calls 'the absolutism of reality' – that is a situation in which he has hardly any control of the conditions of his existence.[7] It is the human response to this primordial state which is recorded in the evidence of history. This response is not merely narrowly practical, directed toward the material modification of the world, as our emphasis on technology may have suggested, but symbolic and cognitive, that is, intellectual, as well. The world interpretations of myth, of religion and of science are, no less than tools and weapons, instruments of human survival; attempts to overcome an initially threatening world by reducing it to a state in which it can be comprehended and so cognitively mastered. At the level of symbolic achievement, man makes himself at home in the world through a process of representation, in which the given data of existence are subjected to interpretation and re-presented as a coherent cosmos, a symbolic universe as Berger and Luckmann put it,[8] in which man has an intelligible place and destiny.

Blumenberg argues that such representations, which are manifest in the typical symbolic forms of myth, religion and science, are, like tools and weapons, subject through human history to a process of quasi-natural selection. That is to say that those which survive are those which prove most effective not only

[7] Hans Blumenberg, *Work on Myth*, Cambridge, Mass.: MIT Press, 1985.
[8] Peter Berger and Thomas Luckmann, *The Social Construction of Reality*, New York: Doubleday, 1966.

in extending man's control over the world but in making sense of the changing existential situations in which he finds himself. Parallel to the perennial march of technological achievement, we find an unceasing 'work on myth' – a reworking of the initial patterns of human self-interpretation to take account of man's increasing sense of responsibility for his fate and that of the world. In his book *Work on Myth*, Blumenberg illustrates this process through examination of the way in which the myth of Prometheus is successively reworked in the cultural history of the West.[9]

In the context of a discussion of technology the Prometheus myth, or rather the successive 'mythologies' that can be drawn from it, may seem to occupy a privileged position. The story of the theft of fire from the gods is the technological myth *par excellence* – a tale of how man aquires the means to overcome his initial state of deficiency – and it is significant that, from its first cultural appearance in the poems of Hesiod, it is fraught with ambiguous implications. Depending on the outlook of the particular mythologist, it can be read either as a blasphemous seizure of powers which are not man's by right or as a praiseworthy triumph of ingenuity over the hostile powers that initially govern the cosmos.

The greater the confidence in technological process as the royal road to human fulfilment the more man identifies himself with the figure of Prometheus as he appears in the second reading. This is the beneficent and guiltless Prometheus who is the boyhood hero of Karl Marx and whose spirit imbues the predominant optimism of the nineteenth-century world-view. From such a 'Prometheanism' the ambiguity of the ancient myth is significantly absent. Of course, in the case of Marx, the other aspect of the myth, Prometheus the blasphemer, the implacable enemy of divine power, is also a central ingredient of the vision of the human condition; but here blasphemy has ceased to be a crime and become the precondition of a truly human existence. Divine power is to be banished from a world in which man alone must be the master if he is to survive and flourish. The pursuit of human fulfilment, as the most all-embracing of the rights of man, is seen as incompatible with recognition of any divine right to order the cosmos – and this because divine right, in nature as well as political

[9] See above, n. 7.

society, is seen simply as the sanctification of given conditions which it is man's destiny to overcome.

The Prometheanism of the nineteenth century disowns the ambivalence of the original myth in an unequivocal assertion of man's right to restructure the conditions of his existence, natural as well as social and political. Though new in its application to the socio-political realm, this 'right' is something that had always been simply assumed in the sphere of technology, in which practical effectiveness is the sole intrinsic criterion of judgement. So long as the balance of power remained tipped in nature's favour the exclusivity of this criterion posed no practical problems. But once nature had, at a certain level at least, been reduced to dependence on man it became a highly dubious guide to action. For in terms of the technological criterion of practical effectiveness we cannot distinguish the point at which transformatory action, without ceasing to be apparently beneficial, begins to undermine the possibility of there continuing to be a humanly habitable world.

Here judgement required a different sort of criterion, one derived from the traditions of practical, political and moral reasoning – spheres in which, formerly at least, man had been all too aware of his responsibilities for conserving the institutions on which the good life depended. But in the intellectual and spiritual climate of the nineteenth century such traditions tended to be undervalued in comparison with what was perceived as a bountiful technology founded in the certainties of natural science. Far from the prudential logic of practical reason finding a place in the projects of technology, the logic of technique was introduced into a political discourse which conceived the purpose of politics, like that of technology, to be the transformation of the world. At the extreme, both were seen as equivalent vehicles of ontological transformation, *metastasis*, whose ultimate purpose was to raise man to a qualitatively higher level of being. Mankind, a collective Prometheus, would be finally unbound from the chains of finitude.

Even in the intrinsically transformatory sphere of technology this involved a grotesquely exaggerated notion of what human action can accomplish. For, in becoming a sphere whose continued existence is subject to the uncertainties of human decision, and thus a human responsibility, nature retains, in full measure, its original ontological primacy over the creatures who depend upon it, including man himself. In overcoming the initial form of the absolutism of reality, in which reality is experienced as a realm of forces utterly beyond human control, man does not thereby overcome the effective primacy of the real. Not only do his actions create new levels of reality which impose upon him burdens of their own; but these spheres, cultural, political and technological, remain ultimately dependent upon the subsistence of the very level, nature *tout court*, against whose threats the 'second nature' of civilization is initially created. The dependence of nature on man, which is such a salient feature of the modern world, and which results from our success in learning to make use of the once incomprehensible forces which threatened our existence, cannot therefore obviate the more fundamental dependence of man on nature, nor abolish the ontological limit that this implies. The extension of human mastery over nature entails not the absolutism of freedom, as technological utopians like Ernst Bloch have imagined, but the absolute burden of responsibility for the survival of a world in which life remains possible. This is the reality of the situation, at once novel and rooted in the primordial imperatives of human life, which underlies our present state of unease.

Existential uncertainty in itself is nothing new. It is inseparable from the reflective life of the members of a species uniquely aware of their own individual mortality and of the dubious effectiveness of the self-created powers at their disposal. What seems to be new about the form of existential uncertainty characteristic of the contemporary world is that its object is displaced from the limited perspective of the present to include all potential futures. Uncertainty has been radicalized to the extent that we have come to recognize that we are capable not only of cutting back what presently lives but of tearing life up by the roots. Unlike our remote ancestors we need no longer doubt the technical efficacy of the powers we have to hand. It is not their insufficiency that we need fear but their extraordinary potency, in comparison with which our inherited powers of judgement seem weak indeed. Existential mastery of nature sits uneasily alongside a renewed sense of ontological dependence.

In the perspective of Gehlen's philosophical anthropology the existential uncertainty of the modern world can be seen to reproduce, on a cosmic scale and in response to a scientifically formulated analysis of the possible conditions of existence, the survival anxiety which has formed part of man's condition from the beginning. In the same light, it may even be that the radical uncertainty which seems uniquely to characterize our present age is also not without precedent. Paradoxically though, we share it not with our immediate historical predecessors, but with the inhabitants of those archaic societies, described by Mircea Eliade,[10] which lived in the belief that cosmic catastrophe was always imminent and could only be held off through the careful and regular practice of rituals of world renewal. In some ways we may be existentially closer to such cultures than to the optimistic world-view of that earlier phase of modernity when recognition of the dynamism of human achievement was taken to imply that the intrinsic risks of life were about to be definitively overcome. If ours is still a 'Promethean' age, its Prometheanism is marked anew by awareness of the profound ambiguities that attend man's assumption of responsibility for his fate.

By this I mean that in the phase of modernity we have now entered our sense of what is at stake in the actions we undertake is closer to that imagined by the men of archaic civilizations, on whom responsibility for political and cosmic order weighed with equal force, than to the characteristic attitudes of the last two centuries, in which trust in technological advance went hand in hand with belief in a form of intellectual progress that was simultaneously scientific and ethical.

If this is so, and if we are right in conceiving our future to be unprecedentedly at risk, then we may find more salutary lessons in archaic conceptions of world order and man's place within it than in the still potent legacy of Enlightenment optimism. In particular, we will find ourselves having to reformulate our ideas of political and ethical responsibility to take account of responsibility for realms of being which, in Enlightenment thought, were considered to be subject only to the automatism of a physical order beyond human disturbance. What this implies is not a revival of archaic myths of the sources of human responsibility for cosmic order, but the formulation of a practical philosophy, an ethics and

10 Mircea Eliade, *The Myth of the Eternal Return*, Princeton: Princeton University Press, 1954.

a politics, that takes into consideration the reality of that responsibility in our age.

In *The Imperative of Responsibility*, Hans Jonas has given an example of the sort of rethinking required. Sub-titled 'in search of an ethics for the technological age', Jonas' book takes as its starting point the situation which I have sought to describe above – one in which the growth in the technological power at man's disposal has reached a point at which the causal reach of human action extends to the question of the very survival of the world. In the past, he writes,

The presence of man in the world has been a first and unquestionable given, from which all ideas of obligation in human conduct started out. Now it has itself become an *object* of obligation: the obligation namely to ensure the very premise of obligation, that is, the *foothold* a moral universe in the physical world – the existence of mere *candidates* for a moral order. This entails, among other things, the duty to preserve this physical world in such a state that the conditions for that presence remain intact; which in turn means protecting the world's vulnerability from what could imperil those conditions.[11]

The field of ethics remains, as it always was, coextensive with the area of reality subject to the effect of human decisions; but since this area now includes the whole natural, organic and inorganic world, an ethics appropriate to the age must bring within its scope a range of issues which previous ethics could, quite properly, ignore. Where, previously, ethics could confine itself to investigation of the conditions of right order among men and to the evaluation of the likely immediate consequences of action, it must now take account of what Jonas calls man's obligation to nature – both in itself and as the precondition for human life – and to the probable long-term effects of human activity. 'We must', Jonas argues, 'educate our soul to a willingness to let itself be affected by the mere thought of possible fortunes and calamities of future generations, so that the projections of futurology will not remain mere food for idle curiosity or equally idle pessimism.'[12]

It is not temperamental pessimism but a carefully calculated awareness of the lack of balance between the scope of technology and the finite resources of nature, including human nature, that

[11] Jonas, *The Imperative of Responsibility*, p. 10.   [12] *Ibid.*, p. 28.

leads Jonas to propose, in explicit opposition to Ernst Bloch's technologically based *Principle of Hope*,[13] an 'heuristics of fear' as the guiding principle in our future conduct. Acceptance of such a principle does not entail abstention from technological innovation but only that we give extra weight to what we can see to be reasonable and scientifically well-founded fears about the effects such innovation may have. In seeming to tip the balance of judgement in this way, an heuristics of fear actually does no more than redress the initial imbalance produced by the inherent innovatory dynamic of technology itself. Seen in this light, the heuristics of fear, which Jonas proposes, is not a recommendation of pessimism but a reassertion of the primacy of prudence among the virtues required in practical reasoning.

The need for such a generalized restatement is a result of what I have called the shift in the balance of power between man and nature – a shift whose most significant feature is that, under the impact of human agency, nature is seen no longer to possess the seemingly inexhaustible capacity for self-regeneration which past generations could take for granted. This introduces a new dimension to what has traditionally been seen as the domain of practical philosophy; a dimension in which, on the one hand, consideration of complex and long-term scientific and technological projections must play a central, informing role in determining political and ethical considerations, and, on the other, where considerations of prudence, the stock in trade of practical decision making, must be introduced into a field of human activity in which previously they played no part at all.

Out of this situation there emerges a whole complex of problems which demand careful investigation by philosophy and the human sciences. Many of them are raised and clarified by Jonas in the course of his attempt to develop the principles on which an ethics of cosmic responsibility must rest. The most significant aspect of his argument, beyond the clarity of the way in which he describes the existential novelty of man's present situation, lies in his elaboration of a metaphysics of morals derived from the philosophy of nature enunciated in his previous work, in particular *The Phenomenon of Life* (1966). According to this philosophy, the

[13] Ernst Bloch, *Das Prinzip Hoffnung*, Frankfurt, 1959.

realm of nature is permeated by teleology, not in the sense that it plays any knowable part in a Divinely ordained scheme of things, but simply because every organism is oriented in its activities toward its own survival. The reformulation of a practical philosophy, a politics as well as an ethics for a technological age is, at root, a practical imperative derived from the orientation toward our own survival which we share with every living being, and which is, as we have seen, at the source of technology itself. As a moral project, a sensed obligation directed toward the maintenance of our survival as moral beings, it is clearly one that has no precise equivalent in the animal world. And yet, in so far as its aim is to preserve ourselves in our ontologically given state of being as moral beings, it is clearly derived from the guiding imperative which runs through the whole phenomenon of life.

As my title suggests I suspect that the intellectual problems raised by the entanglement of technological and ethico-political issues in the present day are problems which, while entailing an extension of human responsibility in general, impose a special responsibility on intellectuals in particular. The source of this special responsibility lies precisely in the fact that our task today involves an attempt to relate spheres of thought and activity which have, until now, been considered separately. We need to consider how the extended range of human agency, which is the consequence of technological progress, affects the classical ideal, recently revived by so many social and political thinkers, of a practical philosophy whose mastery is a matter not of scientific knowledge or technical expertise but of the application of the common sense of an educated citizenry. While the Aristotelian distinction between *praxis* and *techne* remains valid in principle, the relationship between practical judgement and technical knowledge has reached a new level of complexity. In what was traditionally considered the sphere of *praxis* we must take account of a range of scientific knowledge and technological achievement of whose implications and likely effects only the specialist can tell us. In the sphere of *techne* the exclusive dominance of the criterion of practical effectiveness is no longer a sufficient guide for action.

Thus the two elements of the specific responsibility of the contemporary intellectual identified earlier in my paper are drawn together in what is, in terms of the history of philosophy and of ethics in particular, a new project. Let us recall what these elements were. The first related to the intellectual's possession of what I called 'a specialized range of practically effective knowledge' – knowledge which, as we have seen, enters through its effects into the very structure of the environment with which present and future practice must cope. The second, more general, element derives from the skill, developed in the course of intellectual activity, of estimating the likely consequences of complex actions and of communicating these to the population at large. Only acceptance of what Jonas calls the 'heuristics of fear' as an integral part in all such calculations – a premise that we can no longer dare to deny – will serve to prevent such thought experiments from being diverted into what are increasingly dangerous utopian directions.

8

The intellectual and the
imitation of the masses

GRAHAME LOCK

The democratic intellectual, when he comes to reflect on his social role and political responsibilities, does well to measure his position against the strongest arguments bearing on the presuppositions of his position. My object in the present paper is to test out some of these presuppositions against certain arguments to be found in Plato's *Republic*.

In Book II of *The Republic*, Plato makes Socrates relate an account of 'the origin of the city'. This origin, he says, is 'to be found in the fact that we do not each severally suffice for our own needs . . . One man calling in another for one service and another for another, we, being in need of many things, gather many into one place of abode as associates and helpers, and to this dwelling together we give the name city or state' (369B).[1] The 'real creator' of the city is thus, argues Socrates, 'our needs'. And our needs are food, housing, clothes 'and that sort of thing'. The city therefore consists, at a minimum, of a farmer, a builder and a weaver – to which list Socrates, however, adds 'a cobbler and some other purveyor for the needs of the body', the precise function of this last member being left unspecified. So, he concludes, 'the indispensable minimum of a city would consist of four or five men'.

Jacques Rancière has drawn attention, in a recent work,[2] to this phrase: why such imprecision in an author otherwise attached to precise figures derived from rigorous mathematical demon-

---

[1] I make use throughout of the Loeb edition of *The Republic* (trans. Paul Shorey, London/Cambridge, Mass.: Heinemann/Harvard University Press, 1930/1935). With some modifications to the translation.

[2] Jacques Rancière, *Le Philosophe et ses pauvres*, Paris: Fayard, 1983.

strations? Why four *or* five? And why the lack of information as to the function of the possible fifth member? Plato provides no direct answer to these questions. But we can, in the light of the general content of his doctrine, speculate as to his reasons.

We might for example suppose something like the following. The minimal city which Socrates here describes is in fact an ultra-minimal city. For it lacks one element belonging to the essence of a city, i.e. *justice*. A transition must therefore be made from the ultra-minimal city, which operates according to the criterion of physical needs, to the minimal city, which functions according to the principle of justice. But what, in this connection, of the 'fifth man' in the ultra-minimal city? What of the man apparently 'less indispensable'[3] to this city, according to its criterion of needs, than the first four?

We know, of course, from the rest of *The Republic*, that the category of justice will be defined in terms of a certain division of labour. And a certain division of labour is present in the ultra-minimal city. But it is not the same division. Or rather, the principle of the division invoked by Plato is here absent. It must be added; it must be articulated. But there is no one in it capable of articulating the principle. A farmer cannot do it, nor a builder, a weaver or a cobbler. Cobblers, as is well known, stick to their last – or ought to. Weavers stick to their loom, builders to their trowels and farmers to their ploughs. Moreover, the enigmatic fifth man will, if he exists at all, be a purveyor to the needs of the body. So it does not look, at first sight, as if he could be the source of the idea of justice. But his description provides us with a clue. He is the only member of the city whose task is not so defined that it is – again at first sight – evident that it will keep him metaphorically chained to his post. He might for instance be (say) a doctor, or a hairdresser or a manicurist. And in such cases his life, with four clients to look after, is certainly not going to be over-strenuous. He will have – or at least he might have, and Plato does not exclude the possibility – time left over for himself. That is, he might have 'leisure time', time for example *to think*. He might even think about the city, about its principles of social organization and such things. In an anachronistic terminology: he might

---

[3] Rancière, *ibid.*, p. 18.

become an (amateur) intellectual. Would he be in his rights to do so?

This question allows us to draw attention to an important point in Plato's doctrine. Socrates argues as if workmen were constantly busy, as if they never had a free moment for anything but work and sleep. (Indeed, one of the characteristics of the workman is that he even tends to fall asleep at work.) Such a man cannot, for example, afford to 'sit idle . . . and lose time from his own work' (371C). This may well be a plausible claim when applied to an ancient Greek farmer, builder, weaver or cobbler. But it hardly applies to a doctor, and even less to a hairdresser or manicurist. Socrates has, of course, another formula characterizing the duties of a workman: it is not so much, he suggests, that a workman needs to be working all the time; it is rather that he must be permanently available. Yet permanent availability is compatible with having a great deal of free time on one's hands – especially time to think. But if this is so, then there seems to be no serious *practical* basis for Plato's argument that a shoemaker must stick to his last (etc.), where this means that he has no leisure to do anything else, and in particular no possibility of reflection. The conclusion must be drawn from other premises. And of course it is. I shall return to this point in a moment.

Let me first note, however, that the characterization of the ultra-minimal city appears to be deliberately incomplete (since it lacks a principle of justice). The vagueness of Plato's description – four or five members, the fifth purveying to some unspecified need or needs – is, I think, neither accidental nor a matter of lack of interest on Plato's part. He must have had a purpose in view. This may have been to draw our attention to the fact that the difference between the ultra-minimal and the minimal city (the latter being described at 371–4) is not simply that the latter is a city of luxury, as Socrates points out in answer to Glaucon (372E). It is also that, in the former, no provision has been made (as I already noted) for any principle of justice which could legitimate the division of labour to be found in it. That is why this division is first presented as purely practical. But its essence, as we come to understand when we read more about the respective roles of the workman and the philosopher, is not so much the horizontal division between trades (however necessary this is) as the vertical division between tinker and thinker which renders the city possible. This is why Plato does not need to provide a serious specification of the trades required for the functioning of an ultra-minimal city. Any rough list will do. The point is rather that the city needs workmen; but that these workmen must stick to their workbench, in the sense discussed above. Sticking to the workbench means not trying to become philosophers, even if they have time to reflect on philosophical questions. So, for the time being, Plato lets Socrates put forward all kinds of reasons for this restriction, and in particular lets him talk as if the four or five members of the city, given their onerous tasks, obviously could never undertake any other – in the event reflective – task; though this is in fact not obvious at all.

The tacit premise, which is articulated elsewhere, is, of course, that there is a difference *in nature* between a workman and a philosopher. Thus the famous passage at 493E:

Can the multitude possibly tolerate or believe in the reality of the beautiful in itself as opposed to the multiplicity of beautiful things, or can they believe in anything conceived in its essence as opposed to the many particulars? ... Philosophy, then, the love of wisdom, is impossible for the multitude.

And at 495D–6A he adds:

In comparison with the other arts the prestige of philosophy even in her present low estate retains a superior dignity; and this is the ambition and aspiration of that multitude of pretenders unfit by nature, whose souls are bowed and mutilated by their vulgar occupations even as their bodies are marred by their arts and crafts ... Is not the picture which they present ... precisely that of a little bald-headed tinker who has made money and just been freed from bonds and had a bath and is wearing a new garment and has got himself up like a bridegroom and is about to marry his master's daughter who has fallen into poverty and abandonment? ... Of what sort will probably be the offspring of such parents? Will they not be bastard and base? ... And so when men unfit for culture approach philosophy and consort with her unworthily, what sort of ideas and opinions shall we say they beget? Will they not produce what may in very deed be fairly called sophisms, and nothing that is genuine or that partakes of true intelligence?

This is the tacit premise. But, for the moment, the argument about the ultra-minimal city turns around a supposed lack of leisure, as we saw – around the ἀσχολία of the workmen, that is, around their occupation or (the term has both meanings in Greek) their want of time. Rancière (to whose work I am indebted for a number of ideas presented and developed here) points out that contradictory democratic and anti-democratic arguments are to be found in Greek writing concerning the location and consequences of this phenomenon. Thus Xenophon claims that artisans have no free time to devote to politics, and thus have no interest in the subject, whereas farmers do have (sometimes enforced) leisure, and are therefore able to devote time to political thought and action, such that they may even be called the best defenders of the city. Aristotle, in contrast, argues that artisans have too much leisure, too much time to think, and therefore to meddle in politics; while farmers are too busy regularly to attend political discussions in the assemblies, and are consequently of little danger to the city, even when their formal rights are quite extensive. Aristotle writes in *The Politics* (Book vi, ch. 4) that

An agricultural population makes the best demos; so that it is in fact possible to make a democracy anywhere where the population subsists on agriculture or stock-raising and pastures. For having no great abundance of wealth they are kept busy and rarely attend the Assembly . . . They find more satisfaction in working on the land than in the duties of government and citizenship, so long as there is no great profit to be made out of holding office . . . Moreover to have the power to vote at elections and to call to account outgoing officials makes up any deficiency which those who have political ambitions may feel.[4]

The advantage of this kind of democracy, says Aristotle, is that, while everyone possesses formal political rights, in practice those elected to high office will be drawn not from the peasantry and suchlike, but from persons with substantial amounts of property or ability. (One is reminded here of certain realistic currents in American political science.) And 'this form of administration satisfies the men of culture and distinction, [for] they will not find themselves ruled by their inferiors'. There will be government by good men, free from error, and without detriment to the people at large.

In Aristotle, the peasant can be a citizen, indeed a 'good citizen',

---

[4] Penguin edition, Harmondsworth, 1962, pp. 240–1.

just because the exercise of his citizen's rights will for all practical purposes be limited. But Plato cannot accept such a pragmatic compromise. For Plato, on the contrary, each member of the city has one and only one occupation. A shoemaker cannot at the same time be a farmer; a cobbler cannot be a weaver. More important, none of these can be a citizen in any real sense: that is to say, none can be a *philosopher* or an *intellectual*. Nowadays, of course, we should never dream of excluding workmen from citizenship. But by the same token we should never dream of admitting them, as they stand, to the status of intellectual. We obviously no longer apply a condition of origin in this connection. Anyone can become an intellectual, if he spends enough time and energy on the task. We no longer write letters like that sent to Jude the Obscure by the Master of Biblioll College:

Sir, – I have read your letter with interest; and, judging from your description of yourself as a working-man, I venture to think that you will have a much better chance of success in life by remaining in your own sphere and sticking to your trade than by adopting any other course. That, therefore, is what I advise you to do.

Yours faithfully,
T. Tetuphenay[5]

It is simply that, in our time, it is obvious that a workman, unless he gives up his work and enters on a serious course of study, cannot simultaneously be an intellectual (or if he is, he will be called an 'amateur'). He just does not have the time. To be an intellectual – a philosopher, an historian, a writer, a scientist – is to practise a craft. That the problem is nowadays regarded as only or largely one of time and investment of energy is a matter of democratic progress. But this same movement brings with it a problematic aspect. For intellectual activity now becomes, in the practical reality of the contemporary division of labour, what it already was for Plato, namely a protected profession. The difficulty then is: how in these circumstances to maintain the notion of a universal citizenship? For this seems to require us to divorce the concept of the office of citizenship from that of serious intellectual reflection

[5] Thomas Hardy, *Jude the Obscure*, Harmondsworth: Penguin, 1978, p. 167.

on politics in general and the duties of a citizen in particular. And this does appear to be the way in which the idea of citizenship has evolved in recent times: its active aspects have atrophied, and it has become something like a collection of positive rights connected with national status. In our societies, some intellectuals (most of them) are citizens; but by no means all citizens are intellectuals. Most are not.

I shall not here examine the question of the relation of the intellectuals to the class of professional politicians (a matter discussed by Edward Shils in his paper on 'Intellectuals and responsibility'). One point is, however, of importance: namely that both groups work with a concept of 'representation'. Indeed, it is this concept which is invoked in order to resolve the problem of the divorce referred to above. The intellectual claims to represent something else: the conscience of the nation, the latent traditions of a people, the working class or whatever. What interests me here is not so much the various particular claims which have been made and are still made in this connection, but rather the notion of representation itself, as it is used in this connection. For it cannot be taken for granted. And Plato, anticipating its use in something like the above-mentioned sense, proposes a critique of the notion which is not easy to meet.

Plato's critique is, in brief, that representation is *imitation*; and that imitation corrupts. The democratic politician, for his part, will, for example, normally need to speak 'the language of the people', to *mimic* it. He will 'deliver a speech as if he were someone other than himself', as Plato puts it (cf. 393B–C); as if he were himself of lower breeding. But if he succeeds, he must *be* of lower breeding, or so Plato argues. 'Do we wish our guardians to be good mimics?', asks Socrates (394E). Of course not. It 'would not be fitting for them to imitate anything else' (395C), or at least only what is appropriate to them – things brave, sober, pious and free. For such a man 'will not wish to liken himself in earnest to one who is inferior . . . but will be embarrassed, . . . because he shrinks in distaste from moulding and fitting himself to the types of baser things' (396D). The mimetic art 'produces a product that is far removed from truth . . . and associates with the part in us that is

remote from intelligence'. It is 'an inferior thing', appealing to the
inferior part of the soul (603B–C).

How then could an intellectual hope to 'represent' the people, or
any part of it? How could he even want to? He should resist any
temptation to do so. Reason and law are here pitted against bare
feeling (604A–B). For the rational disposition does not allow of
imitation, or only with great difficulty, says Plato. The representation of such a rational disposition by the non-rational man will
involve an imitation of a type that is alien to him, in the same way
as a representation of the non-rational by the rational man.
Representation is only possible within the same type. But there it
ceases to be representation. Imitation or mimicry within a type is a
practical pleonasm.

So far, so good – or bad. If we accept Plato's naturalistic theory
of the difference in human natures, we must, so it seems, draw the
conclusion that representation, because it requires imitation or
mimicry, is either impossible or grotesque and self-defeating. The
intellectual cannot represent the people. Thus it is only to be
expected that the people remains unrepresented, that it is
excluded from citizenship (even in Aristotle's limited sense,
discussed above); and that there is an identification of the class of
intellectuals or philosophers with the class of citizens – or, rather,
of citizens with philosophers. But, it will be objected, most of us
do not share Plato's naturalistic theory of the difference in human
natures. So the rest does not follow, and the topic is of academic
interest only.

If the matter were so simple, we might be quickly reassured. But
it is not so simple. Plato's argument is more complex, and contains
at least one consideration which appears to be independent of his
theory of human nature, and therefore more threatening to our
contemporary view of the intellectual's representative function.
There is, says Socrates, 'a form of diction and narrative in which
the really good and true man would tell anything that he had to say'
(396c). This form is characterized by a preference for pure
narration, and a distaste for imitation and mimicry. But this
distaste is not just a matter of natural disposition. Behind it lies an
argument which might be said to belong to the theory of rationality. What Plato writes is that 'there is *no two-fold or manifold
man* among us [in the ideal city], since every man does one thing'

(397D–E). If a man should arrive in the city 'who was capable by his cunning of assuming every kind of shape and imitating all things', then – though we should marvel at the sight – we should send him away. Why? Because there would be no way of reading off, from his speech and actions, his own thoughts and convictions. Or, in a terminology nearer to that of Plato, there would be no discernible correlation between his speech and his soul. The multiplicity of appearances would obscure the reality. Knowledge and its imitation could not be kept apart.

It is just because the mimetic art is 'far removed from truth' that it can produce anything and everything out of a hat. Now Plato argues at 436B that 'the same thing will never do or suffer opposites in the same respect in relation to the same thing and at the same time. So that if ever we find these contradictions in the functions of the mind we shall know that it was not the same thing functioning but a plurality.' He refers back to this principle at 602D–3A, noting that it is thus impossible for the same thing (soul) at one and the same time to hold contradictory opinions about the same thing. There is no 'two-fold' or 'manifold' man among the guardians of the city because such a man would be of irrational disposition: he would, in his manifold aspects, hold contradictory opinions about the same thing.

One can put the point in another way. One starts out from the problem of the legitimacy of expressing an opinion 'in a capacity'. It is useful to make reference in this connection to an argument of G. A. Cohen's to the effect that there is a serious problem involved in this idea.[6] The argument, in brief, is the following.

It is not possible to provide justification or to give cogent grounds for two contradictory opinions. The holding of a given opinion will be justified by providing good grounds for the proposition expressed in the opinion. The mere fact that the official who expresses such an opinion holds a particular office can never provide a ground for that opinion. The mere fact that one is, for instance, an official of the Ministry of Defence cannot in itself be a ground for the opinion that defence should be allocated a higher proportion of the national budget at the cost of education

6 G. A. Cohen, 'Beliefs and Roles', in Jonathan Glover (ed.), *The Philosophy of Mind*, Oxford: Oxford University Press, 1976, pp. 53–66.

and health. One might perhaps object to this that a Minister of Defence, say, must surely believe some things *ex officio*, for instance that his country ought to be defended in some adequate way. But this is to pose the question the wrong way around. What is true is rather that whoever does not, as an individual, believe such a thing (whether because he is a pacifist, or for some other reason) ought not to accept a senior post in the Ministry.

Suppose that we call this the 'belief requirement' for the acceptance and holding of public office. Now it is in empirical fact likely that the private – but also the public yet personal – opinions of citizens will often fail to meet the belief requirements of the offices or posts to which they have a chance of being appointed. This leaves – if the citizen in question wants to eat – two alternatives: deception of the public, or self-deception.

I think that this argument is near enough sound. If it is, then its consequences are important and far-reaching. They are indeed far-reaching in respect of their application to office-holders: not only to those like ministers, ministerial civil servants and the like, but also to that very interesting category, the judiciary. Can it really be true that a judge can neither believe something nor honestly give his opinion on the relevant point 'in his capacity as judge'? But this is again a misleading way of posing the question. The judge's 'legal opinion' may differ from his personal opinion: but the former ought not in fact to be understood on the model of the former at all. For his 'legal opinion' tells us what, as he – honestly and personally – believes, is the state of the law with respect to some point. It may be that he – honestly and personally – would, for instance, have decided a case differently if he had been the presiding judge in that case. But since he was not, and the presiding judge decided as he did, and our judge is not a judge of a higher court, he is bound to respect precedent and give a 'legal opinion' with which he disagrees, in the sense just indicated. This is not incoherent or irrational, as long as the difference between a 'legal opinion' and a personal opinion is made clear.

But such differences are, of course, not always made clear; indeed, sometimes they seem to disappear entirely. A ministerial civil servant supporting (say) a proposal to increase defence expenditure will not usually restrict himself to a form of words indicating that he is just presenting the arguments, good or bad, which the ministry officially requires him to put forward. For that would not be to *defend* them. On the contrary, he normally does defend them, as the basis of his own, honestly and personally held view. And this is the type of case in which difficulties do arise.

But I leave this problem in its general form, in order to return to the special case which concerns us. For if the above holds, then it must – perhaps *a fortiori*[7] – hold that what an intellectual believes to be true cannot be something which he believes 'in his capacity of intellectual'.[8] It is simply something which he believes. In particular, he cannot – following Plato's argument – mimic the people, attempting explicitly to articulate its beliefs, hopes and aspirations. It may, of course, be that an intellectual happens to hold the same views as certain non-intellectuals; the latter might then elect him as their spokesman. But this is not how intellectuals typically have viewed their representative task. They have rather seen it as requiring them to be, so to speak, in two places at the same time: with and inside the world of the masses, and yet outside of it too, in the world of ideas. This notion is, however, the butt of Plato's critique: a man cannot be in two places at the same time. To try to do such a thing would be to commit an error the opposite of that of the cobbler who wants to be a philosopher: it is to be a philosopher who wants to be a cobbler.

It is not luxury which threatens to corrupt the city; not the extension of the list of needs which Socrates discusses with Adeimantus at 371–4; not the introduction of a sophisticated cuisine, or of feasts with myrrh and incense and girls and cakes, nor the love of embroidery and of gold and ivory ornaments. What threatens to corrupt the city, as it develops out of its ultra-minimal

---

[7] A special problem is posed by the intellectual who – for instance through his appointment to a chair in a continental university – becomes by this title a civil servant. Edward Shils points out that 'the legal status of university professors as civil servants should not obscure the difference between academic and administrative or ministerial civil servants'. But nor should we forget that certain pressures can be exerted on academics with civil servant status.

[8] Shils claims that intellectuals have not on the whole thought of themselves as intellectuals, 'i.e. as members of a category, aggregate or community of intellectuals as such', at least not until recent times. But, as he also notes, when they do identify themselves in this way it is typically when they come to engage in political action.

phase, is the absence of a principle of justice. 'Where ... can justice and injustice be found in it?' asks Socrates. The answer must be: with the arrival of the philosopher, of the intellectual, who can recognize both justice and injustice and distinguish one from the other. But this philosopher, this intellectual, is not a representative of the people. He is no imitator or mimic.

One is not obliged to follow Plato in his general political doctrine in order to follow him on this last point. Let me here draw an illustrative and probably unexpected comparison, drawn from a quite different historical period, and having to do with a quite different political doctrine. Lenin is well known for having defended the position that, within the Marxist movement, intellectuals have nothing to apologize for. It is immaterial, writes Lenin in 1902 (in *What Is To Be Done?*), whether a professional revolutionary has an intellectual or a proletarian background. His task in any case is to bring socialist ideas to the workers. This is how Lenin answers his opponents inside the socialist movement, whom he calls 'demagogues'. For they appeal to the 'masses', whereas Lenin appeals to the truth. The demagogues, he adds, are the worst enemies of the working class, 'because they arouse *base instincts* in the masses'. Lenin prefers to put his trust in a dozen 'wise men' (as his opponents call them) – that is to say, in men who have undergone the training of 'many years' which it takes to become a professional revolutionary; who are not so much representatives of the masses as their leaders. 'I know', he says, 'that exception will be taken to my "undemocratic" views'; but this, he argues, is an unintelligent objection. 'It is not at all our task', he writes, '*to descend* to the level of the "working masses".' Nor, therefore, was it entirely surprising that, after the October Revolution, Lenin should have announced that the Russian proletariat was in large part corrupted, and unfit to hold power; and that in consequence 'all sentimentality and empty words about democracy' must be set aside, so that the party could take upon itself the task of administering a dictatorship of the proletariat in a land in which, as he claimed in 1921, the proletariat had disappeared.[9] Of

9 V. I. Lenin, 'The New Economic Policy and the Tasks of the Political Education Departments', in *Collected Works*, vol. XXXIII, Moscow: Progress Publishers, 1965, p. 65.

course, I am here emphasizing only one side of Lenin's thought. But it is important to note that this side exists – that is to say, that Lenin too does tend to reject both the pretence of representation and the imposture of imitation, which he calls demagogy.

Lenin was, of course, no Platonist. The point of this comparison is only to draw attention to an unexpected parallel. But let us return to Plato, and to the question of the division of labour separating the workman on the one hand and the philosopher on the other. I have suggested that the original argument presented by Socrates to justify this division – that workmen have insufficient free time to indulge in philosophical reflection – is not Plato's deeper thought. This deeper thought has two parts: one founded in a theory of the difference of natures, the other in a (rudimentary) theory of the conditions for rational discourse. And this latter theory does have considerable persuasive power, while being independent of the other, intuitively repugnant aspects of his doctrine. The persuasive power of the theory derives from the kind of considerations which I have sketched out above, together with the fact that the rejection of the concept of the 'manifold man', the polytechnical imitator, is at the same time a rejection of criteria of validity for knowledge which would consist – in Ernest Gellner's formulation – in 'adjustment' and 'effectiveness'. And it requires us to forswear the kind of 'evaluative subjectivism' to which (as Edward Shils points out) present-day social scientists are in practice drawn. It implies an anti-Romantic and an anti-pragmatist position. And it insists in its own way on what Alan Montefiore calls 'the responsibility for the respect of truth', which is itself, he argues, a 'political virtue'.

Now Plato's own conclusion, if I formulate it in my terms, may be said to be that the responsibility of intellectuals lies (at least in part) in their refusal to accept an imitative or representative role, whether the latter is seriously intended or adopted opportunistically as a pose. We now arrive, however, in Plato's account, at certain paradoxical theses. He claims that any technique which is ignorant of its own proper end or goal is itself imitation, and therefore far removed from truth; in short, a lie. This at least is the case as soon as the technician moves outside of his single speciality, and especially when he trespasses in the domain of philosophy. It is just because technique thus has the tendency to become a lie that the workmen in Plato's *Republic* are strictly controlled in this respect. 'If . . . the ruler catches anybody else in the city lying, any of the craftsmen, "whether a prophet or healer of sickness or joiner of timbers" [a quote from Homer], he will chastise him for introducing a practice . . . subversive and destructive of a state' (389D). But the philosopher, quite on the contrary, has a right – indeed a duty – to lie. In particular, he must be ready to tell the 'noble lie' of the metals in the souls of men. 'How', asks Socrates at 414B–C, 'might we contrive one of those opportune falsehoods . . . so as by one noble lie to persuade if possible the rulers themselves, but failing that the rest of the city?' The philosopher, as Rancière puts it, must in fact be 'a specialist of nature and of the lie, an engineer of minds'.[10]

It is not that the lies of workmen are always so very dangerous. 'For cobblers who deteriorate and are spoiled and pretend to be the workmen that they are not are no great danger to the state. But guardians of laws and of the city who are not what they pretend to be, but only seem, destroy utterly, I would have you note, the entire state' (421A). In this case it is the guardians who are forbidden to imitate and to lie. But the exception only proves the rule. For the guardians who fall under this prohibition are, as Plato tells us, false guardians. True guardians, by contrast, do not need to pretend to be what they are not, for they are what they are.

Let us now take up again the question of justice. This is defined at 433A as the situation in which 'each one man must perform one social service in the state for which his nature [is] best adapted'. It is 'to do one's business and not to be a busybody'. (But compare Prof. Szacki's remark that 'interference in other people's business seems to belong to the very nature of an intellectual defined in a certain way'.) The business of the philosopher or intellectual is in any case to rule. In order to rule, he must both know the truth and be ready to lie. But now we are confronted with another paradox: when he tells the truth and when he lies, he does so, apparently, *in his capacity of philosopher*. If this is, indeed, in both cases so, then we face after all the difficulty already alluded to, that which attaches to the expression of views in a particular capacity. If, on

---

[10] Rancière, *Le Philosophe et ses pauvres*, p. 37.

the other hand, he neither tells the truth nor lies in any particular capacity, then Plato's model of the division of labour, together with his connected principle of justice, seems to be rendered vulnerable. For in this case there would be no essential reason why a workman (especially one who disposes of the necessary free time) should not himself try to discover and to teach the same truth – except of course if we refer back to the theory of the difference of natures. In this last case, we can translate the terminology of official capacities into that of natural capacities, and we avoid the difficulty. But we only avoid it in respect to the problem of what it is to express a sincere view. For lying is a different matter. Plato cannot seriously want to claim that lying is a character trait of the superior human being. He must want to argue, rather, that the need to lie follows from the duties of the philosopher as defined by his official capacity. But now we have a hybrid theory of the justification of the division of social labour, which relies at the one moment on a natural principle and at the next on a formal principle. This is not a fatal objection to Plato's doctrine, but it is a difficulty; and I do not know that it has been much remarked on. It is paradoxical, and the paradox would need to be resolved.

'Lying and poetry', wrote Oscar Wilde, 'are arts – arts, as Plato saw, not unconnected with each other.'[11] But Wilde does not entirely approve of Plato's general account of lying. Wilde is in fact thoroughly modern (though he denies it) and a democrat in the matter of the theory of human nature. 'What is interesting about people in good society', he writes (via the character of Vivian), ' ... is the mask that each one of them wears, not the reality that lies behind the mask ... We are all of us made out of the same stuff. Where we differ from each other is purely in accidentals.' And he adds, by way of application of his own doctrine, that 'the crude commercialism of America, its materializing spirit, its indifference to the practical side of things, and its lack of imagination and of high unattainable ideals, are entirely due to that country having adopted for its national hero a man who, according to his own confession, was incapable of telling a lie' (though the whole story of the cherry-tree is, of course, a pure myth). Lying

[11] Oscar Wilde, 'The Decay of Lying', in *De Profundis and Other Writings*, Harmondsworth: Penguin, 1973.

for the sake of the improvement of the young, he notes, still lingers amongst us, 'and its advantages are so admirably set forth in the early books of Plato's *Republic* that it is unnecessary to dwell upon them here'.

Wilde's message is ironic. That of Nietzsche on the same subject is, I think, less so. Nietzsche remarks, for instance, that 'the intellect, as a means for the preservation of the individual, unfolds its chief powers in simulation'. And he adds:

In man this art of simulation reaches its peak: here deception, flattery, lying and cheating, talking behind the back, posing, living in bor-rowed splendour, being masked, the disguise of convention, acting a role before others and before oneself – in short, the constant fluttering around the single flame of vanity is so much the rule and the law that almost nothing is more incomprehensible than how an honest and pure urge for truth could make its appearance among men.[12]

But what is it then to be truthful? In the existing state of things, in any case, it is 'to lie according to a fixed convention'. So Nietzsche could not, on account of his pessimistic position, have accepted the role of the representative intellectual – though of course he was exploited by various political causes. As Ernest Gellner has pointed out in a contribution to the Vienna working group on 'Political responsibility', he certainly understood the irony of his own position. 'Everything profound loves the mask', he writes in *Beyond Good and Evil* – but not the 'new species of philosophers', the 'new friends of "truth"'. These new philosophers are imitators – they are 'slaves of the democratic taste'; they would like to 'strive after ... the universal green pasture happiness of the herd'. Nietzsche characterizes himself as the opposite of all this; as a friend of solitude.

To the extent that there is irony in Wilde and Nietzsche, it is in the content of their claim that what is interesting is the mask: appearance, imitation. This is also true (to take one last example) of Karl Kraus, whose work was described by Walter Benjamin as displaying the 'true mask' of the satirist. In his recent work on Kraus, Edward Timms writes that individuality, with which

---

[12] Nietzsche, 'On Truth and Lie in an Extra-Moral Sense', in Walter Kaufmann (ed.), *The Portable Nietzsche*, Harmondsworth: Penguin, 1976, p. 43.

Wilde was also so concerned, can express itself in terms of 'role-distance', and that 'the attempt to detach oneself from the role required by a given situation may be seen as an inverted form of role-behaviour – an "anti-role"'. Kraus was very fond of Wilde (especially of his essay 'The Soul of Man under Socialism', where he defended socialism as the means to the realization of true individualism). He was more ambivalent with respect to Nietzsche, though both are thinkers of the mask. But Kraus was himself a kind of actor. His acting was, however, not an imitation of the masses, or of mass taste and ideology – except in the sense that, by means of simple imitation, the absurdity of the imitated positions could sometimes be better brought out than by a reasoned critique. Kraus' 'acting' was then – if we follow Timms – an attempt to create that 'true mask' through which a public role could be created, a role which would not be discontinuous with some other, private, role, but in which the public and private spheres would meet.[13]

None of these thinkers – Wilde, Nietzsche, Kraus – thus proposes an anti-Platonic political position based on an imitation of the masses. Indeed, Nietzsche cautions us against the intellectual of the future, who will no longer be able to pretend to leadership unless he is prepared to become a 'great actor', a 'philosophical Cagliostro', a 'pied piper of the spirit' – 'in short a mis-leader'. In this he is at one with Plato. For according to Plato, 'theatocracy' (as he calls it in *The Laws*, 701) lies at the origin of the curse of democracy: it proved to be 'the starting point of everyone's conviction that he was an authority on everything'.

But the critique of the intellectual as imitator of the masses is not intrinsically linked with an anti-democratic position. On the contrary, it can also function as a warning to democratic intellectuals against certain simulacra of democracy. For we now live in a theatocracy (otherwise known as the world of the mass media): of politicians, for instance, whose electoral successes are proportional to the skills of their make-up assistant and their speech-writer, and to their own skill in reading the latter's magniloquent fabrications from the 'tele-prompter'. This is a tendency which is, of course, particularly prevalent in those countries now in process of

13 Timms, *Karl Kraus: Apocalyptic Satirist*, New Haven and London: Yale University Press, 1986, pp. 182, 186 and ch. 10 *passim*.

Americanization, including America itself. I include these bathetic remarks in order to underline what might be called the contemporary relevance of this paper.

Where, in this configuration, is the place of the intellectual? One does not need to be a Platonist to answer: in any case, in the refusal to play the same game; that is to say, in the refusal to play the part of imitator of the masses.

9

Responsibility and the act of interpretation: the case of law

IAN MACLEAN

In most legal situations problems of interpretation do not arise.
(H. McN. Henderson, in *JSPTL*, 3 (1985), p. 353)

Few would contest the view that democratic societies are committed to open, public discussion of issues involving such values as justice, liberty, equality, and that such discussion invokes the notion of truth and truth-telling as one of its guarantees. Yet it is also the case that in the operation of the legal systems of democratic societies, a clear distinction is drawn between arguing a case as persuasively as possible and believing in the veracity of that case; and between using language in a way which commits its user to tell the truth as he perceives it, and using language in a way which recognizes a relationship between words and *bona fides*, but deliberately does not adopt it. This paper sets out to investigate these linguistic practices by examining their components – meaning, mediation, interpretation – and by showing how they relate to law and to the responsibility for a given use of language of the citizen, the legal practitioner and more generally of the academic commentator or intellectual: a responsibility which a divorce of truth and meaning may seem to compromise, if not undermine.

Such an investigation is necessarily concerned with the relationship of the human subject with language on the one hand and broadly political or institutional issues on the other; it involves a study of responsibility for and in language; it presupposes that meaning derives from a set of interpersonally checkable rules or norms, which, by rendering meaning itself diachronic and non-private, opens it to the risks of infinite revision; it assumes that meaning has a relationship to groups and institutions as well as individuals, and that all transmission of meaning whether in spoken or in written form has inescapable moral and political consequences. Such transmission of meaning occurs when persons passing themselves off as competent, perhaps by invoking an institution to which they belong, interpose themselves between a message and its receiver (even sometimes between a message and its utterer, as a solicitor may be said to do to a testator in the drawing up of a will). This role had traditionally been fulfilled by members of the university-trained professions: theologians of certain traditions, lawyers and doctors. The care, direction and interpretation of Holy Writ, of the law, of the body are held not to be directly accessible to the believer, the litigant/testator or the patient, but are made accessible through the intervention of a qualified mediator. A late medieval Archbishop of Florence is recorded as averring that men have only their souls, goods and bodies in this life, and that they are controlled in their enjoyment of even these by theologians, lawyers and doctors respectively.[1] In this lawyers occupy a mediate position between the others, for theologians use words to give access to a sphere (the spiritual sphere) to which words alone can give shared and public access; doctors apply remedies to an organism whose material being is of the same order as the remedies themselves; lawyers, on the other hand, use words to bring about effects or represent the facts of a world and its denizens whose being is by and large not of the order of words. If there is a special nature to be attributed to legal language, it may well arise from the referential, normative and performative problems to which such an asymmetrical relationship gives rise.

All such mediators – and in modern societies they have proliferated beyond cloister, court and clinic – may have recourse to specialized registers of language, the 'terms of the art', which effectively deter or even exclude the layman from direct involvement in their activities. In this way they have sometimes been

---

[1] The anecdote is retailed in Castiglione's *Il Cortegiano* (1528), book ii, paragraph 66. The reference to theologians was excised by the Roman Inquisition (see *Il Cortegiano, riveduto e corretto da Antonio Ciccarelli da Forgligni Dottore in Teologia*, Venice: Bada, 1584, fos. 99v–100r).

described as parasites who live off the body politic rather than as specialists fulfilling necessary functions within it. Of course, such specialized registers may be defended on the grounds that ambiguity and obscurity can be avoided and precision achieved; but they may also be attacked as otiose. Montaigne, himself a lawyer by training, asks testily (and he is not the last to have done so) why it is that our common language 'so easy in all other usages, becomes obscure and unintelligible in contracts and wills', and concludes that it is the very search for precision in language which is the cause of ambiguity, obscurity and unintelligibility.[2] He hints also that legal practitioners act self-interestedly in ensuring that their profession is necessary to the running of society: more recent critics have gone futher, and argued that the conception of law as an autonomous language removed from everyday speech is the product of a society in which only a very limited class of legally competent people can read the texts of that language, and that this is 'geared to the reproduction of an economic elite and the discriminatory values that such an elite serves'.[3]

Specialist registers of speech, whatever interests they may be said to serve, give rise to the need for a secondary mediation of such registers, or a critique of their use, for the benefit of a non-specialist public. This has generally been done by the heterogeneous group which have come to be called 'intellectuals', although in different societies, at different times, they have been characterized in different ways. To speak of intellectuals as the guardians of such values as justice, truth, liberty and equality is either commonplace or misleading; but if one were to generate a Weberian 'ideal type' of the intellectual, he would have this as one of his functions.[4] He would also be associated with a broader group of characteristics, not all of which any one intellectual would have

---

[2] Montaigne, *Œuvres complètes*, ed. A. Thibaudet and M. Rat, Paris: Gallinard, 1962, p. 1043: see also Ian Maclean, 'The Place of Interpretation: Montaigne and Humanist Jurists on Words, Intention and Meaning', in *Neo-Latin and the Vernacular in Renaissance France*, ed. Grahame Castor and Terence Cave, Oxford: Clarendon Press, 1984, pp. 252–72.

[3] See, for example, Peter Goodrich, *Legal Discourse: Studies in Linguistics, Rhetoric and Legal Analysis*, London: Macmillan, 1987, p. 81; also pp. 131, 170ff, 206.

[4] See Max Weber, 'Die "Objektivität" sozial-wissenschaftlicher und sozialpolitischer Erkenntnis' (1904), in *Gesammelte Aufsätze zur Wissenschaftslehre*, ed. J. Winckelmann, Tübingen: Mohr, 1968, esp. pp. 195–6.

to possess: articulateness; access to organs of publication; spokes-manship; disinterestedness; application of, and appeal to, check-able norms such as reason and justice; opposition to the misuse of power. With such characteristics, an intellectual's involvement in the interpretation of law may be expected to bear upon the broad moral and political issues with which the legal system is inter-meshed, and from which it is at the same time distinct. Some of the more impressive recent contributions to jurisprudence (notably perhaps Ronald Dworkin's *Law's Empire*) have been concerned with this topic; they may be said to be mediation of the secondary kind in that their implied readership extends beyond the legal profession and academic lawyers.

The focus of this paper is the interpretation of law. It is not, however, intended as an exercise in jurisprudence. At various times over the past four centuries, the question of the interpreta-tion of law has been debated by academic writers of various facul-ties: philologists, philosophers, political scientists, jurists; my own modest access to this issue is through an interest in the history of interpretation on the one hand and in theories of meaning on the other. For this reason, I have taken as a corpus of exemplary texts a select diachronic series beginning with the Digest and culminating in the most recent studies of this issue. Many commentators on the topic of legal interpretation have noted that it seems to induce irreversible logorrhoea in its prac-titioners; in 1567, 30 pages sufficed to summarize the methods by which English statutes were to be understood; Bennion's book on the subject, which appeared in 1984, is 904 pages long, and only one of a number of extended studies of the topic to appear around that time.[5] My purpose here is not to give an exhaustive account of four centuries of competing theories, but to sketch a configur-ation of problems which, in broad terms, seems to be found in many of them, and to indicate how these give rise to the problem

---

[5] See Francis Bennion, *Statutory Interpretation*, London: Sweet and Maxwell, 1984. Ronald Dworkin's *Law's Empire*, London and Cambridge, Mass.: Harvard University Press, 1986 (hereafter referred to as Dworkin), also offers an interpretation of the law in so far as any person *applying* the law *interprets* what is required in particular cases. The process of citing precedents, hearing appeals, awarding damages, holding parties in con-tempt is interpretation in this weaker sense.

of responsibility to truth in the use of language adumbrated above.

Who is the law's interpreter? In one sense, all of us, for as subjects of the law we are deemed to understand it in order to obey it. Although we have already met the claim that to comprehend the law requires a legal training and cast of mind,[6] it seems that the understanding of the law is a more widespread phenomenon – perhaps even civic obligation – than is generally supposed. In a more restricted sense, the draftsmen serving any legislature are the interpreters of the law, for they must make law as an expression of its will. Again, it may also be said that judges are the interpreters of the law, for they must apply it in specific instances; the legal profession – solicitors and barristers – are responsible to their clients for its interpretation; and it could finally be said that academic lawyers and their pupils are its interpreters, in that they are involved in its explanation and assimilation. In his submission to the Law Commission's Report on the Interpretation of Statutes of 1969, M. Manfred Simon, a former president of the Court of Appeal of Paris, made the point that academic writings about the law exercise a significant influence on the practice of French courts; this is implicitly true in England also in that parliamentary reports on aspects of the law invite and accept submissions from University lawyers. Justinian, it is true, had decreed that only the Sovereign should interpret the law; but his stricture went widely unheeded in countries which practise versions of his Civil Law, and in England it was explicitly rejected.[7] Sir Christopher Hatton, writing about English law at the end of the sixteenth century, refers to judges as 'the Sages of the Law' who 'have the interpretation [of the Law] in their hands, and their Authority no man taketh in hand to control: wherefore their Power is very great, and high, and we seek these Interpretations

---

[6] See the comment of Sir Carleton Allen quoted in the *Report of the Law Commission (no. 21) and the Scottish Law Commission (no. 11) on the Interpretation of Statutes*, London: HM Stationery Office, (hereafter referred to as *Report*), p. 4; and Sir Rupert Cross, *Statutory Interpretation*, London: Butterworths, 1976 (hereafter referred to as Cross), pp. 64–7.

[7] *Codex*, 1.17, *De veteri iure enucleando*; William Blackstone, *Commentaries on the Laws of England in Four Books*, 5th edn. Oxford: Clarendon Press, 1773, vol. I, p. 58; John Austin, *Lectures on Jurisprudence* (1828–32), 4th edn, London: Murray, 1873 (hereafter referred to as Austin), pp. 642ff.

as oracles from their mouthes';[8] but Jeremy Bentham, who asks himself who are the Interpreters of the Law in the 1770s, seems to indicate that they may only be the legislative body. He and all subsequent writers are united in the view that a clear distinction should be maintained between the makers of law and those who apply it, between legislature and judiciary, even if the practice of understanding and expounding laws is a function shared by both these and by others.[9] The doctrine of the separation of powers, however, rests on the assumption that the legislature enacts the law to be applied by the judiciary; this (in England at least, as for the Roman Empire before Justinian) has not been unequivocally the case, for normative expectations such as the performance of contracts, the making good of torts or the prohibition of murder *per se* have never been expressly forbidden by the legistlative body, although murder, the breach of contract and torts of all kinds are manifestly against the law. The only possible sources of such norms are the judges and the textual record of past judgements of particular cases to which they refer; it might therefore be argued that in this way those who apply the law also make it, or at the very least 'find' it. This problem is less acute in legal systems which do not operate both by statute and precedent, but it has always been an issue in the practice of interpretation whether meaning is instituted or recovered, so that even in the West German system, which expresses the separation of powers most forcibly, there is a constant threat of the distinction between application of law and legislation becoming blurred, as will emerge more clearly below.[10]

Just as there is a multiplicity of interpreters of law, so also is there a multiplicity of readers of its interpretation. Private citizens, academic lawyers and judges may all be supposed to be

---

[8] Sir Christopher Hatton, *A Treatise concerning Statutes*, London: Tonson, 1677, (herafter referred to as Hatton), p. 30.

[9] Jeremy Bentham, *A Comment on the Commentaries and a Fragment on Government* (1774–6), ed. J. H. Burns and H. L. A. Hart, London: Athlone Press, 1977 (hereafter referred to as Bentham), pp. 91, 93, 114, 139–40. Also Austin, pp. 647ff.

[10] See *Institutes*, 1.2.3; *De confirmatione Digestorum* (Tanta), 20a; (Deo Auctore) 6; Ralf Dreier, 'Interpretation', para. 3(c), in *Staatslexikon*, 7th edn, Freiburg, Basle and Vienna: Herder, 1987, vol. III, p. 181; I am grateful to Professor Bernard Rudden and W. B. Ewald for having drawn my attention to these texts and arguments.

addressed by books on legal interpretation. Even as early as 1632, a law book appears especially for women readers telling them of their rights; and the Report of 1969 makes clear that law and its interpretation are not just for experts:

A statute is not exclusively a communication between the legislator and the courts. A statute is directed, according to its subject matter, to audiences of varying extent. As it is part of our duty to review the law with a view to its simplification our proposals must aim at ensuring that any statute can be understood, as readily as its subject matter allows, by all affected by it ... the intelligibility of statutes from the point of view of ordinary citizens of their advisers cannot in fact be dissociated from the rules of interpretation followed by the courts.[11]

Bentham also assumed that the reader of both the law and books about the law was the private citizen;[12] but this may be a somewhat misleading or disingenuous assumption. Elmer A. Driedger declares in his *Construction of Statutes* that 'a reader of a statute should be thoroughly familiar with the interpretation act of his jurisdiction';[13] but this can be true of only a tiny minority of citizens. For all the respect shown to the notional figure of the layman, most legal interpretation is addressed to the specialist: whether the student of the law, the academic lawyer, the legal practitioner or the judge.[14] Bentham, is obliged to admit that specialist terms in law call for specialist knowledge, and that the law furthermore makes use of ordinary language in idiosyncratic ways; the the Report of 1969 is forced (ironically) to supply footnotes to explain to *specialists* that it has avoided the use of

---

[11] *Report*, p. 3. The 1632 text is anonymous, and entitled *The Lawes Resolutions of Women's Rights: Or the Lawes Provision for Women* (published at London).

[12] Bentham, pp. 90–1.

[13] Elmer A. Driedger, *The Construction of Statutes*, Toronto: Butterworths, n.d. (hereafter referred to as Driedger), p. 193.

[14] Cross, p. 20, points out that Bentham 'took Blackstone's paragraphs about interpretation to be addressed to the general reader of the statute ... whereas it is tolerably clear that Blackstone conceived of himself as formulating, in an elementary way, rules on which the court should act in the event of a dispute concerning the meaning of statutory words coming before it'. The preface of Sir Peter Benson Maxwell, *Maxwell of the Interpretation of Statutes*, ed. P. St.J. Langan, 12th edn, London: Sweet and Maxwell, 1969, describes it as 'the Practitioner's Armoury'.

terms commonly used in legal contexts in order not to confuse *laymen*.[15] A more telling problem arises when it is not clear whether a handbook of legal interpretation is designed to be prescriptive (to tell judges and other members of the legal profession what they ought to do) or descriptive (to describe to students of the law what judges and others do in fact do); such confusion has arisen in relation to recent controversial books on the topic. It demonstrates the importance of identifying the implied reader of a treatise.

The issue of the language and meaning of the law affects its denizens in different ways. Legislatures have the responsibility for the *drafting* of law: as Felix Frankfurter says, 'they must not be encouraged in irresponsible or undisciplined use of language. In the keeping of legislatures more than any other group is the well-being of their fellow men. Their responsibility is discharged ultimately by words. They are under a special duty therefore to observe that exactness in the use of words is the basis of all serious thinking.'[16] Equally, the responsibility of judges in the *application* of the written law is undisputed: 'Fact situations do not await us nearly labelled, creased and folded; nor is their legal classification written on them simply to be read off by the judge. Instead, in applying legal rules, someone must take the responsibility of deciding that words do or do not cover some case in hand.'[17] A different responsibility lies with those who administer the law, notably policemen, as is recognized by the 'Judges' Rules' in accordance with which they were enjoined to obtain and record evidence. It is worth making a brief excursus to examine these rules in order to expose some of the presumptions about language which they encapsulate. Writing is presumed to be an adequate record of speech, as is made clear from the words of the caution

---

15 Bentham, pp. 100–3, 113–14, 146; *Report*, p. 49 n. 177; the hesitation about readership is also perceptible in Dworkin, pp. 14–15.

16 Felix Frankfurter, 'Some Reflections on the Reading of Statutes', in *Essays on Jurisprudence from the Columbia Law Review*, New York and London: Columbia University Press, 1963, pp. 43–62 (hereafter referred to as Frankfurter), p. 62.

17 H. L. A. Hart, *Essays in Jurisprudence and Philosophy*, Oxford: Clarendon Press, 1983 (hereafter referred to as Hart), pp. 63–4. On the differing role of judges in Europe on the one hand and in England and America on the other, see the comments of Cross, pp. 170–1.

given to suspects ('You are not obliged to say anything unless you wish to do so, but whatever you say will be taken down in writing and may be given in evidence'); it is further presumed that this caution can be paraphased (i.e. that its 'sense' can be given in 'the [police] officer's own words'), but that the evidence obtained by interrogation is relative to the time, place and circumstances of its acquisition; lastly, that any statement made by the suspect can be limited to that which is material to the case in point. This last presumption gives rise to a difficulty with which the 1964 revision of the Judges' Rules attempts to grapple: the police officer 'shall take down the exact words spoken by the person making the statement, without putting any questions other than such as may be needed to make the statement coherent, intelligible and relevant to the material matters' but 'he shall not prompt him'; furthermore 'in writing down a statement, the words used should not be translated into "official" vocabulary; this may give a misleading impression of the genuineness of the statement'.[18] We may sense here a shift between procedural language and ordinary language, and between objective meaning ('sense') and historical or context-bound meaning which will emerge as central problems in the methods by which the law in interpreted.

A more diffuse responsibility rests on the interpreters of the law. According to Dworkin, they are there 'to make the object or practice being interpreted the best it can be' according to the theory of 'best interpretation' which implies the existence not only of past legislative decisions but quasi-objective moral and political norms.[19] For others, legal interpreters do no more than elucidate obscurity and dispel doubt; any legal system, by the very nature of the words in which it is expressed, has, as O. W. Holmes put it, 'a certain play in the joints',[20] which is exacerbated in various ways – by the potential inadequacy of the work of the draftsman, by the

---

[18] The 'Judges' Rules' may be found in the appendix of Geoffrey Marshall, *Police and Government*, London: Methuen, 1967, pp. 127–34; they were superseded by the Police and Criminal Evidence Act 1984, on which see Michael Zander, *The Police and Criminal Evidence Act 1984*, London: Sweet and Maxwell, 1985, esp. pp. 259–304 (the Home Office Code of Practice).

[19] Dworkin, p. 77 and *passim*.

[20] Oliver Wendell Holmes, *Collected Legal Papers*, New York: Harcourt, Brace and Howe, 1920 (hereafter referred to as Holmes), p. 204.

fact that all consequences of a law cannot be foreseen, and by the
fact that a law does not unambiguously and clearly meet all cases
for which it was designed. Some legal commentators and judges
presume clarity in expression unless this is shown not to be the
case; others, more suspicious by nature, assume obscurity or
ambiguity until it is proved otherwise.[21] An extreme version of this
last doctrine holds that the sense of the law can only be discovered
after it has been written; Frankfurter records seeing a cartoon in
which one American senator tells his colleagues: 'I admit this new
bill is too complicated to understand. We'll just have to pass it to
find out what it means.'[22] But in either case – whether the law is
held to be mainly unequivocal or fraught throughout with difficulties of comprehension – the undisputed function of the interpreter seems clear: to dispel ambiguity and doubt from the words
of the law.

This project of understanding the law and making it com-
prehensible for others apparently presupposes that judges, practitioners and citizens will endeavour to understand the law in good
faith: a judge whose judgements bore no relation to the law would
either be thought to be no judge at all or would belong to the realm
of imaginative fiction, like Rabelais' Bridoye, Brecht's Asdak or
Kafka's Untersuchungsrichter.[23] Equally, the citizen as the subject of the law is enjoined to obey its spirit, and not to circumvent
this by subtlety in interpreting its letter.[24] But it has long been a

---

21 Albericus Gentilis, *In titulum Digestorum de verborum significatione
commentarius*, Hanau: heirs of Johannes Aubrius, 1614 (hereafter referred
to as Gentilis), p. 19. Also Bentham, p. 116; *Report* p. 8 (quoting Viscount
Simonds).

22 Frankfurter, p. 61; see also Pierre Rebuffi, *In titulum Digestorum de
verborum et rerum significatione commentaria*, Lyons: Rouillé, 1586, p. 3,
quoted by Maclean, 'Interpretation', p. 263.

23 See Stanley Fish, 'Working on the Chain Gang: Interpretation in the Law
and in Literary Criticism', *Critical Inquiry*, 9 (1982–3), pp. 201–16, esp.
p. 212; it would seem appropriate to establish this point by reference to
John Searle's distinction between regulative and constitutive rules (*Speech
Acts*, Cambridge: Cambridge University Press, 1969, pp. 33–5). It is
constitutive of the office of judge in Searle's sense to pass judgements which
understand the law in good faith.

24 Digest 1.3.29 (Paulus): 'contra legem facit, qui id facit, quod lex prohibet,
in fraudem vero, qui salvis verbis legis sententiam eius circumvenit'
('Someone who does what the law prohibits, but fraudulently, by sticking

widespread practice to employ a legal interpreter to find his way round the strict application of legislation (for example, tax legislation) by insisting on the words, and not the spirit, of the law. In such cases, the citizen endeavours to understand the words of the law expressly in bad faith. Mr Justice Stephen once declared that drafting Acts of Parliament required a remarkable degree of precision because 'although they may be easy to understand, people try to misunderstand [them], and therefore it is not enough to attain a degree of precision [in them] which a person reading in good faith can understand; but it is necessary to attain, if possible, a degree of precision which a person reading in bad faith cannot misunderstand'.[25] The sensitivity of legislatures to this problem is well known and can be easily instantiated: Sir Rupert Cross illustrates it by reference to a statute of Edward VI according to which those who stole *horses* should not have the benefit of clergy: a new Act was procured in the following year to cover the case of 'him that should steal but *one* horse'.[26] Such egregious misreading can also act against the citizen, as in the (possibily spurious) case of a Canadian Indian who was convicted of shooting his horse, which at the time had a feather pillow on its back, under the Small Birds Act which protects animals with feathers and (at least) two legs.[27] Enshrined in Mr Justice Stephen's principle is an interesting reversal of a common presumption about successful communication which will be discussed below, namely that for meaning to be transmitted successfully it is necessary to assume good faith on the part of the participants in the exchange. But more important still, the Stephen principle raises the thorny issue of the relation-

to the words of the law but circumventing its clear sense, contravenes the law'). Also Gentilis, p. 20: 'Sic facit secundum leges qui facit contra legem, qui contra sententiam tantum facit et ... faciunt fraudem legi, qui secundum verba faciunt contra sententiam' ('To act in accordance with the law is to act in accordance with its spirit and not its word. Equally to contravene the law is to act against its spirit; those who act in accordance with the letter but not the spirit of the law act fraudulently'). There is a vast literature on cavillation, deriving from Digest 50.16.177 and 50.17.65. One can of course equally associate 'bad faith' with the interpretation of the spirit of the law (i.e. the egregious neglect of the manifest sense of the law).

[25] Cited by Lord Thring, *Practical Legislation*, London: Murray, 1902, p. 3, and Cross, p. 60.

[26] Cited by Cross, p. 19 (cf. also Cross, p. 52, on the phrase 'any offence').

[27] R. V. Ojibway, 8 Crim.L.Q. 137 Toronto 1965, pp. 21–3.

ship of words to intention or 'spirit' or 'meaning'. How do the
words of the law express the 'meaning' of the law? Under what
constraints, through what authority and by what processes may
meaning be extracted from the words of the law?

In order to tackle these questions, it is pertinent to offer first
an account of 'meaning' itself; then to make explicit some of the
presumptions about the language of the law; next to examine the
methods applied to legal texts to extract sense from them; and
finally to investigate the contentious dichotomy of sense and
intention. A full survey of competing theories of meaning is
beyond the scope of this paper, but a few general and relatively
uncontroversial points need to be made. These are rarely made
explicit in jurisprudential writings; indeed there is a healthy (if
not hoary) disrespect shown for 'theory' and a preference for stu-
dying 'points of law' which can be traced back to the earliest
stages of Roman law; but even practising judges like Oliver
Wendell Holmes have conceded the importance of stating the
premises by which legal science operates, and these concern the
most general features of language as a semiotic system.[28]

A first presumption to be made about the language of law is
that it is a form of intentional communication: that is, that it both
expresses a sense and conveys a given message. H. P. Grice has
codified the principles of conversation which are necessary for
this to be successful as communication; his maxims apply well to
the presumptions made about the use of language in law:

The co-operative principle
make your contribution such as is required, at the stage at which it
occurs, by the accepted purpose or direction of the talk exchange in
which you are engaged

The maxim of Quality
try to make your contribution one that is true, specifically:
1. do not say what you believe to be false
2. do not say that for which you lack adequate evidence

The maxim of Quantity
1. make your contribution as informative as is required for the
    current purposes of the exchange

[28] See Fritz Schulz, *History of Roman Legal Science*, Oxford: Clarendon
Press, 1953, p. 70; Holmes, p. 207; *Report*, p. 5; also Cross, pp. 142–55
(on presumptions).

2.   do not make your contribution more informative than is required

The maxim of Relevance
make your contributions relevant

The maxim of Manner
be perspicuous, and specifically:
1.   avoid obscurity
2.   avoid ambiguity
3.   be brief
4.   be orderly[29]

These maxims specify what participants have to do in order to converse in a maximally efficient, rational, co-operative way. Their relevance to legal science becomes clear if we turn to a recent attempt (that by Robert Alexy) to establish the ground rules of legal discourse: his first four rules are

1 No speaker may contradict himself.
2 Speakers may only affirm that which they themselves believe to be the case.
3 Speakers who apply a predicate F to an object a must be prepared to apply F to any other object which is in relevant ways the same as a.
4 Different speakers may not use the same expression with different meanings.[30]

For our purposes, Grice's and Alexy's insistence on telling the truth (or what one believes to be true) has crucial implications for the language of law, which is presumed to be serious; to make sense; to refer (where appropriate) to objects in the real world; furthermore to be able to refer to objects even when they are not present to the speaker of hearer by 'displacement'; and finally to be consensual. For a contract to be a contract, there must be a

---

[29] H. P. Grice, 'Logic and Conversation' in P. Cole and J. L. Morgan (eds.), *Syntax and Semantics 3: Speech Acts*, New York: Academic Press, 1975, pp. 41–58; H. P. Grice, 'Further Notes on Logic and Conversation', in P. Cole and J. L. Morgan (eds.), *Syntax and Semantics 9: Pragmatics*, New York: Academic Press, 1970, pp. 113–28; see also Stephen C. Levinson, *Pragmatics*, Cambridge: Cambridge University Press, 1983, pp. 100–18; Geoffrey N. Leech, *Principles of Pragmatics*, London and New York: Longman, 1983, pp. 7–10, 79–103.

[30] Robert Alexy, *Theorie der juristischen Argumentation*, Frankfurt: Suhrkamp, 1983, pp. 234–8.

'meeting of minds', a 'consensus ad idem'; in other words, an agreement that the two parties are saying the same thing by the same words.[31] The interpretation of law can only proceed on the basis of these crucial presumptions. They form the link with a number of modern theories which have attempted to codify 'seriousness' under different names – Gadamer's 'Verhältnis zur Wahrheit', Habermas' ideal speech situation, Davidson's principle of charity, J. L. Austin's analysis of speech-acts. Some of these theorists recognize that legal studies have long grappled with these problems.[32]

There are two further general presumptions about language which are almost never stated in law (indeed, they are implicitly repressed). The first is that language is reflexive: that is, that it can refer to itself. The fact that we must use language in order to talk about language (or, to put it in a different way, that we can both use words and mention them) means that language's capacity to refer to objects is not simple and can give rise to confusions of use and mention. It is of importance to legal science that such confusion should not arise, and that where words are used normatively, their use should predominate over their mention;[33] it

---

[31] Holmes, pp. 206–8; cf. Digest 34.5.21 (Paulus): 'Ubi est verborum ambiguitas, valet quod actum est, veluti cum Stichum stipuler et sunt plures Stichi, vel hominem, vel Carthagini, cum sunt duae Carthagines. Semper in dubiis id agendum est, ut quam tutissimo loco res sit bona fide contracta, nisi cum aperte contra leges scriptum est' ('Where there is verbal ambiguity, for example, if I stipulate Stichus and there are several persons of that name, or a man from Carthage and there is more than one Carthage, the intentions of the utterer determine what is valid. In all cases of doubt, the principle to be followed is that except where a provision clearly contravenes the law, any contract made in good faith should be accorded the maximum protection'). On the referential function of language, and its capacity to refer to absent and fictional objects ('displacement'), see John Lyons, *Semantics*, Cambridge: Cambridge University Press, 1977, vol. II, pp. 181–97.

[32] Hans-Georg Gadamer, *Wahrheit und Methode*, 2nd edn, Tübingen: Mohr, 1972, ii.2.1, pp. 275–90, esp. p. 278; Jürgen Habermas, *Theorie des kommunikativen Handelns*, Frankfurt: Suhrkamp, 1985, vol. I, pp. 369–454; D. Davidson, 'Radical Interpretation', *Dialectica*, 27 (1974), pp. 313–28; J. L. Austin, *How to Do Things with Words*, Oxford: Oxford University Press, 1962, esp. pp. 19,36.

[33] There is, of course, a sense in which reflexive language is more commonly encountered in law than elsewhere, namely in those elements of statutes

is equally of importance that the prevaricative feature of language (that is, its capacity to be used to deceive and misinform) should be held in check. However, it is widely recognized in the law that language can be used prevaricatively, although the law itself as a semiotic system could not operate if it did in its own case. Umberto Eco's claim that 'if [a sign] cannot be used to tell a lie, conversely it cannot be used to tell the truth'[34] cannot be held to apply to the language of the law, or there would be no such thing. The importance of the relationship of language to truth, as in Grice's and Alexy's rules, is here made clear.

Another relevant presumption is that which distinguishes 'subjective' sense from 'objective' or 'literal' sense (or 'what the legislature means' as opposed to 'what the words of a statute mean'). This distinction is commonly understood in the context of the rival claims of objectivism and relativism: by these terms I mean (a) the conviction that there is some permanent ahistorical structure or framework to which we can ultimately appeal in determining the nature of rationality, knowledge, truth, reality, goodness, rightness and so on and (b) the opposing view that there is no such structure or framework, and that we are irredeemably caught in a jungle of mutually exclusive values and conceptual schemes, none of which can prove its correctness against any other. In terms of this debate, meaning can be conceived of *either* as that which arises from the words and propositions of an utterance or a text, constituting its 'semantic autonomy', *or* as that which the author or reader as subject means; the first representing the 'objective' fact of the text, the second the 'subjective' act of intending or making sense. Much has been said about the inadequacy of this opposition, and of the opposition objectivist/relativist, but it should be noted that debates about meaning in law are still informed by it. It follows from this distinction that legislatures are supposed to have purposes and that words embody intention – both a general intention (to

which precede the normative sections (definition clauses, interpretation clauses, repealing and codifying enactments, entrenchment clauses, marginalia, etc.).

34 Umberto Eco, *A Theory of Semiotics*, Bloomington: Indiana University Press, 1976, p. 7; on reflexivity and prevarication, see Lyons, *Semantics*, vol. I, pp. 5–10, 74–85.

express a sense) and a specific intention (to convey a given message).[35] Even though intention is always found in the form of words, it is itself not to be identified with a string of words: rather, it is often characterized as a mental state, or ideal object, or force distinct from the words which embody it.[36] Without this presumption, no theory of *mens rea* could work, nor could a distinction between formalism and voluntarism (or *ratio legis* and *mens legislatoris*) be maintained. The presumption of an 'objective sense' in the words of the law further implies that an unequivocal literal sense is in fact possible,[37] and that it may be obtained by recourse to the 'general usages of speech' or 'grammatical meaning' or 'natural sense'.[38]

It is presumed that the written text of the law is the authoritative text and that the written text is only a fixed form of a spoken text or a text which potentially could be spoken.[39] This is often made explicit in Interpretation Acts, as in that of Canada (para. 10): 'the law shall be considered as always speaking, and whenever a matter or thing is expressed in the present tense, it shall be applied to the circumstances as they arise, so that effect may be given to the enactment and every part thereof according to its true spirit, intent and meaning'.[40] The language of law is therefore taken to be performative (in the limited sense of recording verbal acts),[41] and always to relate to the present; as Bentham says: 'If the will of

---

35 Bentham, p. 103. I do not wish here to discuss the argument that intention can be public and knowable as opposed to private, which is invoked to undermine the validity of the objectivist/relativist distinction.

36 Holmes, p. 204; cf. Digest 1.3.17: 'Scire leges non hoc est verba earum tenere, sed vim ac potestatem' ('To know the law is not to know the words of the law but rather its force and power') (cf. also Digest 1.3.19; 50.16.6).

37 Austin, p. 1028.

38 See Cross, pp. 56ff, and his distinctions between primary and secondary meaning and fringe meaning. The role of rhetoric in law (see Goodrich, *Legal Discourse*) and the distinction literal/figurative are major topics not treated here.

39 On this topic, see Paul Ricoeur, *Interpretation Theory*, Fort Worth: Texas Christian University Press, 1976, pp. 25ff.

40 Quoted by Driedger, p. 239; the source of this (Lord Thring, 1884) is given in Cross, p. 45.

41 Hart, pp. 32ff; cf. Digest 1.3.7 (Modestinus): 'Legis virtus haec est imperare, vetare, permittere, punire' ('The force of the law is this: to command, to prohibit, to permit and to punish').

former races of legislators has the force of law at all, it is only because it is tacitly adopted by the present. Will without power to back it is just nothing.'[42] In this respect, the text of the law always addresses the reader, as though in a dialogue.[43]

But as well as being a speech-act or performance, the language of the law also embodies a predictive element, since it is drafted in order to come into effect *after* its drafting, and since it is interpreted in order to obtain an 'intelligent *anticipation* of the way in which it would be interpreted by the courts'.[44] In Frankfurter's words, 'statutes come out of the past and aim at the future'.[45] Thus the language is taken to be present in force but future in intention; this 'future meaning' is the space in which interpretation operates. It is by its nature an hypothetical space, yet it is also necessarily committed to the real and the referential in that it is the language of the law. It is also strongly committed to a separation of past from present in which the past can both authorize the interpretation of the present law and act as the status quo which generates new law.[46] Legal language has therefore a very strongly charged temporal element, which compromises its claim to embody objects and opens it up to an historicist or hermeneutic analysis; it obliges its interpreters to be explicit as to the relationship between the text they are interpreting, the time of its composition and the time of its interpretation. In this respect, Ralf Dreier has identified four possible hermeneutic positions: the interpretation which accepts the historical will of the legislature as binding; that which accepts the 'objective' sense of the words used in their historical context as binding; that which accepts the hypothetical will of the legislature (that which it would intend now if apprized of present conditons) as binding; and finally that which

---

[42] Bentham, p. 102.

[43] Cross, p. 24, quoting Plowden, 1574: 'it is a good way, when you peruse a statute, to suppose that the lawmaker is present, and that you have asked him the question you want to know touching the equity, then you must give yourself such an answer as you imagine he would have done, if he had been present'. Also Robert Alexy 'Problems of Discourse Theory' (unpublished conference paper).

[44] *Report*, p. 3; cf. Bentham, pp. 92–3.   [45] Frankfurter, p. 51.

[46] Digest 50.17.1 (Paulus): 'ex iure quod est regula fiat' ('rules are made from the law as it stands'): cf. Digest 1.3.26, 28; Bentham, p. 102.

is bound by the objective sense of the words of the law in their present usage.[47]

The canons of interpretation which are underpinned by these presumptions have received many codifications: from their earliest methodical exposition (by the postglossators) to the most recent versions – Cross' four basic rules, Dreier's seven principles – there has been little radical change although many shifts in emphasis.[48] In the context of this discussion, four features of these methods are pertinent. The first is their implicit or explicit adoption of the norms of equity, justice, reasonableness (rationality) and common sense (practical convenience). In England, this adoption is enshrined in the so-called 'Golden Rule', as can be inferred from Lord Simon of Glaisdale's account of it:

in statutes dealing with ordinary people in their everyday lives, the language is presumed to be used in its primary ordinary sense, unless this stultifies the purposes of the statute, or otherwise produces some injustice, absurdity, anomaly or contradiction, in which case some secondary, ordinary sense may be preferred, so as to obviate the injustice, absurdity, anomaly or contradiction or fulfil the purpose of the statute.[49]

Lord Simon refers also here to the 'Literal Rule' and the 'Mischief Rule' which we will consider below: but he implies that these can be overridden by an appeal to notions of justice, reason and so on.

The second feature is their recourse to context. This may mean no more than the preamble, punctuation, headings and marginalia of a statute (most attention being paid in determining sense to the preamble, the 'key' to the purpose for which the statute was enacted); it can embrace parliamentary material written prior to the enactment of *travaux préparatoires*; it can even extend beyond the legal domain into the wider social and political context.[50] Crucial to the determination of context is the intention

---

[47] *Staatslexikon*, vo. III, p. 181.

[48] *Ibid.*, vol. III, p. 182 ('Wortlautinterpretation; logische; genetische; historische; systematische; komparative; teleologische'); Cross, p. 43; also Maclean, 'Interpretation'.

[49] Cross, p. 43, and *passim*.

[50] Hatton, p. 17; Frankfurter, pp. 44, 54; *Report*, pp. 8, 25–6, 31–7; Bentham, pp. 104–5; Austin, pp. 1030ff; for the *in pari materia* rule, see Cross, pp. 127–9.

said to be the *vis motrix* of the statute; a classic formulation of this is found in the frequently adduced 'Mischief Rule' cited in Heydon's case of 1584 (3 Co. Rep. 7a):

And it was resolved . . . that for the sure and true interpretation of all statutes in general (be they penal or beneficial, restrictive or enlarging of the common law), four things are to be discerned and considered:
1st. What was the Common Law before the making of the Act,
2nd. What was the mischief and defect for which the Common Law did not provide,
3rd. What remedy the Parliament hath resolved and appointed to cure the disease of the commonwealth,
And, 4th. The true reason of the remedy; and then the office of all the Judges is always to make such construction as shall suppress subtle inventions and evasions for continuance of the mischief, and *pro privato commodo*, and to add force and life to the cure and remedy, according to the true intent of the makers of the Act, *pro bono publico*.

One may note here the imputation of a judicial duty to correct laxity on the part of draftsmen, the allusion to the practice of *non-cooperative* understanding in the fourth clause, and the presumption that the 'true intent' of the makers of the act is unequivocal. But as we have seen, the 'non-cooperation' in fulfilling the intention of a speaker or a text poses a problem at the level of language – the *bona fides* inherent in its uses and this element of good faith is not easy to codify or translate into a formal description; and the 'true intent' of the legislator may either be irrecoverable, incoherent or even contradictory.[51] Its status as a guarantee of meaning is therefore not very secure.

The third feature is their recourse to 'general usages of speech' or 'grammatical meaning'. In a sense, this is also contextual, for it implicitly recognizes a distinction between 'legal speech' and 'ordinary language' which exists beyond it. Gentilis provides as an example of the former the Latin pronominal phrase 'si quis', which although in ordinary speech is masculine, can refer in legal texts to both male and female.[52] In this case legal speech takes priority

---

[51] Austin, pp. 652–3; Hatton, p. 26; Frankfurter, p. 58; *Report*, p. 33; also Digest 1.3.20 (Julianus): 'non omnium, quae a maioribus constituta sunt, ratio reddi potest' ('it is not possible to give the reasons for all the laws laid down by our forebears').

[52] Gentilis, pp. 1–2; Interpretation Act, 1889, para. 1(1)(a).

over ordinary speech; but the recourse to the latter implies that it has its role to play within the sphere of the law. The sense of this 'ordinary speech' is taken to be that which a 'normal speaker' would have construed from the circumstances of its utterance;[53] but as Holmes points out, the 'normal speaker' is not any native speaker of a language but a special case, the 'prudent' or 'reasonable' man; furthermore, he is a 'prudent' or 'reasonable' man capable of distinguishing dictionary meanings from meanings of words embedded in a rather special sort of discourse, namely a legal document; in short, he is an interpeter of the law.[54] Thus interpretation of the law by recourse to 'grammatical sense' threatens to become the pursuit of a principle of validation which is already presupposed in the making and reading of the law: in other words, no sort of validation at all.

The fourth feature is their recourse to historical sense. In broad terms, interpreters of the law have the choice of determining the sense of a statute by asking the question: what did the legislator mean when he conceived of this law? Or by asking: what would the legislator have meant if he had made the law in the circumstances which prevail now? This choice is particularly difficult in jurisdictions which have both statute law and case law, under which judges decide on case law effectively by extracting rules from precedent.[55] The risks of such interpretation are clear: judges, by construing the law, *make* the law; by 'extending' interpretation, they improperly take on the role of the legislature.[56] But even in the case of statutory interpretation, their acts of construction can be seen to be acts not of application but of legislation. All jurisprudential writers are agreed that judges do not have the authority to 'use words as empty vessels into which they can pour anything they will';[57] many unite in the explicit hope that their

---

53 It is presumably for this reason Cross (p. 52) makes the assertion that 'the ordinary meaning of words, a matter of obvious concern to the law of interpretation, is a question of fact' where 'question of fact' indicates that it is for the legal layman to determine the sense of words (such as 'dishonest' or 'insulting': contrast the interpretation of such words as 'embezzlement' or 'contempt' or 'theft').

54 Holmes, p. 204; cf. Bentham, pp. 107–8.   55 Hart, p. 99.

56 Austin, pp. 469ff (the classical discussion).

57 Frankfurter, p. 45; cf. the category in literary theory of 'subjectivism' as described by E. D. Hirsch, *Validity in Interpretation*, New Haven and London: Yale University Press, 1967, pp. 155–63.

interpretative methods will act as constraints on the judiciary
(Blackstone, Bentham, Austin); but the methods they offer all
seem in the last analysis to offer no secure and objective guidance
in interpretation, and they can all be shown to depend on the
determination of norms which may be historical in character.

It may be helpful to examine one case of jurisprudential
reasoning to show how this impasse is reached: that of Jeremy
Bentham, who in writing a commentary on Blackstone's *Commentaries on the Laws of England* in the 1770s, dismisses derisively the
method of interpretation offered by Blackstone and offers his own
which he expresses thus:

A Law is made: it is made to a certain end. The intention is manifest:
it is to attain that end. It is improvidently penned: the effect is, that
there is a case in which complying literally with its directions would
not contribute to the attainment of that end. It is plain therefore that
such compliance was not intended to be enforced at the time the Law
was making. Exact it not, then, I say to the Judge: and to the citizen,
suppose not that it will be exacted. To this case the Law is not to be
interpreted to extend. For to this case the will of those who made the
Law *never* did extend. The words of a Legislator are no[t] otherwise
to be regarded than inasmuch as they are expressive of his will . . . The
question is concerning the intention (viz. of those who made the Law)
at the time of making it: not what at a subsequent time, ought to be or
may probably be their intentions. For that these supposed subsequent
intentions are not turned contrary must be taken for certain, since
they have not changed the expression of them: and to change their
intentions to what it is conceived they ought to be, belongs to them
only, and to no other person: for that other person who should do so
would be himself the legislator.[58]

Crucial to this interpretative method is the identification of the
purpose of the legislator: his subjective intention (or the intention
analogically embodied in the legislature).[59] Access to this intention
(which will overcome the problem of the 'improvident penning' of
the Law) is made through words, which in some way are thought
to be neutral or objective signs of the will of the legislator. Ideally,
the intention would be able to pass directly from legislator to
reader: 'If a legislator means to be understood, he must call up
directly [my emphasis] the ideas of those actions he would have

[58] Bentham, p. 115.   [59] On this see Cross, pp. 34–40.

done or not done' (p. 116): but there is no such thing as an expression of written intent which is not couched *indirectly* in the form of words: and, furthermore, words which are not objective counters but indices subjectively realized by readers. Elsewhere Bentham acknowledges that words are detours through which mental objects and states pass from one mind to another (p. 99); but in his own method he chooses to disregard this problem. This is all the more surprising in that he submits the word 'reasonable' to an analysis which shows that the same slippage from subjective to supposed objective status occurs in Blackstone's text (pp. 158–9); and in that Bentham recognizes at another point in his argument that 'grammatical' or 'literal' meaning is no more than a consensus as to what the meaning of a word or phrase is, and cannot be demonstrated formally or logically (p. 98).

The foregoing analysis is not intended to belittle Bentham's text, but to show how difficult it is to establish some sort bedrock in the shifting sands of verbal interpretation, because the reflexivity and prevarication which are features of the language system inhibit the establishment of external or objective guarantees of sense. A similar configuration of problems appears in John Austin's lectures on jurisprudence of the 1830s in his distinction between 'ratio decidendi' and 'ratio legis'; it may even be detected in recent debates between Dworkin and Stanley Fish in which the claims of rival schools of legal thought have been debated and the questions asked whether there are objective moral and political criteria which can be applied by judges, derived from such abstractions as 'liberty', 'equality' and 'justice', or whether such values are always relative to the community in which they are used and to its own interpretative rules.[60] These problems are most clearly perceived when the distinction between the purpose of the statute (the 'mens legislatoris') and the 'verbal meaning of the statute' (the 'ratio legis') is investigated; my last comments will be devoted to this issue.

By 'mens legislatoris' (the intention of the legislature, which although not a human body is nonetheless given a 'will' by analogy), a historical, quasi-subjective meaning is designated, which can be cross-checked by reference either to an extra-legal

60 Austin, pp. 640ff, 1024ff; and the debate between Dworkin and Fish on this issue (reprinted in the *Texas Law Review*, 60 (1982)).

context, or to material embodied in the law – preambles, definitions, interpretation acts and so forth. Thus far it is able to be
verified and given an ideal status (that is, it is taken to be
transferable from one context to another without loss or alteration
of sense).[61] It is, however, in the form of words or of implications
of words, and if pursued to its limits, it comes back to the analysis
and determination of the express words of the statute or law itself,
as one judge, Lord Watson, pointed put:

'Intention of the Legislature' is a common but very slippery phrase,
which, popularly understood, may signify anything from intention
embodied in positive enactment to speculative opinion as to what the
legislature probably would have meant, although there has been an
omission to enact it. In a Court of Law or Equity, what the
Legislature intended to be done or not to be done can only be
legitimately ascertained from that which it has chosen to enact, either
in express words or by reasonable and necessary implication.[62]

Yet we all manifestly believe that a distinction is possible between
our words and our intention: as one ancient legal maxim has it,
'who says something other than that which he means, neither says
what the words mean, because he does not mean them, nor what he
means, because he does not say it'.[63] By saying what the words of a
law mean (that is by assigning an intention to them), the interpreter following the 'mens legislatoris' rule can do no more than
adduce supplementary textual material in a process of demon-

[61] Frankfurter, p. 55; Driedger, pp. 191–2.
[62] *Report*, p. 31. Lord Watson does not specify what logic would be employed
to obtain the 'necessary implication'.
[63] Digest 34.5.3 (Paulus): 'qui aliud dicit quam vult, neque id dicit quod vox
significat, quia non vult, neque id quod vult, id non loquitur' ('who says
something other than that which he means, neither says what the words say,
because he does not mean it, nor what he means, because he does not say
it'). Cf. such English law maxims quoted by Hatton (pp. 14–19) as 'ut
verba serviant intentioni et non intentio verbis'; 'in dubio haec legis
presumitur est sententia quam verba ostendunt'; 'ubi manifeste pugnant
legis voluntas et verba, neutrum sequendum est. Verba quia non congruunt
menti, mens quia non congruit verbis' ('words are the servants of intention,
and not intention of words'; 'in cases of doubt the sense of a law is presumed
to be that which is evident from the words'; 'whenever there is an obvious
conflict between the sense and the words of the law, neither is to be
followed; neither the words, because they do not agree with the sense, not
the sense, because it does not agree with the words').

stration which is probable at best, and which may have to suppress conflicting accounts of the intentions of the law-makers or even supply them by supposition when they are absent or lost.

The procedures followed by those who choose to concern themselves only with the 'express words of the law', in which the 'ratio legis' is to be found, are no more certain. The 'semantic autonomy' of legal texts, their 'grammatical meaning' is a hollow principle of exegesis unless some guarantee can be found of its validity, and this cannot be supplied by a formal semantic analysis without the provision of a broader verbal context which is implicitly historical. Even recourse to equity as a principle or interpretation cannot release the process from the threat of infinite regress.[64] The 'objective meaning' which in theory can be extracted from the words alone of the law is, in one sense at least, no more than that meaning assigned to them by the interpreter or judge, even if both of these figures try in good faith (that unquantifiable factor) to justify such assignation. The historical school of law inspired by von Savigny implicitly recognized this by arguing that the law once published detaches itself from its originators and their intentions to take its own course according to the evolution of the social context; we may recall also the hermeneutic solution to this problem expressed in Gadamer's stricture: 'each age has to understand a transmitted text in its own way, for the text is part of the whole of the tradition in which the age takes an objective interest, and in which it seeks to understand itself'.[65]

Where has this examination of legal interpretation left the issue of responsibility which falls to interpreters of law? Few would agree that the claim of one prominent judge – that 'the meaning of a sentence is to be felt rather than proved'[66] – settles the issue: certainly the host of jurists who have attempted to lay down canons of interpretation cannot have thought that their labours could so lightly be dismissed. The *vis motrix* of interpretation is the need to dispel ambiguity and doubt about meaning arising from features of the language system itself: reflexivity; prevarication; displacement (the fact that language refers to objects which need not be present); the combination of synchronic and diachronic

---

[64] Hatton, pp. 28–9; Bentham, p. 158.
[65] Gadamer, *Wahrheit und Methode*, p. 280.
[66] Holmes, quoted by Frankfurter, p. 47.

elements; the inscription of temporality. The language of law is normative, and is structured in the form of commands and general maxims; but it is also often context-specific, and thus brings together uneasily, as we have seen in the case of Judges' Rules, depragmatized and pragmatic aspects of communication. Therefore, for both general and specific reasons, precision, formal demonstration, correctness are exceptionally difficult to achieve, if achievable at all, as the most recent German jurist to have attempted a logic-based account of legal discourse has conceded.[67] Yet the law works: as Dworkin points out, 'Law is a flourishing practice, and though it may well be flawed, even fundamentally, it is not a grotesque joke. It means something to say that judges should enforce rather than ignore the law, that citizens should obey it except in rare cases, that officials are bound by its rule.'[68] Furthermore, it is widely held that there is a close relationship between the law and concepts of fairness, justice, equality, due process and so on. Even though firm ground may be difficult to reach, it seems wrong to abandon the attempt altogether under the aegis of hard relativist arguments.

One way forward might be to distinguish the responsibility to language and truth in law according to the function of its denizens. Draftsmen, judges, officials, academics, even intellectuals writing about legal issues from outside the law, can be said to bear different responsibilities, but all to have a commitment to truth and to believing what they say in respect of the law: to describe how their functions differ in this, one might have recourse to the historical distinction in hermeneutics between the *subtilitas intelligendi* (applicable to all), the *subtilitas explicandi* (particular to draftsmen, academics and intellectuals) and the *subtilitas applicandi* (particular to judges and officials).[69] Whichever function is fulfilled, these interpreters of the law are obliged to read it in good faith, to read it disinterestedly and, in the case of textual exegesis, to act humbly as the servants of a text by mediating its dictates to others.[70] But the process of interpretation is not a humble one at all: rather than being the servants of the text, interpreters threaten to become its masters by devising and applying the rules by which

---

[67] Alexy, 'Problems of Discourse Theory'.   [68] Dworkin, p. 44.
[69] See Gadamer, *Wahrheit und Methode*, pp. 290–1.
[70] See Frankfurter, pp. 49–50; Maclean, 'Interpretation'.

sense is made of it; indeed, they threaten to become its masters to the point of laying down the law themselves. This effect is produced because whether the 'objective sense' or the 'subjective sense', the 'ratio legis' or the 'mens legislatoris' of the law, is sought, no absolute guarantee of meaning can be produced. The best that can be hoped for is an intersubjective or consensual agreement as to the rules and conclusions of textual analysis which can never aspire to formal demonstration, and in which the contextual and performative features of such agreement are made explicit: who did it, for whom it was done, when it was done and in what context. Law-makers themselves often do this in preambles, definitions and marginalia. A commitment to seriousness and to truth-telling may not be susceptible to adequate codification, but an explicit recognition by interpreters of the historicity of their role may go some way towards reducing the authoritative claims of any act of mediation, even if this seems to compromise their allegiance to concepts such as justice, equality, fairness and so on which are often held to be universals.

The legal practitioner (particularly the advocate) and the citizen, however, are not enjoined to marry truth, meaning and belief in the same way: it is open to them to read and interpret the law in bad faith, in their own interest or in the interest of an argument. But this may not be as calamitous for democratic societies or for such values as civic virtue, truthfulness, justice and reason as might be supposed. The process of reading in bad faith lays bare the features of the language system which themselves give rise to instability of meaning and obscurity, and in so doing it forces upon succeeding generations of legal interpreters the task of clarification, which itself produces a distinction (whether universally valid, or historically contingent does not here matter) between disinterested and interested argument, between a commitment to truth and a use of discourse which is irresponsible in terms of truth.[71] The constant testing of linguisitic meaning by

---

[71] It should, of course, be pointed out that if truthfulness were a requirement in defendants, then every one who was found guilty would have subsequently to be indicted for perjury; and that there is a limitation of the 'irresponsible' use of language and disregard for veracity in respect of advocates, who may not state what they believe not to be the case as regards matters of fact; they are merely entitled (indeed, some would say obliged)

argument in this way is a feature of an 'open' society which recognizes the potential disjunction of truthfulness and meaning in its members, but monitors this by continuous inquisition. That this claim about 'open' societies should have been made independently by a jurist dealing with the logical problem of legal discourse and a philosopher writing in defence of analytical philosophy in the last few years seems to me to indicate its importance,[72] and to demonstrate the weakness of any account of language which excludes from consideration either the notion of truth and the aspiration to its formal demonstration or the historical, contextual and consensual aspects of discourse.

to put forward what it will be in their clients' interest to say on matters of law, irrespective of their own beliefs.

[72] Alexy, 'Problems of Discourse Theory'; L. Jonathan Cohen, *The Dialogue of Reason: An Analysis of Analytical Philosophy*, Oxford: Clarendon Press, 1986, esp. pp. 190–1. I should like to thank Geoffrey Marshall for his most helpful advice and criticism in the preparation of this paper.

The Hungarian intellectual and the choice of commitment or neutrality

MIKLÓS MOLNAR

(*translated by Ian Maclean*)

Intellectuals without political responsibility are members of a category defined by education and profession which occupies an increasingly important place in society. They have their own sphere of responsibility which is perhaps even better defined than that of Benda's clerk, namely responsibility for technical competence. If an engineer designs a dam, it must be strong enough for its purpose; he will be held responsible if it bursts. If a surgeon leaves a pair of scissors in his patient's stomach, he will have to answer for it.

On the other hand, the intellectual who is thought to carry a political responsibility and who is the subject of the papers of this volume is defined by a tautology. He is an intellectual, a clerk, a man of letters who, whether he likes it or not, carries political responsibility either because he commits himself to a cause or because he refuses to do so. One might quote in this regard the great Hungarian poet laureate Mihály Babits who was the *arbiter elegantiarum* of the 1930s. This lord of the ivory tower, having remained silent in the face of the rise of fascism, was at last brought to sound the following warning in a poem: 'he who remains silent in the midst of the guilty is their accomplice'.

A passive sense of responsibility of this kind has always existed: in the course of the twentieth century with its characteristic totalitarianism, it has become more acute. The lived experience of history has not, however, for all that caused it to be defined more clearly. One is responsible, yes: but for what? To whom? Before which tribunal or assembly? According to which notion of rationality? Or even, according to which version of history, if indeed history is the supreme tribunal?

Should we not rather admit to ourselves that in the absence of an agreed norm the political responsibility of the intellectual is an irresponsible sort of concept? Without a norm, only myths can legitimize different modes of behaviour such as the myth of Prometheus, of Socrates, of Galileo, or of Dostoevsky's Grand Inquisitor. It is in the name of such myths that the only competent tribunal – that of the dominant community of intellectuals – passes judgement on its peers for having failed in their duty as men of letters. In their turn, the members of such a tribunal are open to similar condemnation: nothing is easier than to set in motion proceedings on the charge of intellectual misconduct, or of the treason of the clerks.

I should not like these cynical remarks to mislead the reader. They do not mean that 'anything goes' because 'nothing is true'. Rather, I wanted to highlight both the quasi-epistemological difficulty of producing definitions in this domain, and the wholly empirical difficulty of producing a normative ideal attitude which conforms to the necessity of acting responsibly. A man of letters will not, as we know, be condemned for writing a bad book in the same way as our surgeon will answer for his forgetfulness. Moreover, commandments such as 'thou shalt not kill' or 'thou shalt not lie' are general moral rules which say nothing about the specific moral code of the intellectual.

There are, however, two criteria which might be invoked. The first is that of conformity to historical circumstances. This is, I confess, a fragile criterion, but it is only concrete historical situations which can engender the imperatives of responsible behaviour. In the face of fascist totalitarianism, for instance, the intellectual can only become like Camus' *homme révolté*: a man who says no.

Camus it is also who defines the second criterion which I am inclined to call the 'duty of neutrality': that is, moderation in the face of immoderate behaviour; or rather, as Camus says, the awareness of limits: do not go too far; do not be overzealous; do not be dogmatic; do not be fanatical.

In the history of intellectuals in Hungary there are, I must confess, very few examples which correspond to these criteria, perhaps because the duty of neutrality and of reserving judgement has too often been in conflict with the duty of commitment, which has, in the course of the last two centuries, become the first commandment of responsible intellectuals. It is true that one can find a few examples of poets subscribing to the doctrine of 'art for art's sake', and a handful of philosophers and aesthetes who have refused to commit themselves to a party (or to a practical course of action, as Julien Benda would have said): but they are rare.

As in other countries defined as Eastern European, national and social conditions have perhaps played their part in this development. In Hungary in particular, the problem of nationhood has never ceased to preoccupy – not to say obsess – the minds of thinkers; and not only in its primary dimension, namely independence. The size of Slavic, Romanian and German ethnic minorities placed Hungarians, who *vis-à-vis* Austria were proponents of independence, in the inverse position *vis-à-vis* the other national groups in the kingdom. The problem of nationhood became enmeshed also with class structures, with the economy, with the language, with public education, with culture and with the army. In the end it was even impossible to ask the great metaphysical questions about mankind without referring to the problem of nationhood.

This odd state of affairs with its unfortunate mixture of ingredients held even the best minds such as Oszkár Jászi in its thrall. One way to escape it was found by those (such as the young Georg Lukács in his *Cercle du dimanche* period) who opted for 'a kingdom not of this world'.

Furthermore, the lack of modern institutions or their inadequacy may be said to have set the Hungarian intelligentsia on its characteristic path. This is a difficult hypothesis to support in the light of the fact that the backward state of bureaucratic institutions, of public life and of a civic sense in society may just as well have played a positive as a negative role. On the one hand it was responsible for what István Bibó has called 'the distorted Hungarian conformation'; on the other, it acted as a constant challenge and stimulant to intellectuals, inciting them to take the place of defective institutions and to assume the role the political classes had failed to assume either because of their inability to do so or because of their archaic character.

This situation gave rise to a sense of prophetic vocation and an ethic of responsibility for the *res publica*, particularly among poets. Endre Ady, a poet who died at the age of forty-two during Count Károlyi's democratic republic which lasted some 150 days, wrote the following: 'I have not come to be a poet, but to be all things'; and long before his time Hungarian poetry – the major literary genre – was particularly political in nature, characterized by commitment if not militancy. When, towards the middle of the nineteenth century, the secular social group of men of letters came no longer from the fringes of cultured aristocratic society but rather were composed of a mixture of *raznotchintzi*, it was already more of a community bound together by a common cultural and spiritual vocation than a simple socio-professional group. Its self-image is recalled in the title of Paul Bénichou's excellent work: *The Coronation of the Author: An Essay on the Accession of Lay Spiritual Power in Modern France*.[1]

It is for these reasons that I believe that the political responsibility of Hungarian intellectuals lies closer to the model of the first half of the nineteenth century than that of Benda, whose advice is to set oneself above or apart from partisan emotions and commitment to practical causes. The Hungarian intellectual cannot say with the clerk living under different skies: 'my kingdom is not of this world'. It is also difficult, if not impossible, for him to follow the path laid down in Camus' journal *Combat* in 1945 in the following words: 'if one wants to pass beyond simple opportunistic measures, it is necessary to justify one's actions by arguments from general principles which can only be established by recourse to theory'.

How can such advice be followed in a country in which for centuries intellectuals have, from the moment they leave their studies, been caught up in tasks which if not opportunistic have at least always been of a practical and urgent nature?

The conflict between committing oneself on the one hand and remaining neutral or transcending the particular on the other places intellectuals in any country during a period of high tension in a difficult position. But in a society such as that of Hungary in which social institutions suffer from chronic inadequacy, it is even more difficult to strike a balance between these two duties – a balance between being a citizen and being a mere subject or

---

[1] The original title reads *Le Sacre de l'écrivain: essai sur l'avènement d'un pouvoir spirituel laïque dans la France moderne*, Paris: Corti, 1973.

Untertan; a balance between being a responsible member of the intelligentsia and setting off on a crusade. The danger either of shutting oneself up in an ivory tower of abstract ethics or of straying on to the dangerous terrain of extreme left-wing or right-wing millenarianist ideology is all the more acute.

It would be easy to censure Hungarian intellectuals, especially those of the present century, for having followed one or the other of these extreme courses or for having stood on the side-lines in a country in which their historical situation and their traditions placed them in a position of responsibility. The treason of the clerks – either by omission or by commission – is in fact as widespread a phenomenon as the proper accomplishment of their duty. I need only mention the rise of Hungarian fascism and the coming of war which found them to be either lacking in a spirit of resistance (as was the case of the majority) or seduced by the fallacious promises of Nazi demagogues to create a new European order in which Hungary might hope to regain its lost grandeur. The numbers of real collaborators and of anti-Semitic and nationalistic activists may have been small, but there were concomitantly very many passive spectators. Fewer Hungarians were disgraced or condemned to prison after the war than in France; but there were also many, many fewer who took part in the resistance than in France, or, for that matter, in Poland. To produce an explanation for the passivity of the majority of Hungarian intellectuals would require a far more detailed analysis than is possible in the scope of this paper, but on the one hand, nationalism paralysed the minds of intellectuals and, on the other, the political culture of the Hungarian elite which seemed so promising in the nineteenth century came to suffocate and atrophy because of the static nature of Hungarian society.

I have not the space here to say why this political culture ran out of steam: others have written at length on this topic without suggesting any reasons other than the political classes and conservative intelligentsia bear the responsibility for having used their power to reduce 'progressive' intellectuals to impotence. All that these 'progressives' were able to do was to develop a separate political culture and a separate literary and artistic world, designed for the consumption of literate city-dwellers who were more cosmopolitan than the traditional middle classes and marked by the presence of Jews. These factors made the culture of such 'progressives' suspicious in the eyes of public opinion, thus hindering the process of democratization and modernization in Hungarian culture as a whole.

In a recent work the Hungarian historian István Nemeskürthy paints a picture of this culture in the last decades of the nineteenth century, characterizing it as the beginning of the decline of the liberal tradition. The work has a somewhat mystifying title to non-Hungarian readers: *The Grandchildren of the Stone-Hearted Man*. To understand it, it is necessary to know that in his novel entitled *The Sons of the Stone-Hearted Man* Mór Jókai, sometime friend of Petöfi, draws a picture of a family, a father and his three sons, who were heroes in the struggle for liberation, but also heroes of the 1867 compromise in which the national-liberal mode of thinking remained unchanged. Nemeskürthy shows in his study that the 'grandchildren' – that is, the generation of 1870–96 – far from betraying the ideals of their fathers and grandfathers, remained loyal to them, if not in the political arena itself, then at least in their intellectual and cultural activities. Nemeskürthy's argument is convincing in that he is able to produce endless examples and quotations to support it. At the end of this period, however, to mark the point at which the decline begins, the historian can do no better than to quote a contemporary poet:

> Mi az életnek rabjai vagyunk
> Körülmények pórázán ballagunk.
>
> (We are life's prisoners
> Trudging along on circumstances' lead.)

This is not altogether similar to the explanation of Jacobinism by the 'theory of circumstances', but it does leave unanswered in a similar way two fundamental questions. First, how and why might circumstances be said to change so radically at the end of the nineteenth century? For the Hungarian economy and Hungarian society were flourishing at that time. Secondly, why did the great-grandchildren betray their national heritage of liberalism of preceding generations (if in fact they did) and adopt more and more aggressively conservative and nationalistic attitudes? These are complex questions. Another historian, Miklós Szabó, throws light on an important dimension of the problem in his study of the 'agrarian' wing of Hungarian conservatism, but the general turn towards anti-liberal attitudes remains a little-investigated historical episode. If one 'acquits' as it were the generation of the grandchildren of Kossuth, Széchenyi, Wesselényi, Ferenc Deák, all that happens is that the problem of accounting for the change is carried forward to the next generation, that of the beginning of the twentieth century. At that time, while still responsible for its once archaic nature, Hungary enters the turbulent period marked by anti-Semitism, the Dreyfus affair and the pogroms, the rise of anti-liberal totalitarian ideologies and similar phenomena which belong to a world not limited by Hungary's frontiers. István Bibó, the lucid and courageous intellectual who has pursued further than anyone else the analysis of the 'deformations' of Hungarian thought and public opinion, and of the relationship between these deformations and the confused political history of the Danube region, also offers no satisfactory answers to these questions.

What type of man of letters, and what intellectual current, emerge as exemplary, I wonder, from this tormented period of history? What counts as exemplary, of course, is a matter of dispute as much as personal taste. In respect of the grandchildren of 1848, I would have been inclined for myself to mention the great Hungarian historian Gyula Szekfü who wrote a famous study entitled *Three Generations* in 1920, in which he arraigns revolutionary thought, progressivism and liberalism and accuses them of the same evils as the left-wing historian accuses right-wing movements. History remains in large part an ideological discipline. For all that, I would like to point to three exemplary figures who without being uncontroversial nonetheless manifest attitudes which if not necessarily 'right' from a political point of view, deserve to be described as 'intellectual'.

In 1801 Ferenc Kazinczy, a learned nobleman who owned an estate of modest proportions, was released from prison having served a sentence of 2,387 days for the crime of rebellion. In fact, Kazinczy played a relatively passive part in the 'Jacobin conspiracy' in which he was involved and which earned him such a heavy term in Habsburg prison. After his release, he returned to his estate and up to his death thirty years later devoted himself passionately to the movement concerned with the reform of language and literature of which he was the instigator and indefatigable organizer. It was indeed a genuine movement.

He recruited his sympathizers, collaborators and correspondents from the ranks of men of letters, mostly of noble origin, with some high-born aristocrats and a few city-dwellers of modest birth: in other words, from the emergent intelligentsia which fulfilled the role of the cultivated bourgeoisie in all Central-Eastern European countries.

What was unique to this Hungarian intelligentsia was its conscious choice of a model of cultural development both as, and in the place of, a political programme. Its most urgent self-imposed task was to modernize the language and literature in order to make them suitable media for the expression of the ideas of European Enlightenment and revolution. The best way to grasp the importance of this linguistic and literary movement is to compare it with other contemporary cultural trends.

Cultural life may be somewhat arbitrarily divided into five currents: the patriarchal and conservative current; the current of economic reform; the Jacobin movement; the linguistic and literary reform movement; and the less coherent movement of opposition, members of whom were known as the 'orthologues', who acquired this name to distinguish them from the 'neologues' of the linguistic and literary reform movement.

The principal strength of this movement lies in its refusal to be drawn into other intellectual currents or movements. Kazinczy himself, having been embroiled in the trial of the Jacobin conspirators, was excellently placed to be able to judge how unsuitable Jacobinism was to Hungary, and particularly to its culture. On the other hand, he was repelled by stagnant conservatism and purely economic reform. If Jacobinism was a foreign and inappropriate ideological model, economic reform *per se* would have led to the subjugation of Hungary to its stronger neighbour, Austria. The proponents of linguistic reform realized, unlike their orthologue adversaries, that the only way to prepare the minds and spirits of the people was through reform of the language. The importance of their activities can best be seen in contradistinction to the movements around them. How, they asked, could commerce be promoted in a country which possessed no word to denote this activity? How could industry be developed if there was no term for industry in Hungarian? Or how could one engage in revolution without knowing what the concept meant? Commerce, industry, revolution, together with several thousand other notions or linguistic nuances had no equivalents in Hungarian. Kazinczy and his friends set out, as their first and most vital task, to create these equivalents, and to inculcate them into the whole of the literate section of the Hungarian population (the orthologues excepted).

This was a genuine cultural revolution. All linguistic conventions were broken; vocabulary, grammar, orthography, style, form, register and semantics were all subjected to change. In theory the same modernizing effect could have been obtained through administrative and educational reforms, but no institutions existed which were capable of effecting a cultural revolution of this magnitude, other than this union of linguists and writers. Furthermore, a reform movement imposed from above by the Diet or by Vienna would never have penetrated the very mentality of the people. Linguistic evolution reflected a social need which was not merely material or technical. No parliament or government could have created a new language and through it the new system of concepts and values which the country needed. This was a cultural undertaking in the full anthropological sense of the word 'cultural'.

The results of this enterprise cannot be described in a few sentences. The linguistic reform movement created in different ways at the very least 4,000 words if we are to believe the great linguist Bárczi who, without giving precise figures, speaks of several thousand words now integrated into modern Hungarian as well as several thousand others which have fallen out of use. The movement reformed and codified the grammar of Hungarian which up to then had been imprecise and variable. It brought to the fore hitherto unknown forms of literary expression of great richness, subtlety and variety. It assisted from the 1830s onwards the policial activities of the 'generation of reforming Diets' and of the 1848 revolution. Finally it laid the cultural foundations for the generation of Petöfi which completed the task of fusing popular language and literature with that of elite culture: that final stage in a long journey. Hungary remained, it is true, a backward country in many respects, but it succeeded in completing a task which other great Western democracies might well have envied.

The second case I would like to refer to is that of Count István Széchenyi: but not to become embroiled in the interminable debate about the relative merits of Kossuth or Széchenyi, nor to give a full intellectual portrait of this remarkable figure. Széchenyi's journal of some several thousand pages, rather, provides us with an example of a text which reflects the anguish of an intellectual politician when faced with his duty of commitment on the one hand and his fears of revolutionary zeal and excess on the other. Few texts are as moving as this journal. Széchenyi read everything, visited every country, met every serious thinker. He was a close associate, one might say favoured son, of Metternich, and yet he vigorously opposed his system. He sat on the same benches in the Diet as conservative aristocrats on the one hand and reformists on the other, whom he considered demagogues and subversives; he never ceased to fight against both parties. As a man of action he engaged in a number of public campaigns to modernize legislation, the economy, commerce, transport, scientific and cultural life, even horse breeding. Restlessly active, he suffered from psychic and physical illness and from his sense of isolation throughout his life, right up to his death in a mental institution at Döbling. 'You declare yourself to be committed to Hungary, yet you pay court to Crescence [his future wife, to whom he paid court for fifteen years]: you won't get very far like that.' 'She was right', Széchenyi commented, 'my country marches inexorably on, and I am inexorably propelled forward by my destiny.' Hundreds or even thousands of times he recorded in his diary his premonition that he would one day be crushed between the irreconcilable forces of attachment to Hungary and of his desire for neutrality and moderation in the face of political evolution which he believed was leading the country towards the catastrophe of revolution. His journal extends over forty-six years from 1814 to 1860, with occasional long interruptions. The most anguished pages are those he wrote in 1848. On 15 March, the day the revolution started, he commented: 'Hungary is slipping towards total dissolution . . . it's like a bad dream! Saint Nemesis, pray for us! A Pole and Kossuth are pouring petrol on the flames. The first is perhaps the spiritual heir of Sobieski . . . the second has been martyrized and considered to be insane.' On 20 March he wrote: 'Jews are being persecuted at Pozsony/Presburg/Bratislava. It's nightmarish', and later 'Kossuth at least will die for his "beliefs", but I will die for a faith I have never ceased to oppose.' For Széchenyi assumed his full political responsibility: he entered the Battyányi–Kossuth government in spite of his disapproval of its policies. In one of his speeches in July, Kossuth proposed that 200,000 men should be conscripted but said in a slip of the tongue '200 million soldiers'. Széchenyi records the slip in his journal, finding it to be 'hyperbole on the Chinese scale' and an excellent satirical barb. In August and September, as the conflict between Vienna and Budapest grew worse and war threatened to break out in a matter of weeks, Széchenyi suffered a nervous breakdown: 'I have only slept for four hours. The Eumenides are pursuing me. Interview with Kossuth. I have decided [Széchenyi puts a question mark after this word] to live and die here ... no man has brought as much chaos to the world as I have. God have mercy on me.'

The journal stops here, and there are no further entries for eleven years: Széchenyi himself was transported to Döbling.

My third example is that of Károly Eötvös, a lawyer and writer, who was born into a family of the minor nobility in 1842. He belongs to the teeming generation of the grandchildren of those ancestors we have already mentioned. Like many of his educated contemporaries, he was a liberal; but he found himself almost completely ostracized when, in 1882–3, he undertook the defence in a notorious trial, in which the Jews from the village of Tiszaeszlár were accused of ritual murder. A young servant girl called Eszter Solymosi had died; she had either committed suicide or drowned accidentally. When her corpse was recovered from the water, it bore no mark of injury; the accusation itself was in any case absurd. Nonetheless, the trial took its course under the pretext that the identification of the victim was not beyond doubt and the fifteen-year-old son of the principal defendant, little Móric Scharf, heaped implausible accusation after implausible accusation on his family, having been set up as the main witness for the prosecution. It should be noted that his evidence had not been obtained by torture but by a kind of brainwashing during which he was led to believe that he would enjoy a brilliant future as a converted Christian; and indeed little Móric expressed the desire to break all links with the Jewish community, including his family.

The trial caused great excitement throughout Hungarian society and in the Jewish population which made up more than 4 per cent of the total population at that time (just before the First World War this figure had risen to 5 per cent, that is, almost a million people). It caused anti-Semitism to flare up in Hungary which before this had had a record of tolerance; indeed, it flared up to such an extent that a group of men founded an anti-Semitic party which gained seats in Parliament, published a newspaper and nurtured great political ambitions; ambitions which were frustrated when feelings subsided once again. But the trial left behind it an uneasiness which presaged the post-war rise of anti-Semitism and the fascist agitation of the Hitlerian epoch. The defendants from Tiszaeszlár were in fact acquitted thanks to the tribunal's rigorous adherence to the law and the indefatigable efforts of their advocate, Károly Eötvös. Everything was against him, except justice and truth, whose champion he was. Even the members of the tribunal (though not the attorney-general) were convinced of the guilt of the accused; it was only the absence of proof which led them to acquit the defendants. A fine victory for the rule of law! But it was a terrible defeat at the level of collective mentality. The majority of the intelligentsia revealed itself to be anti-Semite and 'anti-Dreyfusard' in its heart and mind, even if its thin veneer of liberalism and civilization did not actually crack. The verdict was accepted, but not the man who had won the case for the cause of justice. Eötvös was ostracized by his own class and by the intellectual community at large. For a decade or so, he remained in Parliament as a deputy, and enjoyed some success with his writings; he was, however, no longer a member of his own cultural milieu, but rather of that of the Jewish intelligentsia.

No general conclusions may be drawn from these examples chosen at random; they can be no more than illustrations of different intellectual attitudes adopted at critical moments during which the path of the man of letters is not set out clearly for him to follow, and he is threatened by isolation, hostility or even madness and death.

I I

The political responsibility of intellectuals

ALAN MONTEFIORE

There is, no doubt, something not wholly responsible in the idea of writing on the political responsibility of intellectuals without first examining the range of possible senses of each of the terms contained in this phrase. But there already exists, of course, a vast and heterogeneous literature on the nature of the political, and another on what may be taken to be the peculiar characteristics of intellectuals as such – not to mention that which is devoted to the notion or notions of responsibility. In this paper I propose to start from rather simple, rough and ready accounts of the political and of what constitutes an intellectual – or, better perhaps, of what may constitute an intellectual attitude or interest. As for responsibility, the development of the argument itself will, hopefully, bring into gradual focus the sense or senses that may here be at stake.

Briefly, then, I propose to regard as political all that characterizes or touches upon the domain of public policy, leaving undetermined for the moment what may variously be meant by such reference to the domain, or overlapping and intersecting series of domains, of the public. By 'an intellectual' I mean here to refer to anyone who takes a committed interest in the validity and truth of ideas for their own sake, i.e. for the sake of their truth and validity rather than for that of their causal relationships to whatever other ends. Against this general background I shall argue for the thesis that while it may indeed be true that, as thus understood, certain intellectuals at least bear a special responsibility within or for the nature of the sphere of the political in their respective societies, it is first and even more importantly the case that everyone has in a sense to recognize himself or herself as bearing some small share of this responsibility. This may be taken as tantamount to arguing, somewhat surprisingly, perhaps, that everyone must be considered, to some small extent at least, to have something of the intellectual in them.

What are the lines along which one may hope to make this thesis seem more compelling? One of their starting points may be taken to lie in the facts that to engage in meaningful discourse (or indeed in any form of meaningful thought) is *ipso facto* to engage in normative or partly normative activity; and that to engage in normative activity is *ipso facto* to engage in activity that must in principle admit first to the possibility of proving on any given occasion to have been 'objectively' mistaken, and secondly to recognition of itself as being in general involved in networks of interpersonal interaction. The nature of such interaction may be expressed by saying that within the interplay of discursive communication everyone has some basic share of responsibility towards everyone else for the maintenance of its overall meaningfulness, and that the basic reciprocity of this interplay is such that it also includes a certain degree or kind of responsibility of self-respect *vis-à vis* himself or herself; and, furthermore, that these responsibilities carry with them a certain not wholly determinable responsibility for the respect of truth and its expression. Truthfulness is thus, in this sense and from this point of view, a political virtue – political in as much as the nature and degree of truthfulness within a community (whether within or across the lines that may divide one social sub-grouping from another) is a major determinant of the nature of the public or political space in which the community conducts or contests its affairs. Indeed, it may even in the last resort figure among the criteria of the boundaries of a community as such.

In what follows I try first to sketch out the arguments to the fundamentally normative nature and reciprocally intersubjective responsibilities of language and thought, whether as conceptual structure or as discursive activity, under three heads, or in three versions, and by more or less allusive reference to three writers who had or have their roots firmly in central Europe: Kant, Wittgenstein and Vàclav Havel. (This should in no way be taken to mean that there are not other major writers in whose writings I might equally well have sought to anchor my arguments. Habermas provides one example; so, in another and earlier way, does John Stuart Mill.) I shall then try, even more sketchily, I fear, to bring out and together some of the morals of these arguments.

I

We may start, then, with the 'old' Kantian argument to the inescapably dual perspectives of Transcendental Idealism and Empirical Realism, an argument that remains as deeply controversial as it is deeply familiar.

On any view of the matter, no doubt, and there exists a notorious diversity of views on it, Kant's own arguments are, in their precise detail, exceedingly hard to make out, perhaps the only thing obvious about them, indeed, being the degree of their complexity. On *my* view, and quasi-exegetically at any rate, the matter may be seen to stand roughly as follows.

As we try to make sense of the facts and nature of our experience, we (human beings in general) find the whole content of the world of our cognitive awareness to be given to us through our senses – that is to say, putting it in the most general possible terms, in spatio-temporal form. But our discursive awareness of this our world, our ability both to recognize one aspect of it or another, as we discriminate between them, and to reflect upon them, is not thus given to us. On the contrary, it is we ourselves, through the exercise of our own rational and conceptualizing powers of judgement and of our creative imagination, who introduce into the otherwise 'blind' data of our senses those relational structures and continuities by virtue of which alone we may identify and recognize any one item of experience as being either similar or dissimilar to any other.

Nevertheless, although our ability to think our experience, and ourselves as subject(s) of it, is not given to us along with its content or as part of it, it is yet crucially dependent upon the existence of this given content. For it is only in so far as we both can and must think of what is given to us (i.e. given to our consciousness) as being 'objectively' of one sort rather than another, that is to say as being whatever sort of thing it may be independently, or at least in part independently, of whatever on any given occasion it may *seem* to us to be, that any judgement we may make as to its nature can have any determinate content at all. Thus, it is only in so far as we are able, through our active employment of the most general concepts or categories of our understanding, so to structure the otherwise meaningless jumble (or 'manifold') of our given sense impressions as to constitute it a world of empirically objective reality that we are capable of any discursive awareness of anything whatsoever, including even any conceptually articulate awareness of ourselves or our own states of consciousness. Yet without the given content of our sense experience to work upon, the categories of our understanding, lacking anything to get to work upon, would remain totally empty and we should remain wholly devoid of any experiential self-awareness.

It is for this reason that our own self-conscious awareness of ourselves has from the beginning its characteristically radical and radically perplexing duality. On the one hand, we can neither find nor give any determinate content to our own awareness of ourselves as the particular individuals that we are other than that which lies in our awareness of belonging to (or forming part of) the spatio-temporal and causally determinate world of nature, all of whose contents are thus given to us through our senses. (On Kant's view, the strictly causal structure of the knowable world has to be presupposed as a necessary aspect of its necessarily to be presupposed objectivity.) On the other hand, we are also, in the very act of sensory self-awareness, so to speak, non-observationally but inescapably aware of ourselves as belonging, through our share in or of the powers of rationality and conceptual understanding, to a domain or 'world' that, *qua* rational, carries with it nothing of time or space or causal determination – and, consequently, nothing by way of any principle of observable or even clearly thinkable individuation. For time and space are, to repeat, but the forms of our sensory experience, and, as human beings, we can think of ourselves as individually distinguishable or distinct from each other only in so far as we think of ourselves in our spatio-temporal (and causally determinate) embodiments.

We human beings are thus bound to a complex awareness of ourselves as each one of so many particular and contingently different actual or possible embodiments of a principle of rational activity, which, as such and abstracting from its divers embodiments, is itself not particular but universal. Such radically dual aspect beings as ourselves have, then, to think of themselves – we are inescapably aware of ourselves – as subject to two quite different sorts of motivation. As members of the animal kingdom and belonging to the world of nature, we know ourselves to be subject to the drives of our causally determined desires and appetites; and even though we may, on other grounds, have to presume these drives to be organized in the light of certain functionally appropriate ends, they are nevertheless only to be *known* as constituting part of this causally determinate domain. At the same time, as thinking and conceptually self-aware beings, we find ourselves *ipso facto* committed to the recognition and would-be fulfilment of the demands of our own rationality as they may present themselves in whatever context we may find ourselves. The problem is, of course, to determine what, in any given context, the appropriate content of these demands might be.

How, in principle, is this problem to be tackled? In so far as the goals of action are in fact given to us by our own natural needs or desires, that is to say in all cases of so-called hypothetical imperatives, the problem is evidently a 'merely' technical one of working out the means best adapted to the achievement of our given ends. On any Kantian view of the matter, however, our rationality is not to be thought of as nothing but some technical tool or device, to be used, if we so choose, in the better ordering of our thoughts or for the more efficient satisfaction of our natural desires. On the contrary, as the source of our own conceptual awareness and self-awareness, as the principle of all our own consciously deliberate activity, it demands overriding respect for the norms, standards and embodiments of itself as, to borrow a Heideggerian term, our ownmost principle of rationality, whatever the situation in which we may find ourselves. This principle of rational self-respect and of respect for others – that is to say, of reason's respect for itself in all its self-embodiments – is, indeed, intrinsic to reason itself; it is intrinsic to our own self-awareness as (in part) rational beings. But here, of course, when it comes to determining the content at any given moment and in any given context of this 'Categorical' demand for human self-respect that, *qua* rational beings, we find ourselves making upon ourselves, something more is needed than 'mere' technical judgement, formidable though the problems of technical judgement may only too often be. What is needed here is something more akin to what may be called moral and political wisdom.

On my view, for what it is worth, the evidence of the various Kantian texts shows his own grip on the further implications of some of his own most central and fundamental principles to have been at times (and altogether unsurprisingly) somewhat slipping and uncertain, as he struggled with this problem of the determination of the content of that moral imperative which, at all times and of our own rational nature, we lay upon ourselves. Sometimes he seems to yield to the temptation, as it were, of seeking to derive from the pure rational demand for respect for rationality itself something like a specific code of conduct. To that extent he seems to me to be embarked on a project that must of necessity fail – and fail, moreover, for reasons that are themselves deeply embedded within the Kantian framework of thought. But this is not the place for any attempt at a detailed exegesis of these struggles. For the moment it must suffice to claim, dogmatically if need be, that the demands of Kantian rationality are surely best understood as commands to the adoption of certain underlying attitudes rather than as instructions for the observance of any specific, or, indeed, fully specifiable, code of behaviour.

Our own self-awareness, then, as human beings and the only principle of individuation that we have appropriate to our condition are alike bound up with the conditions of objective, spatio-temporal and causally determinate embodiment. We human beings are, as it were, caught in the very condition of morality; for this condition just *is* that of such dual aspect creatures as ourselves, unavoidably aware of ourselves as such, and thus subject to seeking the satisfaction of the demands of our own rationality in a context where we must know ourselves to be also and always causally bound by the natural or animal side of our being to pursuing the satisfaction of natural desire. If this is indeed a proper characterization of the human condition, it is clearly one that defies complete understanding. As Kant himself says in effect, in that famous last sentence but one of the *Groundwork to the Metaphysic of Morals*, all that we may hope in the end to comprehend of our own condition are the parameters of its own incomprehensibility.

If the radical duality of our nature thus sets limits to whatever degree of theoretical self-understanding we may aspire to achieve, we are not thereby dispensed from the ever-insistent practical necessity of seeking practical answers to the problems of embodied and, therefore, practical or moral reason. These problems have, as we have just noted, their endlessly technical aspects; but they are also and above all those of giving content to the demand that our own rationality makes upon us as rational beings for respect for rationality, its norms and its embodiments, itself – that is to say, with Kant himself, for respect for persons. For persons are, precisely, just so many different individual embodiments of that very universal principle of reason. Seen in this light, self-respect and respect for others are but two different sides of the same coin, namely, of reason's universal respect for itself wherever and in whatever particularization it may find itself. Moreover, and the point is crucial, to say that reason demands of us this form of reciprocal self-respect is in effect to say that we together demand it equally of ourselves and others. For, as so many embodiments of reason, we are, in one aspect of our common duality, together tied to the conceptual impossibility of outright denial of our own share in rationality, without, in the very act of seeking to give conceptual expression to that denial, giving it, by the same token, the lie.

What, then, should be our approach to the problem of determining in any given situation the particular forms of behaviour by which, in that situation, respect for the norms and embodiments of reason may best manifest itself? Not, surely, by the formulation and attempted enforcement of would-be rigid codes (appropriate though the formulation and implementation of such codes may be for the satisfaction in given circumstances of certain other social needs). Indeed, Kant himself had some very pertinent remarks to make on the impossibility in principle of being able to draw up rules for the invariably proper application of rules, and on the ultimately inescapable need for a wisdom born of experience or for what he called 'mother-wit'.[1] But this lack of invariably determinate content does not mean that reason's command to respect for self and others is vacuous. It means simply that there can be no directly guaranteed way of reading off from the observable surface of people's behaviour just what degrees of respect or lack of respect

---

[1] See the *Critique of Pure Reason*, A.133/4–B.172/3.

that behaviour might represent. There can likewise be no book of rules by which to determine just what gesture or act one has to perform by which to give due respect to others or even to oneself.

That this is so is, surely, in general unsurprising – if, indeed, to treat people with respect, in the sense of respect with which we are here concerned, is to treat them as if from a certain point of view and with a certain quality of intentional understanding; and certainly no one would suppose that intentions are invariably or even often displayed with incorrigible evidence in the immediately observable behaviour of one moment or another. This does not, evidently, mean that just any form of behaviour will do, that just any form of behaviour may succeed in embodying respect, provided only that the 'inner' intention is alright. It does mean, however, that the characterization of any form or instance of behaviour as an act of respect for self or others must always involve appropriate reference, direct or indirect, to the relevant intentionality.

This is, of course, a familiar point. So too is the closely associated – and characteristically modern – insistence on the fact that not even the agent himself or herself can have any guaranteed assurance as to the precise balance of his or her own motives or the exact moral significance of his or her own behaviour. This latter point takes on a deeper and more complex poignancy within the framework and perspectives of Transcendental Idealism. For from these perspectives even the most rationally self-conscious of agents must know that his behaviour, even when produced in accordance with his most rationally deliberate intentions, must always in principle allow of a dual reading – one, certainly, in the language of rational intentionality, but the other, in accordance with the inescapable presuppositions of his radically dual nature, in the language of natural desire.

However this may be, and whatever the acceptable strengths or unacceptable weaknesses of Transcendental Idealism as such, it goes without saying that no form of empirical description can be made so determinate as to have unambiguously certain applicability or non-applicability to all borderline cases. Moreover, the higher the level of generality or abstraction, the more open the range of potentially contestable judgement when it comes to the subsumption of the particular instance or case under the relevant universal, or to the giving of specific content to essentially formal injunctions. For example, if we have to recognize, according to the terms of the preceding argument, that our own individual capacity for self-consciousness and self-recognition is but a manifestation of that universal principle of reason that lies within us, thus playing its indispensable part in constituting us the peculiar human beings that we are, we have by the very same token to acknowledge our own constitutive self-commitment to unremitting (universal) respect for those values of truth and validity that are themselves constitutive of the principle of reason itself. Respect for such values, in the context of respect for persons as the very embodiments of this principle, must amount, *inter alia*, to respect for truthfulness in interpersonal relations. But if Kant thought, as some of his arguments seem at times to suggest, that respect for truthfulness in human affairs is to be sought and secured by an invariable speaking of what presents itself in the moment as being 'literally' true, he was surely caught up in a mistaken oversimplification – mistaken, moreover, in terms of the further implications of Transcendental Idealism itself.

What are these further implications? A thoroughgoing Transcendental Idealist, it would seem, must always remember that all actual deployment of reason, all acts of communication, development of argument or transmission of information, are, in their expression and reception, of necessity bound to the spatio-temporal conditions of human existence and human self-awareness. Our thought and our communication of it are always mediate. This means that while it is, of course, but a striking exaggeration to proclaim that the medium *is* the message, it has, nevertheless, to be recognized that the two are not entirely separable from each other. Or rather: whenever a (conceptually structured) message is transmitted, it is necessarily the case that certain physical events, articulated in space and time and that may be presumed to constitute its transmission, will in fact take place.

Moreover, our knowledge, in Kant's strong sense of the term, is as always and of necessity limited to the domain of such events. This means that there must always be some residual doubt, some irreducible penumbra of indeterminacy , as to what exact message may have been conveyed through the medium of any given transmission; *à la limite* there is no such thing as an exact message.

We cannot but take ourselves to have the power of reason within us; but we also know that we can have no direct or immediate access to it. Furthermore, and again the point has a very modern ring, these residual doubts, this irreducible penumbra of uncertainty, must affect our own thought, our own communication with ourselves, if not to the same practical extent, at any rate in principle in the same way as they affect our communication with each other. The truth and validity of Pure Reason can never be captured and enshrined, as if with timeless certainty, within the purity of some wholly transparent formulation. We are not such timeless creatures, and our access to our own reason does not have that kind of transparency.

It follows from this that a proper respect for truthfulness in human affairs demands a constant vigilance as to the given state of the medium of our thought and to the conditions of its transmission. Our essentially inescapable and ultimately self-imposed obligation of respect for reason and its embodiments, and hence for truth and truthfulness, involves an ever ongoing commitment to look to the well being of the conditions of communication. Such a commitment inevitably includes a concern with, first, the conditions, both physical and mental, in and under which human beings, whether individually or together, may come to maintain and enhance their best capacities for all forms of reason and rationality; secondly, the living state of available forms of discourse, the language, the arts, the prevailing culture; and, thirdly, all those conditions that may either favour or constrain the public pursuit, affirmation and communication of truth as any and all may best perceive and express it. It is evident that all three of these concerns are mutually involved in and with each other.

It is likewise evident that the Categorical Imperative to rational self-respect, both personal and reciprocally interpersonal, when understood in this way, must involve a whole programme of not only moral, but also educational and political reflection and practical action. Within such a programme particular attention will, of course, have to be given to the variable interplay between the demands of the particular moment and those of the longer term, between occurrent and dispositional fidelity to the law of reason, even, if one likes to put it that way, between the sometimes rival claims of truth and truthfulness.

However, although the potential conflicts associated with these distinctions present themselves often enough as painfully real, they are seldom, if ever, absolute. Reason's demand of the moment may be to speak the truth as one sees it at that moment; but it can surely not be to speak it simply in the first formulation that comes into one's head, irrespective of where or with whom one may happen to find oneself. Is that first formulation the one best adapted even to one's own understanding of the truth? Has one in any case one's own certain vision of the truth prior to and independently of one's formulation of it – and if not, does one not need often to be cautious before assuming the adequacy of the first formulation that occurs? How is one's chosen formulation most likely to be interpreted and received by those to whom it is addressed, and, beyond them, by those whom one must responsibly suppose to be likely to encounter it? May not an encounter with some truth of the immediate moment, particularly one that is enforced or imposed, sometimes impair or distort the ability to receive and to assimilate other more far-reaching and perhaps far more important truths of far more enduring significance? May there not even be occasions when a certain 'economy with the truth' may show a more sensitive respect for a humanity that is of its embodied nature limited in its capacity to deal with certain truths by the contingent conditions of its particular embodiment and of the context in which it may find itself, than would an insistence that the truth be made explicit and faced here and now?

To none of these questions, and to the many others of the same general order to which the command of respect for embodied reason must properly give rise, can there in principle be straightforwardly codifiable answers. Angels, if there are any such, may be deemed to know what they are about, When we human beings have, as best we may, to adjust the universal to the particular, we have to rely on judgement. But whatever the nuanced uncertainties of particular acts of judgement may be, there can be no doubt as to the direction of the overall command: rational self-respect and respect for others, respect for reason in all its embodiments and therefore for its embodiments as such, respect for truth and for whatever may be the prevailing conditions of its expression, communication and receivability, respect for truthfulness and for honest thought and inquiry as guiding features of human life in all its interlocking personal and social dimensions.

If the term 'intellectual' is indeed to be taken, as I suggested at the outset, as applying to all those who 'take a committed interest in the validity and truth of ideas for their own sake', then intellectuals have surely to recognize themselves as having a very special concern and responsibility for watching over the conditions and observance of rational self-respect as I have tried to elucidate them above. However, I have also tried to argue, in outline sketch at least, that there are broad Kantian grounds for holding that this concern and this responsibility are rooted in the very conditions of human knowledge and human self-awareness; they must to that extent be viewed as the properly inescapable concern and responsibility of every rationally self-conscious human being. In that very fundamental sense everyone must be considered to have, to some small but crucial sense at least, something of the intellectual in them, and should be treated morally, educationally, socially and politically as such.

2

I turn now to what may be called, in even more broadly allusive terms no doubt, the Wittgensteinian thread of my argument.

Let us start from the assumption that a subject capable of self-awareness and some degree of self-understanding as the producer of its own discourse must itself be able to understand the marks or noises that it produces as being symbols or bearers of meaning, and must, moreover, be presumed to have at least some putative understanding of the meaning that they bear. (This assumption, no doubt, needs arguing for, as does my here undefended use of the much-contested concept of a 'subject'. The arguments can, I think, be provided; but it would take rather too much space to try and do so here. Let me therefore here be allowed the assumption as an assumption.)

What, then, is it to produce a mark or a noise as a symbol or bearer of meaning? We do not, in fact, need to presume that every producer of a sequence of marks or noises that may be taken to be interpretable as an instance of meaningful discourse must himself/ herself/itself be explicitly self-conscious of his own behaviour as meaningful at the moment of its production. (Very small children, for example, may well be recognizable as participants in meaningful discourse long before they are in any position to conceptualize it as such.) What we do have to suppose is that the producer of meaning is seeking to produce some differential effect in his situation or in his audience by his production of a mark or noise that may be taken, by himself or by others, as being in some recognizable way more appropriate to his general intentions or appreciation of the situation than would be almost any other mark or noise that he might have produced. If we do not ascribe any purposiveness to his behaviour at all, then while it may be possible to take it as sign or symptom of the state that he is in, it will make no sense to suppose that it has been produced as a symbol of it. For it to make any sense to treat a mark or a noise as a meaningful symbol, one must be able to make sense of the supposition that, in its production, there is or was some distinction to be made between 'getting it right' and 'getting it wrong'. In other words, one must be able to suppose the mark or noise in question to be or to have been produced under the general governance, however flexible or imperfect, explicit or implicit, of some linguistic norm.

We do not, we have just noted, have to suppose every producer of what we may take to be meaningful marks or noises to be himself or herself explicitly conscious of them as meaningful. However, we are here primarily concerned with the situation of those participants in discourse who, to some extent at least, are aware of themselves as such, and who, as they strive to work out what to say to themselves or others, or to understand what they hear being said to or around them (or 'going on', as it were, in their own heads), have to decide on their own production of whatever marks or noises, and to assess the significance of those that they encounter, in terms of their apparent appropriateness or inappropriateness to the presumed demands of the situation. All those, then, who find themselves in any way participating in the production or interpretation of meaningful discourse, find themselves *ipso facto* bound to the observation and/or observance of norms and, by the same token, to the associated assumption that all whom they take to be either knowing or unknowing fellow participants must likewise be acting as so bound.

It is, however, a central thesis of the so-called anti-private language argument, associated with the name of Wittgenstein, in virtually any of its versions that it is impossible to conceive of an act as being under the governance of a norm except in so far as it is possible at least to conceive of some way in which one might encounter or establish a check on whether and when the norm has been respected or not. This does not, of course, mean that a check must be in practice available for every occasion of meaningful utterance. It does mean, however, that it must be possible in principle to conceive of an occasion and a way in which the observance of the relevant norm might be subject to such a check. But this, according to anti-private language arguments, must mean in further crucial turn that not only the meaning, but the very meaningfulness itself of any speaker's discourse, or even that of his or her own 'internal' thinking, must in the last resort depend on or presuppose his being able in principle to conceptualize the possibility of encountering another speaker of his language, another participant in his discourse, and of them both being able to recognize each other as such.

For present purposes I must in effect take it for granted, even if with all reasonable confidence, that in one version or another an anti-private language argument of this sort can indeed be made out. It is at least partly rooted, no doubt, in the already noted Kantian consideration that 'it is only in so far as we both can and must think of what is given to us . . . as being "objectively" of one sort rather than another, that is to say as being whatever sort of thing it may be independently, or at least in part independently, of whatever on any given occasion it may *seem* to us to be, that any judgement we may make as to its nature can have any determinate content at all'. To this, however, we must now add the further considerations, first, that there could be no content to this first consideration were we not able to conceive of the possibility of being faced on occasion with at least *prima facie* grounds for having to regard such a judgement as being mistaken; and, secondly, that only an encounter with some fellow classifier of the world of nature could provide us with such a ground. For the world of nature in itself remains silently unable to resist any classification whatsoever that we may seek to impose upon it in accordance with the fancies of one passing moment of our private consciousness of it to another. Only the encounter with another speaker can present us with the challenge that our attempted classification may have deviated too far from the appropriate norm.

(It is often objected that we have but to refer to our own memory for a check on the correctness of any present attempt at recognition; and that not only must our memory suffice, but that we are in any case dependent upon it for recognition and interpretation of the noises or gestures that any apparent other speaker may make, should we encounter one. It is, of course, true that memory is in one way or another involved in *any* act of recognition or interpretation. But the point is not and cannot be that the check provided by encounter with another speaker provides a somehow surer guarantee of correctness than memory or vice versa. The clue may be found rather in the fact that the English word 'check' may mean not only a test of some sort, but also something that may hold one up. If it was not in principle possible to envisage any check on the correctness of a memory claim, every memory claim would simply go through as correct by mere virtue of the claim being made, and there would be no difference of principle between a genuine memory claim (which as such may be either correct *or* incorrect) and any old statement about the past with no pretensions to truth value at all. The point is, then, that, taken together, memory and encounter with other speakers provide the possibility, neither of infallible assurance, but each of some *prima facie* check on the other.)

But how does this redeployment of the anti-private language argument lead back to the notion of some sort of fundamental reciprocal responsibility for respect and the maintenance of meaning and truth? The ideas lying behind this claim are in essence simple enough. For first, if, in producing a mark, noise or gesture, my intention is to produce it as a bearer of meaning, then I have to recognize myself as acting under the broad governance of some linguistic norm. (This will be true even for the cases in which I take some share of responsibility for creating or at least for modifying the norm in question.) In so doing, I am *ipso facto*, and other things being equal, in effect committing myself to – making myself responsible for – the repetition of appropriately similar tokens in appropriate contexts on appropriate future occasions. Secondly, if some version of the anti-private language argument is indeed correct, then I must in principle be looking to similar consistencies of commitment from all my possible interlocutors, all my potential fellow participants in discourse. For if I am to take their apparent responses to my own attempts at the production of meaning as capable of functioning as the necessary checks, I must presume their production of marks, noises and gestures to be likewise under the governance of the relevant linguistic norms.

In the overall networks of our actual and possible responses to each other we are thus together reciprocally responsible, to ourselves and to each other, for the establishment and upkeep of the practices and structures of meaning, within which our productions of mark, noise and gesture acquire and hold their status as symbols. In this area of characteristically human activity we may say that total irresponsibility is not even a possible option. For genuinely total irresponsibility in the observance of linguistic norms would lead to a total loss of grip on meaning. It would thus fall out of the field of assessment of responsibility and irresponsibility altogether.

Nowhere, incidentally, is the force of the preceding argument more apparent than in the field of basic language teaching and learning to and by very small children. If those who precede them in their command of the language did not observe a reasonably high degree of fidelity to its norms of meaning, validity and truthful reference, the newcomers to language would be deprived of that necessary stability of practice, whose patterns they have to internalize and make their own, if they are themselves to acquire any determinate basis to their own growing participation in meaningful discourse.

These arguments should not, of course, be misunderstood as suggesting that I must or even coherently could regard myself as totally responsible for all my own meanings. On the contrary, the anti-private language argument is in important part directed precisely against any such misapprehension. I do, however, have to regard myself as bearing my own share of responsibility for them. That is to say that I have to regard myself as responsible for myself and before or to others for my own status as participant in a common universe of meaningful discourse; and they, in reciprocal turn, have to be regarded as responsible for themselves and before or to me.

The general force of these arguments, then, is to show certain fundamental commitments of responsibility, towards oneself as well as towards others, for the respect of truthfulness and valid argumentation to be grounded in the practices that constitute the production of meaning and meaningful discourse itself. Once again, the detailed working out, in all their ramifications, of the further implications of these commitments would lead on to consideration of whole programmes of moral, educational, social and political reflection and practical action. Respect for truth and for truthfulness is to be sought for and can only be secured in the practices and institutions of society at every level and of every kind. For the moment, however, it must suffice to note that here too we find ourselves confronted with commitments to normative consistency and to truth deriving from the nature of meaningfully human self-awareness itself; and that once again these character-istically 'intellectual' concerns turn out to involve responsibilities common to all participants in meaningful discourse as such – that is in effect to say, common to all human beings.

3

I turn finally to certain considerations drawn from the writings of Vàclav Havel.[2] First, I should say a word about the nature of this book. It was, to quote from the Preface by its editor, John Keane,

the fruit of a 1978 initiative of Czechoslovak and Polish citizens committed to the defence of civil rights. In that year they prepared a joint seminar on the aims, problems and possibilities of their respective democratic movements ... However, the original venture was jeopardized by the arrest, in May 1979, of ten members of VONS (the Czechoslovak Committee for the Defence of the Unjustly Prose-cuted) of whom four are contributors to this somewhat selected and shortened English edition of the original collection. As a consequence of this state interference, the original project had to be hurried forward, and it was decided by the authors to publish the Czechoslo-vak contributions separately. This original volume was introduced by an extensive essay by Vàclav Havel, who had earlier agreed to write a kind of discussion paper for the seminar participants. This very fine

---

[2] Vàclav Havel et al., The Power of the Powerless, ed. John Keane, New York: M. E. Sharpe, Inc., 1985.

and innovative essay by Havel, reproduced here in full, was subsequently made available to the other contributors, who in turn
responded to the many questions raised by Havel about the potential
power of the powerless under neo-totalitarian conditions.

Havel's essay may be read at one level as a remarkably perceptive
and sensitive description of what it had been like for the most part
to live in the Czechoslovakia of his time. At the same time this
description proposes a powerful and suggestive analysis of what it
was that had produced and maintained the quality of that life. In
doing so, it offers not indeed a programme for political action or
change, but rather a way of how to set about the difficult business
of living a 'truly human' existence in the situation as it was (which,
if adopted, might after all have constituted itself a factor of quite
fundamental potential change). It also, and perhaps above all, presents the elements of a way of thinking about politics and individual
responsibility in any society, and not only in that out of which and
about which Havel was writing and was primarily concerned.

One of the most striking features of Havel's analysis lies in the
fundamental role given to the concepts of truth and reality and, by
way of contrast, to those of illusion and lie. He was writing, of
course, out of his direct experience of living within the bounds of
what he calls a 'post-totalitarian' state, a term that he uses to
characterize a state of affairs not of 'simple' repressive domination
and exploitation by one group in society of all the rest through the
straightforward exercise of superior sectional power, but rather
that state of affairs which arises when the ongoing system of
repression has, because of the sheer complexity of its tasks,
become so institutionalized that individual occupants of even the
most strategically influential of its roles may be virtually powerless
to bring about any serious change in its ways of functioning. Havel
argues that in such a system 'that complex machinery of units,
hierarchies, transmission belts, and indirect instruments of manipulation which insure in countless ways the integrity of the
régime, leaving nothing to chance, would be quite simply unthink-
able without ideology acting as its all-embracing excuse and as the
excuse for each of its parts' (p. 29). Ideology as the 'metaphysical
order [that] guarantees the inner coherence of the totalitarian
power structure' (p. 32) 'is, in the post-totalitarian system, something that transcends the physical aspects of power . . . and . . . is

one of the pillars of the system's external stability. This pillar, however, is built on a very unstable foundation. It is built on lies. It works only as long as people are willing to live within the lie' (p. 35).

Why should people – many of them highly intelligent and even more of them, and more importantly, possessed of a perfectly robust everyday common sense – be willing to go on living in such a way? One good reason is, of course, a perfectly commonsensical fear of the consequences, to their families and even to their friends as well as to themselves, should they make themselves conspicuous by seeking to do anything else. Havel takes the example of a greengrocer who 'places in his window, among the onions and the carrots, the slogan: "Workers of the World, Unite"' (p. 27). The greengrocer has no interest in the semantic content of the poster, in so far, indeed, as he is even consciously aware of it; it was delivered to him by headquarters 'along with the onions and the carrots', and 'he put them all into the window simply because it has been done that way for years, because everyone does it, and because that is the way it has to be' (p. 27). But one should not suppose that headquarters has any more interest in the semantic content of the poster than he does, in so far, indeed, as anyone there is consciously attendant to it. (In any case, greengrocery headquarters will in their turn have received a supply of such posters from somebody else, who in further turn will have been ordered to produce and to distribute them by somebody whose routine job it is to be functionally responsible for such things, but who has not actually *thought* about the meaning of the posters that he orders to be printed for a very long time – if, indeed, he ever has.) The 'real' meaning of the poster and of its slogan has anyhow very little to do with its overt semantic content. It is that of a sign of participatory obedience to the system, but one that nevertheless 'helps the greengrocer to conceal from himself the low foundations of his obedience, at the same time concealing the low foundations of power. It hides them behind the façade of something high. And that something is *ideology*. Ideology ... offers human beings the illusion of an identity, of dignity, and of morality while making it easier for them to *part* with them' (p. 28).

Fear of the consequences of opting out of the lie, though real and justifiable enough, cannot, however, be the whole story. What happens if 'one day something in our greengrocer snaps and he stops putting up the slogans merely to ingratiate himself ... He begins to say what he really thinks at political meetings ... He rejects the ritual and breaks the rules of the game. He discovers once more his suppressed identity and dignity ... His revolt is an attempt to *live within the truth*' (p. 39)? As Havel says, 'The bill is not long in coming.' But hardly any – *if* any – of those who apply the inevitable range of sanctions, both direct and indirect, will do so out of inner conviction. Rather 'they will persecute him either because it is expected of them, or to demonstrate their loyalty, or simply as part of the general panorama, to which belongs an awareness that this is how situations of this sort are dealt with' (p. 39).

Moreover, though, on the one hand, that virtually ineliminable residue of respect for the truth and for their own (however shop-soiled) dignity which most people at least carry somewhere within them will bring or even force them to have respect and admiration for the greengrocer for his rebellious rejection of 'the lie', on the other hand 'the alienating presence of the system in people' will also produce in them feelings not only of fear but of resentment. Fear, because to the extent that one has adapted to such a system through the detailed functioning of everyday life, one finds oneself, willy-nilly, apprehensive, threatened by any threat to *its* stability. And resentment because, in the first place, one naturally resents those who cause one to feel apprehensive and threatened, and, secondly, because one resents them all the more if the admiration which one nevertheless cannot help feeling for their behaviour makes one feel guilty and ashamed not only for not doing likewise (even though one may judge the price to be too high and the benefit at best uncertain), but also for feeling resentment against them under the first heading. Admiration, respect and good wishes; fear, resentment and the feeling that they, the rebellious greengrocers of society, deserve whatever is coming to them for having been so foolishly self-regarding as to give way to a spasm of what, in the common context of their and each other's lives, may be seen not so much as honesty – for who was ever *really* deceived? – as a misplaced and childish desire to stick out their tongues whenever and just because they feel like it. (And also, no doubt, in some cases at least, something that goes beyond a mere anxious sense of where one's own material interests and security lie to a certain powerful fascination with the idea of being on the side of power.)

The situation, as Havel presents it, seems, then, highly paradoxical. On the one hand the system appears to possess all the resources of power necessary to the repression or suppression of any threat to itself, even, in most cases, to the undermining of any such threats from within the threateners themselves, so to speak, so that they are alerted to the defusing of their own threats even before their fuses can be lit. On the other hand, it is everywhere and at all times utterly vulnerable to truth, even the most banal of everyday truths. But why is it thus so vulnerable? Why, if it is so powerful, can it not afford to rely on its power alone, why should it not content itself with commanding and enforcing obedience in all effective practice, and simply not care about whether people name its sword a ploughshare or, quite simply and starkly, a sword? Why does it have to commit itself to seeing itself – and thus to being seen – as discredited and enfeebled whenever people, who may indeed acknowledge its power, simply refuse in so doing to pretend to consider its exercise of that power to be just?

To this question Havel (and his fellow contributors) present a number of different answers, all of them, no doubt, containing some share of a complex overall truth. First, most people need to be able to offer some sort of justification to themselves for behaving in otherwise humanly unacceptable ways. Secondly, a system of such complexity as is necessary for dealing with the modern world cannot function successfully without some sort of common code for the commonly recognizable allocation of roles, obligations and privileges, a code which in the nature of the case must embody rules for the justification (or injustification) of all those forms of behaviour to which it may apply. The law must obviously constitute a peculiar and peculiarly important part of such a code.

There is, thirdly, an answer which remains perhaps more implicit than explicit throughout most of the essays of Havel and his colleagues. Even a regime (or a system) whose ordered functioning is commonly recognized to rest on relations of power alone needs and, indeed, will actually produce and insist on a code of ritualized demand and acknowledgement of such relations of fealty and obeisance. In feudal society, for instance, the serf learns very early the ritual signs and gestures of homage to his lord that must accompany and complement his actual services to him – that often, indeed, do no more than (re)signify his standing practical readiness to provide appropriate services if and when called upon to do so. There are those who would argue that this has by now become the main effective function of the official ideology, and that nobody, or virtually nobody, any longer pays any attention whatsoever to its overt semantic content. Be this as it may (and one would naturally suppose it to be a matter of degree, varying, as it seems in fact to vary, from one local instantiation of the system to another), it is a notable and surely far from merely accidental fact that the rituals of homage developed within these 'post-totalitarian' systems include an essential linguistic component, a component, moreover, of explicitly formulated affirmations couched in such language and to be produced in such contexts as to bring them into repeated and unavoidable confrontation with the social realities to which these affirmations ostensibly apply. In this way the official ideology is quite unlike a code whose actualization 'simply' consists in such non-linguistic gestures as, for example, touching one's forelock. One might very well object to touching one's forelock, holding it to be an absurd and even humiliating thing to have to do, but as a gesture of subservience it does not have to make claim to be *true*. When, on the other hand, factory workers are called upon to repeat the slogan that all power lies with the workers, they are constrained not only to the ritual gesture of obeisance, but to the additional and quite peculiarly self-denying humiliation of affirming that which they know in their own living existence to be false.

Of course, an 'ideology' whose effective social role has been reduced (or has naturally evolved) in such a way is no longer an ideology in any traditional Marxist or sociologically familiar sense of the word. Its terms and theses no longer provide the people, of whatever social class, with the means through which to conceptualize, to represent to themselves, the meaning of their own lives and of the society in which they have to live them. The terms of any such ideology in this more traditional sense (and the importance of *its* function should still not be underrated) have to be sought elsewhere – in those of a traditional church, for example, of one nationalism or another, of fragments of an older Marxism perhaps. But even if the official 'ideology' no longer has any 'properly' ideological function, even if its only major contribution to the on-going functioning of the system is that of a ritualized code of recognition of the ruling relations of power, its very capacity to function as such a code commits it to a continuing pretence to be a 'genuine ideology' and depends on a common connivance in the reciprocal imposition of and acquiescence in such a game of make-believe. Nobody may in fact believe its 'affirmations' to be genuine affirmations, still less that they are true; but those who are subject to its constraints have to pretend to such a belief if it is to retain its 'true' ritualistic value as dominant constituent element of the public code of power.

This, then, is why the system, with its dependence on the continuing functioning of its ideology as a code of ritualized communication and mutual recognition within the structures of power, is so vulnerable to every expression of truth and to every explicit appeal to the explicit provisions of its own law. Moreover, the threat of truth is one that can *never* be completely suppressed. Havel quotes Jan Patocka as saying that 'the most interesting thing about responsibility is that we carry it with us everywhere' (p. 80). For Havel, and for the supporters of Charter 77 in general, this presents itself as an essentially moral thesis about the fundamental nature of man, who, each within the terms of his or her own individual identity, carries, in however damaged or distorted a form, the ultimately inalienable capacity for the recognition of truth and of his own individual dignity as bound up with his own responsibility for relating to others on the basis of giving recognizable expression to that recognition.

'By "an intellectual"', I noted at the outset, 'I mean here to refer to anyone who takes a committed interest in the validity and truth of ideas for their own sake.' In terms of any such 'definition' it should be clear how such a thesis leads directly to an understanding of the intellectual's peculiar commitment as having an immediately moral and an always at least potentially political dimension; and clear also in what sense everyone is to be seen as having, if not quite so insistently and unremittingly, a yet unrenounceable something of the intellectual in them. In contemporary society, no doubt, there are many who might feel less than wholly confident about such direct appeals to the *moral*. In that case we may return to our approaches to the same point through the theory of the conditions of self-awareness or through that of language and meaning. If, for instance, as we have already tried to show, no man can actually generate meaning by or for himself alone without at least the possibility in principle of its referral to the response and responsibility of others, each has nevertheless to conduct himself as individually responsible, for and to himself, for sustaining the meaningfulness of his own discourse – for sustaining it, precisely, through his (not necessarily, of course, invariable, but nevertheless paradigmatic) recognition of his discursive responsibility to others. As Patocka said, it is indeed the most interesting thing about responsibility that we carry it with us everywhere – everywhere, at least, that we go as meaningfully thinking and communicating beings. It is not surprising that even a system of the most thoroughgoing lie and illusion should be nevertheless inextricably committed to a certain respect for and recognition of the truth, and to a certain irremediable vulnerability to it.

At the end of his introduction to *The Power of the Powerless* Steven Lukes rightly makes the point that 'these essays are all, in different ways, reflections upon the links between morality and politics'. He goes on: 'All see a line between morality and politics, though they draw it in different places' (p. 21). Though I should not wish to argue that this is actually wrong, there is, I think, one way in which it could be importantly misleading. One major line of Marxist and Marxist-inspired argument has been, as is very well known, that morality, and more particularly the morality of individual dignity and individual responsibility for respect for other individuals and for the truth, is but a characteristic part of bourgeois ideology; and that, on a proper understanding of the matter, the so-called sphere of morality is to be seen as contained within the all-encompassing sphere of the political. In this book, so it seems to me, an almost exactly inverse lesson may be read: namely, that on a deeper understanding of the matter, the sphere of the political is to be understood as contained within that of the moral, and that certain types or aspects of moral behaviour or attitude are of their very nature also profoundly political.

By this I do not have primarily in mind the possibility that what present themselves as essentially moral imperatives may issue at times in indisputably political programmes, though this, surely, is often indisputably the case, but rather the fact that, if the domain of the political is (whatever for relevant purposes may be considered as) the public arena, the effective nature of that arena is as much a function of the moral quality of its individual members in their reciprocal interactions as the moral sense of their own individual lives is a function of the political quality of their common public space. From this standpoint, while there is certainly a distinction to be made between the senses of the *concepts* of the moral and the political, *no* determinate line can be drawn between morality and politics themselves. The nature of the political system determines that of the space of individual moral identity within it; the ways in which individuals, taken together, realize their different identities within the space thus available to them determine the nature and functioning of the political system – not directly, through the pursuit of one political programme or another, but indirectly, through the determination of the nature of the public space in which all political action must take place. In good times, no doubt, when the overall system of moral-political space is in balanced equilibrium with itself, the mutual interdetermination of its two indissolubly associated aspects may work so effectively as to remain almost entirely beneath the noticeable surface of people's lives. At such times people may or may not perceive the moral and political as impinging upon each other, but find it in any case hard to remember in what sense they are, even more fundamentally, each aspects of each other. Yet though this is a truth that it may often be more comfortable or convenient to overlook, it is one that men only forget at their peril.

Havel and his fellow contributors were, of course, writing out of their experience of living within the bounds of one very particular 'post-totalitarian' state. Nevertheless, it is also evident that Western societies too have their problems with the distinctions between lies and illusion on the one hand and truth and reality on the other, including problems – even fundamental ones – with the very concepts through which one may try to think the distinctions between the one and the other. It has by now become something of a commonplace that truth and reality are never delivered to human understanding as they are 'in themselves', so to speak, that is to say in conceptually free independence of the forms of thought of each one's own particular language, culture, society and what may (with all due caution) be called its most general metaphysical perspectives. All the same – and this too may be seen to be a lesson of the theory of meaning and of language – any culture whatsoever will have in one way or another to come to terms with its own version of these fundamental distinctions. No truth may be known as being absolute; but no one is thereby dispensed from the responsibility for recognizing the distinction, within her or his own context, between relative truth and, relative to that truth, indisputable lie and illusion – or from the further responsibility of testifying, when necessary, to it (and the art of identifying that necessity is one of both moral and political judgement).

4

Three different arguments to the political responsibility of intellectuals or three different versions of the one argument: what, in either case, do they add up to?

One way of summing up the matter might be as follows. Everyone, whether they like it or not, whether they are explicitly aware of it or not, bears a certain fundamental responsibility for truthfulness and to truth. This responsibility is rooted in our human capacity for rational reflection, a capacity not merely for thinking and acting rationally rather than irrationally, but rather the prior capacity for thinking at all. Or to put it another way: it is a responsibility that is rooted in our capacity for language and discourse, for reflective awareness of ourselves and of our own states at the same time as for communication with others. Such a responsibility is not, of course, indefeasible. To affirm it is not to maintain that there may not be times when deliberate avoidance or concealment of the truth may be proper or even in effect obligatory. Still less is it to suggest that there need be anything in any way irresponsible in any of those multifarious uses of language or forms of discourse in which fidelity to factual truth or to logical validity are not what is primarily at stake, or perhaps not even what is at stake at all. Many such uses are in any case in no way damaging to truth or truthfulness, even if truth and validity may not be their main concern. Still, the basic responsibility is clear enough, and a genuine underlying respect or concern for it need be in no way incompatible with a playful neglect of truth, or even its deliberate avoidance, on particular occasions. One might put it this way: the fact that this our constitutive responsibility to truthfulness is not one to an absolute truth does not absolve us from the recognition that the responsibility itself is absolute.

This fundamental responsibility for truthfulness and respect for truth, to respond truthfully and thus to provide reliable checks on each other's understanding and use, is, then, one that we all carry with us everywhere. It is not possible to abandon it altogether without abandoning the realm of human discourse as such, the only realm within which we have potentially self-aware access to our own essential humanity. But if this responsibility is indeed partly constitutive of our very background to ourselves, that does not mean that it must form the main explicit focus of interest for everyone in the main preoccupations of their lives. Those whom I have here called intellectuals, however, are bound always to find themselves among the first to be called upon to confront the implications of this responsibility by virtue of their central commitment to an interest in validity and truth for their own sake. But it is, of course, very much part of my thesis that intellectuals in this sense form a far wider class than ever one might normally suppose. All genuine educationalists, for example, may be counted as intellectuals in this sense; but in the last resort, so I have argued, everyone and anyone must expect to find themselves put, at one time or another, to the test. It is in this sense that everyone must be considered to have *something* of the intellectual in them.

This common responsibility for the general reliability of truthful response is not, of course, 'merely' or exclusively political. Indeed, there must be many societies in which the vast majority pass the major parts of their lives without ever being forced to take heed of the political parameters or dimensions of their most ordinary and most fundamental human responsibilities, even when circumstances *do* bring these responsibilities willy-nilly to the central focus of their attention. Nevertheless, when what is in question are truths and lies, realities and illusions concerning either the structure or the content of the public domain, the responsibility for respect for truth becomes *ipso facto* one for the nature of the public domain as such, and thus *ex hypothesi* a political responsibility. Here, once again, one may well say that, just as everyone has *something* of the intellectual in them, so too everyone shares in responsibilities that are always of at least potential political significance. And once again, for the reasons already given, those whom I have here called intellectuals are bound always to find themselves among the first to be called upon to confront the political implications of these responsibilities. For not only are they bound to be among the first to find themselves threatened to the very core of their central commitments by any power that seeks to involve them, whether explicitly or implicitly, by enforced declaration or by the complicity of default, in illusion or outright lie; they must likewise be among those best equipped for and those most committed to the recognition of lie and illusion, as well as recognition, when it is the public domain that is involved, of the political nature of what is at stake.

I return, thus, to my starting point. Truthfulness is, among many other things, a political virtue. It is political in as much as the nature and degree of truthfulness within a community is a major determinant of the nature of the public or political space in which the community conducts or contests its affairs. And it is a virtue of especial significance to whoever may be regarded as an intellectual. In the last resort, indeed, it is rooted in that irreducible share of intellectual commitment that is the ineliminable mark of the human being as such.

12

Intellectuals between politics and culture

JERZY SZACKI

My paper is not mainly intended as an historical or sociological inquiry (very necessary though that is) into the nature of intellectuals as a group and their social history. In any event it seems to me that without comprehensive studies not much can be added to the existing literature on this subject, which expresses diverse opinions and a multitude of possible points of view.[1] I intend to take up such problems only in as much as this is necessary for outlining my main topic. This can be briefly expressed as follows: what is the basis for the common belief that some special responsibility for the fate of the world, society, nation, etc., rests on intellectuals (or the intelligentsia)[2] and on what basis are some special obligations generally assigned to this group?

Since, as is only natural, questions of this kind are asked mainly by intellectuals themselves, one might just as well say that the main subject of my paper will be the group 'ideologies' created by them or, to put it another way, how they justify claims to a special place in society or even to spiritual leadership within it. If such a claim is not common to all intellectuals, it appears often enough to be worth pondering. Even when intellectuals are accorded no special rights whatsoever, one senses that underlying this refusal is the assumption that the group to which the term is used to refer, is

---

[1] See Robert J. Brym, *Intellectuals and Politics*, London: Allen & Unwin, 1980.

[2] 'Indeed, I see no reason for not using the two terms, "intellectuals" and "intelligentsia" as interchangeable except for a slight difference in emphasis due to historical factors . . .' (Paul Hollander, *Political Pilgrims. Travels of Western Intellectuals to the Soviet Union, China, and Cuba 1928–1978*, New York: Harper and Row, 1981, p. 43).

in some way exceptional. 'No ordinary man could be such a fool', said George Orwell.[3] Intellectuals are a group exceptionally difficult to define. It is always timely to question their calling, mission, historical role, and so on, regardless of the different answers given to this question and of the diverse ways in which this group is usually divided. 'This sense of mission is intrinsic to the consciousness of the intellectual.'[4]

Let us reflect on what may be the basis of this special belief – which is so difficult to justify when missionaries of God's word are not involved.

First, however, I have to take up a possible objection. This involves a matter which in any case seems to require discussion quite apart from its relevance to the main concerns of this paper. It is unquestionably disputable to what extent deliberations on intellectuals are allowable which omit, or relegate to the background, fundamental historical, cultural, national, etc., differences which we encounter when we study intellectuals as a group or their ways of thinking. I am not minimizing these differences. On the contrary, I deem it highly desirable to develop comparative studies that would reveal their full importance. But I am assuming here that the basic problems about the role of the intellelctual in modern society are universal. This belief is not based on any belief in the similarity of all societies that could be the object of inquiries on this subject. The point is rather that in all modern societies intellectuals are the most 'cosmopolitan' group. (Even intellectuals with an intentionally nationalistic orientation do not seem to be an exception to this rule.) They are the most susceptible to the infiltration of foreign ideas. One of the reasons for this is surely that quite a few of them have been educated abroad and, even in 'closed' societies, have privileged access to information about the outside world. Some metropolises, moreover, have long retained the capacity for emitting to the world at large the questions and ideas born within them (Paris, for example). Much more interesting than diffusion obviously is the convergence of views that is sometimes observable. One becomes aware of this in comparing,

---

[3] See Robert Conquest, 'The Role of the Intellectuals', *Encounter*, 2, 2 (1978), p. 29.
[4] Lewis S. Feuer, 'What Is an Intellectual?', in Alexander Gella (ed.), *The Intelligentsia and the Intellectuals*, Beverly Hills, Col.: Sage, 1976, p. 43.

for example, the Russian *Landmarks* (1909) by N. Berdayev with
J. Benda's *La trahison des clercs* (for a discussion of which, see
Chapter 2 above). Though very probably Benda did not read the
earlier book he addressed exactly the same basic problem. I cannot
explore these issues in detail here. I mention them simply to justify
my penchant for generalities, perhaps excessive for an historian.

The subject which I have roughly sketched is just as old as (if
not older than) the term 'intellectual' itself, which did not enter
common usage until the time of the Dreyfus affair, when the
unjustly sentenced officer's defenders presented themselves publicly as 'intellectuals' (in the *Manifeste des intellectuels* of 1898).
The conservative spokesmen of the 'social order' immediately questioned this group's right to say what is and what is not just.
Ferdinand Brunetière – one of the critics of this manifesto from the
extreme right – spoke of it then as 'one of the ridiculous eccentrici-
ties of our time ... the pretension of raising writers, scientists,
professors and philologists to the rank of supermen'.[5] One may not
sympathize with the publicist cited, but it is hard to deny that he
touched on an essential issue, namely, the question why the voice
of 'writers, scientists, professors and philologists' should have
some special importance – more than, for example, the voice of
generals, priests or professional politicians. This same doubt was
expressed with exceptional clarity in Warsaw in the spring of 1968,
when anti-government demonstrations were broken up with trun-
cheons under the slogan, 'Writers to their pens! Students to their
studies!' Responding to a challenge from critics of the political
activity of intellectuals, J.-P. Sartre wrote quite aptly: 'Now, it is a
fact that an intellectual is someone who fails to mind his own
business.'[6]

This interference in other people's business seems to belong to
the very nature of the intellectual, defined in a certain way. The
word 'intellectual' is often not applied to all people doing intellectual work or attaining a high degree of intellectual skill, but only
to a certain segment of them, namely, those who have decided to
come out of their 'laboratories or libraries' into the political

[5] See Daniel Bell, *The Winding Passage. Essays and Sociological Journeys
1960–1980*, Cambridge, Mass.: ABT Books, 1980, p. 131.
[6] Jean-Paul Sartre, *Plaidoyer pour les intellectuels*, Paris: Gallimard, 1972,
p. 12.

market-place, into the forum of public life. An intellectual thus understood always appears in a *double social role*: the role of specialist in one or other field of intellectual work (writer, scientist, professor, philologist) and the role of one who for some reason feels the call to active participation, or even leadership, in some *supra-professional* community.

For this reason disputes about intellectuals are not generally disputes over the place of this group in the social division of labour or in the social structure. From such an angle the matter not only looks much less interesting, but, one might say, even turns out to be an entirely different question. Hence, the term 'intellectual' seems to have a primary *political* sense: it refers to people who *behave* in a special way, though who, as far as their social position is concerned, belong to a more numerous class of members of a particular (though not very distinct) category of professions having special education and so on. 'Intellectuals' are only a minority of a larger population, the rest of which does not always sympathize with their activities or regard them as its representatives. As A. Besançon writes, 'not all men of thought have been intellectuals: many have managed to avoid it'.[7] He adds that, among the latter, 'are to be discovered the best of our writers and our philosophers'. Perhaps yes, perhaps no. I mention this only because one should be aware that this group of 'intellectuals', which has been distinguished according to political and not professional or social criteria, is often the object of criticism or sneers – even by those who themselves, by the right of other definitions, are called 'intellectuals' and supposedly have the same grounds for 'interfering in other people's business' as their politically active colleagues.

There is no doubt, however, that this group has played a considerable role in our century. A stereotype of the intellectual is deeply rooted in common thinking: as a professor, writer or artist, who signs appeals, protests and manifestos, speaks his mind in public on every more or less important occasion, participates in congresses, expresses his concern for the fate of humanity, goes on 'political pilgrimage', etc. One hardly need add that this group tends towards leftist radicalism, according to whatever the word

[7] Alain Besançon, 'Les Intellectuels', *L'Express*, no. 1834 (5 September 1986), p. 37.

'left' has meant in different periods. Let us leave this aside. It is not my intention to classify the political activities of the intellectuals of some one, strictly defined, orientation. I am speaking about *political intellectuals* in general. This is the first *type* of intellectual about which I will speak in this paper. The first but not the only one.

As I have already mentioned, this conception of an intellectual, widespread as it may be, is not universally accepted. Quite a few authors who do not accept it nevertheless avoid using the appellation 'intellectuals' as the name of a socio-occupational category, referring to all people who are educated and/or doing work of a particular kind. They introduce this term with the clear intention of limiting its widest semantic sense. It would serve no purpose here to review the multifarious definitions and pseudo-definitions of intellectuals that can be found in the overwhelmingly vast literature on the subject. It suffices to say generally that perhaps the most frequent practice is to accentuate the *creative* role of this group as interpreters of the world, producers of ideas, depositories of cultural values, etc. As L. Kolakowski says, they should be not guardians of the world but its creators. According to Max Weber, intellectuals are seen from this point of view as 'a group of men who by virtue of their peculiarity have special access to certain achievements considered to be "culture values", and who, therefore, usurp the leadership of a culture community'.[8]

This way of putting the matter seems to have very important consequences. First, it means distinguishing intellectuals as an *elite group*, that lays claim to leadership, from all the other consumers and popularizers of culture values who, though they participate in a given cultural community, cannot claim to play any serious role in it.[9] Second, introducing *culture values* (whatever this word might mean) into the definition of intellectuals as the basic field of their activity separates this group from all those whose main task is the carrying through of 'practical' undertakings. Intellectuals appear as those who 'live for and off symbols' (Kornhauser), who feel the 'interior need to penetrate beyond the

[8] H. H. Gerth and C. Wright Mills (eds.), *From Max Weber: Essays in Sociology*, London: Routledge & Kegan Paul, 1961, p. 176.
[9] See Leszek Kolakowski, *Czy diabel moze byc zbawiony i 27 innych kazan*, London: Aneks, 1984, p. 124.

screen of immediate concrete experience' (Shils), 'whose business
was thought and culture not administration or production' (Seton-
Watson),[10] 'whose activity essentially is not the pursuit of practical
aims, . . . who seek their joy in the practice of an art or a science or
metaphysical speculation, in short in the possession of non-
material advantages, and hence in a certain manner say: "My
kingdom is not of this world"'.[11]

To be sure, not everyone realizes that activity in this sphere also
has its material consequences and in this respect is not necessarily
high-minded. One can say in general that there is quite a bit of
idealization and wishful thinking in descriptions of intellectuals as
creators of culture. J. Carroll is surely right when he says that
'reality has been somewhat different, presenting a bizarre array of
types, in fact quite a pantomime of clowns, mountebanks, lunatics
and obsessives'.[12] I am not concerned here with an evaluation of
this group or even with the aptness of all its details, which goes
beyond the scope of this paper. My sole aim for the moment is to
show that there is a notion of intellectuals which is *neither
sociological nor political* in the above senses. One can call it
cultural, where the essential feature of an intellectual is a certain
relation to *culture values*. For quite obvious reasons I will not
embark on a serious description of these values, hoping that this
general expression is sufficiently, if only intuitively, understandable.

This cultural notion of an intellectual obviously differs from the
political notion discussed earlier. First, a person is an intellectual
regardless of whether or not he enters the political market-place.
The quality of being an intellectual is ascribed to a person because
of what he does as a writer, philosopher, scholar or artist. If any
question of leadership is involved, his right to it is based on this
'normal' activity and not public acts of another kind. Moreover, in
this case entering the political market-place may even be regarded
as a threat to the true calling of an intellectual, which exists, so to
say, in another dimension than politics, even though it may have

10 Hollander, *Political Pilgrims*, p. 44.
11 Julian Benda, *The Betrayal of the Intellectuals*, Boston: The Beacon Press,
    1955, p. 30.
12 John Carroll, 'In Spite of Intellectuals', *Theory and Society*, 6 (1978),
    p. 133.

political consequences. (For example, Znaniecki credits intellectuals with a decisive role in shaping national consciousness.) Second, the phenomenon of the cultural intellectual is suprahistoric in a certain sense, while the phenomenon of the political intellectual is of rather recent origin: his prototype is probably the French *philosophe* of the eighteenth century. Third, cultural intellectuals obviously do not have to be political intellectuals and, contrariwise, not all political intellectuals deserve to be called intellectuals in this second sense. I do not quite mean that the cultural intellectual is necessarily apolitical. For reasons that I will explore later, the complete isolation of culture from politics is inconceivable in today's world. What seems characteristic of the cultural intellectual can be illustrated by a remark of Orwell's: 'When a writer engages in politics he should do it as a citizen, as a human being, but *not as a writer*.'[13] In other words, the cultural intellectual eventually involves himself in politics with the awareness that he thereby changes his social role, *begins to do something else*.

These two notions of an intellectual that I have tried to outline seem to carry with them two different ideas of his responsibility. In the one case responsibility is essentially identical with *political involvement*, with coming out of 'laboratories and libraries', and in the second it consists primarily in absolute loyalty to oneself and to values that determine the identity of literature, science, art, philosophy, etc. The political intellectual feels responsible for the entire world; the cultural intellectual feels responsible for his own field, dealing with other fields only in so far as they have direct consequences in the sphere of culture values.[14] I think that in every country one can easily find examples of these two postures, which are represented on a wider scale by, say, Sartre and Chomsky, on the one hand (not to mention 'party' intellectuals in the literal sense of the word), and, on the other hand, by Ortega y Gasset, T. S. Eliot and Husserl (as author of *Die Krise der europäischen Wissenchaften*). We have, on the one hand, the

---

[13] George Orwell, 'Writers and Leviathan', in George B. de Huszar (ed.), *The Intellectuals: A Controversial Portrait*, London: Allen & Unwin, 1960, p. 267.

[14] See T. S. Eliot, 'The Man of Letters and the Future of Europe', in *ibid.*, pp. 256–60.

advocates of some political cause or other and, on the other hand, 'functionaries of humanity' (Husserl) involved in the defence of cultural values of which they regard themselves as depositories; they do not declare this side or that side to be in the right', but simply defend their own argument. There seems to be a traditional hostility between these two camps. The first charges the second with hypocrisy, duplicity, exclusivity and 'intellectualism'; the second charges the first with betrayal, disloyalty to those values adherence to which determines an intellectual's identity. We should note that what is involved is not just a conflict between two different ideas about the social role of an intellectual, but also the *internal conflict* continually faced by an intellectual in his efforts to define his place on earth.

On the surface everything seems to speak in favour of the cultural intellectual's posture. He has a solid basis in the tradition of European thought, which is simultaneously modern in the sense that it simply requires that he do well what he does, without usurping any special rights for himself in fields where, as in politics, everyone is assumed to be equal. The hitch, though, is that adherence to this attitude requires absolute faith in *the independence of culture values from politics*, faith in the sovereignty of literature, art, science and philosophy. After all, the fear of the 'betrayal of the intellectuals' is grounded in the belief that there exists something to be betrayed, that is, a realm of *universal* values, be they supra-national, supra-class, supra-party or whatever; this is the belief in the existence of a culture which is not just the super-structure above the sphere of material interests, but which constitutes its own *kingdom of ends*, which are capable of uniting every one.

For quite a long time we have unquestionably been faced with a deepening crisis of faith in culture values in this sense, leading, if not to extreme nihilism, at least to the view that they cannot any longer remain aloof from the struggles of this world, but can at best be reborn on some new level – thanks to a radical change in the entire social order. The birth of the political intellectual is one of the consequences of the discovery that 'a transvaluation of values' is essential and that this can come about not solely – not even primarily – through patient work in the realm of pure spirit. More and more often the only idea taken seriously is one that can be 'translated' into the language of 'practice' (which is most commonly associated with politics): an idea which can become an *ideology* and have an impact on people who are motivated by interests as well as by ideas. The political intellectual is convinced (using Berdyaev's description) that 'truth is not to be looked for in culture and its objective aims but in the "people", a stream of organic life'.[15] In short, the basic reason for 'the betrayal of the intellectuals' turns out to be the *crisis of culture* in Hannah Arendt's sense. The basic question for the political intellectual is how to leave the 'ivory tower' and enter some social Church. It is not so important to write well as to have readers; not so important for one's discoveries to be true as for people to believe them.

I am hardly saying that these are conscious aspirations. The political intellectual may believe that he is the best defender of culture (and quite often refers to himself as such) and one who, moreover, brings it closer to the average person, supposedly ignored by the earlier 'clerk'. The point is, though, that if you enter the political market-place where there is no place for culture values as such, you inevitably submit to its laws. Making politics more scientific turns out to be making science more political and nothing more; making politics more moral turns out to be making morality more political, etc. Hence the great act of creating a new culture easily turns in the end into an act of self-destruction. Political intellectuals, as Benda says,

have not been content to adopt political passions, if by this one means that they have made a place for these passions side by side with the activities they are bound to carry on as 'clerks'. They have introduced these passions into these activities. They permit, they desire them to be mingled with their work as artists, as men of learning, as philosophers, to colour the essence of their work and to mark all its productions.[16]

It is not my intention to 'debunk' intellectuals of this type. Enough bad things have already been said about them for one to be able to exempt oneself from criticism of them (in the most superficial sense of the word 'criticism'). Besides, I am not inclined to gainsay their contributions, still less their good intentions, or to

---

[15] N. Berdyaev, 'The People vs. the Intellectuals', in *ibid.*, p. 110.
[16] Benda, *The Betrayal*, p. 50.

minimize the problems they have addressed. There is something else that merits our primary attention. The politicization of intellectuals (whatever we may think of its consequences) in no case consists simply in their capitulation *as intellectuals*. Quite the contrary, their desire, in entering the political market-place, is to preserve their identity and to be something different (something better in fact) than the man in the street, whom they might in other contexts regard as the salt of the earth. The intellectual is also commonly welcomed by politicians *as an intellectual*, though there are also cases of opposition to 'encumbrances' of this kind and of glorification of less literate people's 'instinct'. The intellectual is inclined to believe that he brings to his wedding with politics a dowry which entitles him to be the family head in the marriage. Feuer may be quite right when he says that 'the intellectuals were that section of the educated class which had aspirations to political power either directly by seeking to be society's political rulers or indirectly by directing its conscience and decisions'.[17] One may debate whether political power is really involved, but there is usually no doubt that there are some aspirations to leadership. We might well ask on what they could be based since, as we said earlier, the intellectual's entering the political market-place resulted from doubt in universal culture values, privileged access to which traditionally distinguished him from the crowd.

Wanting to remain someone special, not wanting to be just a citizen like other people, the intellectual had to demonstrate his usefulness to them in the area in which he found himself, to prove that he had some unique and socially indispensable skills. It is said that intellectuals whom I call political became the creators of *ideologies*, i.e. systems of beliefs up to the standard of politically divided societies in which few people take seriously universal cultural values. This is true, of course. What requires deeper reflection, however, is the degree to which ideologies can be and are accepted as an equivalent of those values, their adaptation to new conditions, perhaps even their development and enhancement by virtue of overcoming a former elitism and bringing them closer to 'life'. For the most part ideologies are not a simple

[17] Feuer, 'What Is an Intellectual?', p. 49.

negation of those values but an appropriation of them for political use by attaching to them adjectives of one kind or another. Thus we have 'scientific' ideology or 'socialist' humanism, 'socialist' or 'national' art or science, etc. Such expressions are supposed to be bridges linking politics with culture; thanks to them the political intellectual remains an intellectual and simultaneously participates in political passions. It depends on the circumstances and field whether the adjective or the noun is the more important. The *raison d'être* of the political intellectual, however, is based on their connection: losing the adjective, he once again becomes a 'clerk'; losing the noun he loses any special rights in comparison with his countrymen. In any case the position of the political intellectual is ambiguous in the highest degree. He has to combine two sets of loyalties, without being sure whether a combination is at all possible. It is hardly surprising that the political career of an intellectual so often turns out to be brief or marked by changes of political trappings and loyalties.

The situation is further complicated by something else. The political intellectual is not only a producer of ideas but also tries to find a 'material force' to embody these ideas in life. Gouldner described these efforts as 'shopping for an agent'.[18] It is very interesting to see what this 'shopping' looks like: an enlightened ruler, the people, industrialists, the nation, the working class, the new working class, students, Blacks – this is a long list of solutions to the same problem of building a bridge from theory to practice, using knowledge that supposedly already exists to reconstruct the world from its foundations. As a rule this was obviously not just a search for instruments, but also for *an object of faith* to replace the lost faith in absolute culture values. The group selected had only to be convinced that its task was to realize the ideological project; it had to be convinced that this project was consistent with its interests and that it was worth listening to those who had created it. It is apparent that an intellectual cannot rely on his own power; for he has none and is simply looking for it; he cannot appeal to tradition for he is in the nature of things an innovator who rejects the old idea of the calling of men of knowledge; and this is all the

[18] Alvin W. Gouldner, *Against Fragmentation. The Origins of Marxism and the Sociology of Intellectuals*, New York: Oxford University Press, 1985, pp. 22ff.

more reason why he cannot expect his leadership to be accepted without reflection as something natural.

The solution that suggests itself is for him to present himself as someone who *knows, or can do, better*, that is to appeal to a truth which he alone possesses. The paradox is that truth as a value without an adjective, such as is appealed to by the non-committed or non-party scholar – the former 'clerk' – is called in question by the political intellectual, yet he cannot avoid appealing to it himself. The ideology of the political intellectual turns out to be simultaneously a rejection of 'academic' science, knowledge as absolute value, and an affirmation of the need for knowledge, for some different truth which he alone supposedly possesses. Sometimes he even believes that political involvement gives him some special 'cognitive opportunity', inaccessible to his opponents and to non-committed people. The political intellectual, like the cultural intellectual, then appears as a person *in the know*. His knowledge at a given moment may be esoteric, but it can and should be disseminated: to say 'I know' is at the same time to declare oneself ready to instruct others. Kautsky's (and later Lenin's) statement about the intelligentsia's *contribution* of consciousness to the workers' movement is perhaps the best example of this kind of thinking.

The nature of the knowledge to which the political intellectual thus appeals requires thorough analysis. To say that this is *ideological* knowledge is undoubtedly correct, but does not explain very much. This is not only because the word 'ideology' is one of the most ambiguous terms in the humanities today. It is above all because its use can sometimes make it difficult to see to what a great extent this knowledge is the product of a selective processing of contents derived from 'ivory-tower', 'adjectiveless' or 'non-ideological' science. In other words, while the expression 'ideologicality' may seem very useful, this is only on the condition that the assumed understanding of ideology is to be considered not only as differing from science, but also as benefitting from science in a certain way or, if one prefers, as sponging on it. The history of ideologies is, among other things, the history of the introduction into the political market-place of the products and side-products of the development of knowledge. It seems that ideologies try to use for their own benefit the still great authority of knowledge and of scholars as such – while attacking such authority if it cannot be used. For the moment I leave aside the otherwise very important question of whether one is justified (and if so, to what extent) in speaking of social knowledge without additional adjectives to indicate its supposedly unavoidable 'ideological' entanglements. What seems important to me is that, regardless of what sociologists of knowledge may say on this subject, the view has been and is commonly held not only that such knowledge is possible, but also that it actually exists on some scale. As I have tried to show, it is to this belief that the political intellectual owes his position as a person who knows better, even though he is at the same time himself inclined to question this belief.

It is impossible in this paper to make a more thorough analysis of any concrete ideology from this angle. Were I to undertake such an historical analysis, I would concentrate on three notions which, though originating far from politics, seem to have played the greatest role in the history of the ideological and social career of the political intellectual: *nature, history* and *method*. The first two probably require no comment. They have received attention enough in the literature of the history of ideas and political and social philosophy. The knowledge to which political intellectuals most often appeal concerns the laws of nature or history – laws, which, by ideological alchemy, have frequently turned out to be *rules* to act in this rather than some other way. The faith of intellectuals in their possession of knowledge of another kind, namely knowledge of *method*, has attracted much less interest. Its unquestionable attraction is that, though acquired in any area of special studies, it usually has universal application. Any one who has been initiated into the arcana of method gains thereby the right to profess opinions on any subject, even if he has never dealt with it before. This probably explains why many scientists believe that, thanks to the discoveries they have made in their own field, they have gained a mandate entitling them to express opinions in other fields, especially in political and social matters. Important here is also the common-sense belief that someone who is very good in what he does in his own field will not be a fool in any other. In any event, the intellectual who appeals to knowledge of method certainly has a better chance today of finding followers than the intellectual who presents himself as the discoverer of the 'code of nature' or the 'riddle of history'.

Intellectuals, however, are commonly not satisfied with claiming to possess knowledge which should be 'introduced' to the consciousness of less learned people who are incapable of going beyond the horizon of their daily lives and ascending to a view of the whole. They claim also to have an entirely different skill: that of *articulating* what such unsophisticated people feel or think unclearly, but which they cannot put into words or properly classify. Hence the intellectual, whose raw material is *words* may be called upon to act as spokesman for the point of view of his 'clients' – those people who constitute his ideology's reference group. I will here leave on one side the, nevertheless interesting, matter of 'introducing' knowledge as the 'potential consciousness' of the group concerned. Such an imputation (made in an exceptionally subtle way by Lukács for example) seems to be one of the ways of legitimizing the political intellectual's aspirations to leadership of a mass movement. I want here to do no more than indicate this function of the political intellectual, which may consist in supplying non-intellectuals with the language for communicating on a scale wider than that of their daily lives,[19] and for expressing their feelings and almost 'instinctive' aspirations. Mannheim wrote that 'empathy' for circles to which he does not belong is one of the special qualities of the modern intellectual.[20]

A separate analysis would be necessary of the view that intellectuals deserve to be distinguished and play a leading role of one kind or another in society by virtue of representing *special moral values* to a higher degree than other social groups: unselfishness, the capacity for making sacrifices, responsibility, and so on.[21] I obviously do not intend to reflect here on whether such idealizations of intellectuals (or the intelligentsia) are or have been justified. Perhaps they do not distort reality any more than the

---

[19] *Ibid.*, 30ff.

[20] Karl Mannheim, *Essays on the Sociology of Culture*, London: Routledge & Kegan Paul, 1956, p. 118.

[21] See Simon Karlinsky (ed.), *The Nabokov–Wilson Letters 1940–1972*, New York: Harper & Row, 1979, pp. 194–5. Nabokov writes to Wilson: 'The main features of the Russian intelligentsia ... were: the spirit of self-sacrifice, intense participation in political causes or political thought, intense sympathy for the underdog of any nationality, fanatical integrity, tragic inability to sink to compromise, true spirit of international responsibility' (23 February 1948).

pamphlets against intellectuals written at the same time and in the same countries. I want to do no more than draw attention to the possibility of justifying in this way the privileged position of one's own group. One does need to stress, though, that (as in the case of knowledge) the political intellectual does not appear as the exponent of *universal* morality: on the contrary he most readily appears as the defender of a *new* morality, which he opposes to the 'hypocritical' traditional morality. Virtues are also defined ideologically.

This profile of the political intellectual makes clearer the nature of the opposition between him and the cultural intellectual. It also helps us to understand why the career of the political intellectual seems so unattractive to many people despite the rewards it promises. The most important of these rewards is presumably liberation from the feeling of impotence which threatens anyone in our politicized world who seeks independence and who concentrates on matters which – though important from his point of view – are not an object of general interest: science, philosophy, art, etc. But it does not seem possible to react to the failures of the political intellectual by simply returning to the canons of the cultural intellectual. In any case, this would not obviously be a solution. First, the crisis of faith in absolute culture values, which lies at the root of the 'betrayal of the intellectuals', seems a long way from being overcome. Second, even if this faith has not died out completely, or can be rekindled, it is highly debatable whether such values can be served in the same way as before – according to the ideal presented in Benda's book for instance. In a nutshell, is it possible, in 'our age of politics', to be an intellectual on that classical model and is not that model an anachronism?

The political intellectual's negative answer to this question is well known and need not be recalled here. Let us consider instead the possible doubts of a sympathizer with the cultural intellectual's posture. The source of such doubts is primarily the observation that, as T. S. Eliot wrote: 'nowadays ... "culture" attracts the attention of men of politics: not that politicians are always "men of culture", but that "culture" is recognized both as an instrument of policy, and as something socially desirable which it is the business of the State to promote'.[22]

[22] T. S. Eliot, *Notes towards the Definition of Culture*, London: Faber & Faber, 1972 (1948), p. 83.

In other words, the cultural intellectual's relative independence of politics was not just a result of his own choice of this rather than some other posture, but also of the fact that, *in the past*, he could live happily for a long time without ever having to defend this posture against the state, whose requirements on him were entirely different. Unquestionably, this possibility has been drastically reduced. Communism and fascism, which negate, so to speak, all culture values that cannot be politicized and nationalized, must have been especially difficult trials for the cultural intellectual. For the more intense are the state's efforts to control all the activities of its citizens and all areas of life, the more difficult is it to remain a traditional 'intellectual'. The totalitarian state enforces the *politicization*, as it were, of all intellectual activity. Either one accepts the imposed ideological norms and, under pressure of circumstances, adopts the career of political intellectual (quickly transforming oneself into a state official and losing the right of personal initiative) or one sticks heroically to one's opinions and thereby moves into some form of political opposition in spite of oneself. With total state management of culture almost everything takes on political meaning: scientific investigations in genetics, empirical sociological inquiries, sympathy for 'degenerate art', composing a symphony inconsistent with the favoured canons. Any defence at all of the elementary conditions of intellectual work, even if based on the most 'apolitical grounds', inevitably draws the intellectual into political conflict with the state and the ruling party. (Consider, for example, the case of Boris Pasternak who, in a Western country, would have been a classical apolitical intellectual.) He easily becomes a *political* hero in the eyes of all those who, for whatever reason, are *against* the prevailing system or state of affairs. It is easy to see that we have to do here with a 'politicization' of an entirely different kind from that involved when an intellectual decides for himself to engage in a political act of one sort or another, even though there is nothing in the situation which threatens him in his activities as an intellectual. That is why it seems very sophistical to say that an intellectual should be political because he cannot escape from politics. This is indeed sometimes difficult, or even impossible, but from this it does not logically follow that he should give up the fight for absolute culture values.

The situation described above is obviously extreme though, unfortunately, it has not been invented. Moreover, liquidation of the excesses of totalitarianism, such as we seem to be observing in at least some countries, does not necessarily mean a return to the original state of innocence. Everyone is probably aware that the merging of culture and politics that has taken place in our century is irreversible. Even if complete isolation was possible at all in the past, it now seems inconceivable. Even T. S. Eliot, who protested strongly against the politicization of culture, wrote that the intellectual 'should be vigilantly watching the conduct of politicians and economists, for the purpose of criticizing and warning, when the decisions and actions of politicians and economists are likely to have cultural consequences. On these consequences the man of letters should prepare himself to judge.'[23] This posture is certainly no longer that of the old 'intellectual', who imagined that he could simply ignore politics.

Unquestionably this change was brought about by the totalitarian experience, which made intellectuals aware that standing on the side-lines gives no guarantee of safety from the ever more ubiquitous consequences of politics. No less important, however, seems the ever increasing dependence of the condition of culture in today's world on financial decisions which, in one way or another, are political. This is true apart from the fact that the products of culture, whatever their creators' intentions, are becoming stakes in political games between parties, states and camps. All this makes the cultural intellectual more 'political' today than, let us say, one hundred years ago. But that does not mean that this group is dying out. I am even inclined to think that the utopia of absolute culture values has greater chances of survival than its ideological surrogates, created by impatient political intellectuals, who fling themselves into ever more reckless adventures outside the limits of what an intellectual should, and really can, do. The point is, though, what this utopia is and can be today – after all the trials to which it has been subjected.

The dilemma of politics and culture, which I have tried to outline above along with some of its consequences, hardly exhausts the problem of the position of the intellectual in society.

[23] Eliot, 'The Man of Letters', p. 259.

In the opinion of some authors, both the notions of an intellectual discussed here are more or less anachronistic. The future is supposed to belong simply to the *specialist*, who claims no great mission and owes his privileged position solely to the fact that he is so good in some limited field as to be indispensable. Both the cultural and political intellectual were, as M. Foucault says, 'universal' intellectuals, whereas the new type is a 'concrete' intellectual.[24] This vision is unquestionably attractive and it is hardly surprising that so many educated people succumb to it. It supplies the intellectual with an absolutely unshakeable justification for the privileged place he occupies, while at the same time defining realistically the limited influence he can have on the fate of society. While it is true that an intellectual should be an *expert* on something, the reach of his expertise has been continually shrinking as a result of the division of labour and will continue to do so in the future. Even traditional humanistic disciplines, philosophy included, are becoming specialized. Today there is no place for Hegel or Marx, Comte or Spencer. However, I am not certain whether specialization will deliver the intellectual from the dilemma discussed in this paper or will only modify it in some way. In any case this seems not totally to exclude the possibility of a conflict between service to particular political interests (even without claims to leadership) and the defence of absolute culture values such as truth. I leave this question unanswered, since it would require a separate paper. I confine myself to the problems of the 'universal' intellectual which, I believe, are still a vital issue.

[24] See Charles C. Lemert (ed.), *French Sociology. Rupture and Renewal since 1968*, New York: Columbia University Press, 1983, p. 303.

13

The political irresponsibility of intellectuals

G. M. TAMÁS

> When the rain raineth
> And the Goose winketh,
> Little wotteth the Gosling
> What the Goose thinketh.
> Anon.

Responsibility is usually held to be something you may find yourself mixed up in when under some sort of acknowledged contractual obligation. The exercise of many trades involves responsibility, frequently modelled on the idea of promise: the timely supply of goods, the observance of the advertised parameters and the like. Many trades do indeed have quite precise standards of excellence. Quality, for example, can be and often is defined so exactly that the failure of a tradesman to live up to it can be and often is considered to be a case for the courts or as something that should be covered by insurance.

Now our trade notoriously lacks this kind of clearly circumscribed standard. In a way this want of standards is our pride: it is mysterious and it is one of our main arguments against censorship. Modern intellectuals, with the exception of some ill-famed oddballs like Dostoevsky, will unambiguously claim that they are irresponsible. The legal pursuance of an interference with the

This paper was prepared for a conference about 'The Political Responsibility of Intellectuals' organized by Mr Alan Montefiore and Prof. Jerzy Szacki on behalf of the Institut für die Wissenschaften vom Menschen in Vienna, autumn 1987 (and which the Hungarian authorities prevented me from attending). I would like to thank Mr Montefiore (Balliol College, Oxford) for his helpful critical comments and Dr Ian Maclean (The Queen's College, Oxford) for his attempts to improve my exotic English.

content of their speech or writing is said to be an infringement of a fundamental right, a serious limitation of liberty. We customarily demand boundless freedom even for overtly seditious utterances. We all know the familiar dilemma: pamphlets advocating terrorism are instances of free speech and so privileged, while *acts* of terrorism are punishable by law. The feeble-minded bomb-thrower is therefore answerable and the learned demagogue is not. I shall not discuss this paradox because I, too, tend to believe that intellectuals are on the whole irresponsible and thus it is probably for the best that they are not taken to account for what they say.

The problem is, rather, why people in the modern age have come to the conclusion that, in spite of everything, intellectuals might be responsible after all. I would like also to find out whether such – presumably moral – responsibility and freedom of speech are at all reconcilable.

First, let me say that I do not deny that intellectuals *ought to be* responsible. It would be nice if, indeed, they always were. Being responsible pertains to one's dignity, to one's moral adulthood or *Mündigkeit*. Political responsibility would be spiritual culture's coming of age. This pious wish, however, cannot alter my belief that this, alas, is impossible.

It seems obvious that one can think that intellectuals are somehow responsible for their work if one is inclined to believe that he has found solid independent criteria for a standard of excellence in things spiritual, i.e. if one thinks he knows or at least means to discover what, say, truth, beauty and the good are. Not surprisingly, those who are ready to persecute intellectuals for their opinions, or who would at any rate be quite prepared to join in blaming them for the lamentable state of the world, are seldom sceptics or relativists. Let us call them, following the usage, dogmatists. (I am sorry I cannot invent such pretty labels as Professor Gellner does: see his 'narodniks of North Oxford' or 'Mayflower casuistry'.) Dogmatists come in many guises; let me name a few.

Rationalists like Sir Karl Popper apparently think that, since reason is the most widely shared human attribute if intelligent people advocate bad causes, this can only be a sign of their inherent malice or wickedness. I do not deny that political Platonism can have disastrous consequences; the question is whether its proponents are wicked or just mistaken.

Conservative defenders of natural right like the late Leo Strauss apparently think that there is one tradition regarding what is right for Man which it is impossible for anybody to ignore; people feigning this sort of ignorance must be cheating or must be downright hostile to what is self-evidently laid down as moral by the Ancients.

Romantic populists like Aleksandr Solzhenitsyn will go even further. They apparently think – and theirs is a very influential view in Eastern Europe – that there is such a thing as a *calling* for anyone engaging in intellectual pursuits, and the core of this very calling is nothing else than responsibility itself. The soul of a real intellectual is lit from inside: his whole being consists in feeling responsible for the fate of mankind; the outward signs of this condition are, as expected, depth, conviction, lack of frivolity. Those who fail to hear the call and write nevertheless, are demonic traitors. This call gives special rights to the intellectual: the privilege to lead those who have not seen the light. He who is not a prophet is a rascal.

Religious seers like the late Mlle Simone Weil are even simpler than that. The extreme Cathar or Albigensian doctrine of free will leaves us the choice between salvation and damnation; disgrace (like being born Jewish, according to her) can make us ignore the promise of redemption of the One True Church, no doubt. Too bad. But people knowingly resisting our Saviour and offering sophistry instead are justly damned and justly pursued in their this-worldly life, too. No rights, only obligations. Everything else is foul pride.

It is, of course, easy to criticize dogmatists during the dominion of sceptical ideologies. All the same, however much one would like to avoid relativism, political responsibility, we are told, is a 'sort of social idea' and is in sore need of consent. If accepted, I think it would clash with values we generally cherish, values which could make our laicized and unbelieving era tolerable – provided always we do not think that our age's character is the best one could imagine. Let us imagine what would happen if dogmatists had their way in the *contemporary* world. It is plain that we are living among a plurality of beliefs and indifferences. This, I think, is a very poor substitute for true intellectual freedom, because parallel soliloquies will not give us – or so I believe – a culture worth its name. Still, I presume everyone in his right mind will prefer this to Mgr Torquemada or Chairman Mao Zedong. If we introduce into this state of affairs a strong idea of the political responsibility of intellectuals, of their work or of the consequences of their work, *among unbelievers* we shall probably limit the scope of their inquiries, frighten them off fundamental problems, discourage the one remaining kind of professional honesty: unbiassed research. I do not think that striving for objective and universal truth (even in ethics) is a foolish endeavour. But if this is only tolerated in the context of some emotivist or subjectivist outlook, then we must be on our guard. Nobody is more jealous than the tolerant man.

If truth has an authoritative source – scripture, revelation, faith – then there is a right opinion, an *orthodoxy*. Deviating from it in connivance with others is a *heresy*. A heresy, unlike a 'lay' conflict of ideas, can be corrected. Heretics are able to make amends, to repent, to reform. Truth in Christianity can be arrived at by consent, since its truth criteria are criteria of interpretation, and thus depend on the construal of a narrative. The right sense of the latter is established by tradition. The right sort of tradition is established and upheld by an institution endowed with super-human authority. In a true-believing, that is, orthodox Church a Christian scholar is not responsible because the consequences of his teachings may be unpleasant for his fellow men, but because first, since truth for the Christian *is* salvation, false belief is *ipso facto* morally wrong; secondly, since truth *can* be discovered and be known – for example, through miracles and martyrs – and since to those who may be too dense to discover it, it may be given by grace, it would require a certain stubborn malevolence to persist in falsehood; thirdly, since it is certain that error *can* be corrected – the Church as a whole is of one mind *and* is right – persisting in error is resisting revealed truth, i.e. condemning oneself. One is, therefore, responsible for oneself and before God. But this is, beyond doubt, no *political* responsibility. The heretic will, of course, have misled his flock, but heresy is sin regardless of the consequences. The kingdom in question is not of this world, the destiny of 'the community' (*pace* the 'Social Gospel') is of no Christian concern. It seems clear that political behaviour can be heretical: but most heresies have nothing to do with politics, although they might be the causes of political phenomena.

Thus, we could not find political responsibility among believers, either. The Church is a polity, intolerant of error and legislating against it, but – at least ideally – it is not legislating for its own good and in its own name. This is true even in cases where its head is a secular monarch like in England. The immense task of illustrating and defending the teachings of the original, of the primitive Church – hence the commitment to a kind of history – allows of error. This is a huge risk for one's justification, *ergo* salvation, but it does not affect the common good. Paradoxically, if Christians fail to defend Christian civilization, they may be politically responsible towards *the unbelievers* who might be fond of it, because they fail to preserve something they are perceived to be entrusted with and which is judged *by others* to be conducive to the public good.[1] (Likewise, somebody who has inherited a valuable collection of paintings is expected to show them to the public and not to sell them abroad, because we have come to regard his collection as a symbolic part of our common inheritance.) But they will not be politically responsible *as* Christians. Similarly, Christian scholars are not *politically* responsible to their Church if heretical, but they may be regarded as such in a pluralistic society *as citizens*, squandering a precious heritage – therefore not in their capacity as intellectuals. Their responsibility will not depend on whether the Christian doctrine is true, nor will it depend on the adequacy of their hermeneutical work upon it.

If contemporary sceptics think that a fair amount of Christianity is good for us without, however, believing in it, they can indeed claim that churchmen have a kind or responsibility. But if those sceptics would think that those churchmen *qua* churchmen are politicially responsible, they should demand that the latter ought to be orthodox, which for a sceptic would be patently absurd. We may wish in the interest of our civilization that churchmen be so, but our wish is alien to the specific standards of sound theological argument. Churches can – and perhaps should – be forced to do their traditional duty in society, but it is none of the sceptics' business to hand-pick dogmas to suit their social aims. However devastating the impact of the Churches' leniency on dogma might

---

[1] I wrote this and the following with the debate on the ordination of women priests in the Church of England in mind.

be, theologians are responsible only to their spiritual polity, that is, not in a lay political sense.

Let us now briefly consider what would happen in a polity which is ecclesiastical and secular at the same time offering, as it were, dual citizenship – as it would if following the Gallican-cum-Jansenist ideas of Saint-Cyran and of the Arnauld clan and the original Anglican idea. In this kind of polity every citizen is supposed to be a true believer. Is unsound theological argument a matter for political responsibility in such a polity? A Hobbesian, intent on the peace of the realm and terrified by factionalism and religion-inspired civil wars (and Hobbes is *the* political response to the Anglican idea), will have to say that it is. But any theology is all right with a Hobbesian provided it is able to bring about unity and peace. For him, the persuasive and legitimizing *force* of theology is the aspect to be considered. For the Christians themselves this is naturally not so. Their solution will be a recourse to natural religion and natural theology or else, to Scripture and faith. They will prefer – as they have indeed done – strife to peace, since if we choose that dual citizenship, truth has to become a political matter. But political struggle cannot decide where truth lies: that is decided beforehand by other methods. Religious matters are decided in that polity by decree or common will, that is, the rational spiritual, intellectual side of theology will elude political responsibility, unlike religious inspiration or choice of denomination. This is, by the way, why ultramontanes like Joseph de Maistre are Hobbesians at the bottom of their hearts.

If the responsibility of intellectuals – in the absence of orthodoxy – is to be taken seriously, one cannot morally excuse error. Why can one not err in good faith? Because the idea of responsibility apparently presupposes an agreed standard of excellence. In what else, then, can irresponsible intellectual behaviour consist in, other than in failing to live up to this standard? Given the importance of choices (decisions) and procedures in the intellectual pursuits, self-contradictory argument should be morally reprehensible. A *fortiori*, demonstrably harmful hypotheses in politics should be seen as evil counsel and the thinkers in question condemned. But what if the relevant scholarly community and the larger society cannot agree about what to consider harm? I think that if a standard of excellence in *litterae humaniores* cannot be established, a strong doctrine of political responsibility is at best presumptuous. But the search for such a standard seems to run counter to the spirit of the age. One cannot speak of this kind of responsibility except in the name of some truth acquired, taken into possession.

One might say that the obviously evil consequences of holding or propagating a given theory will inevitably compromise the theory whose consequences they are deemed to be. But will our knowledge of social causation account for this? To repeat the old questions: is Houston Stewart Chamberlain responsible for Auschwitz? Is Karl Marx responsible for the Gulag? Are all those half-forgotten doctrinaries enumerated in Hannah Arendt's *Origin of Totalitariansim* responsible for the horrors of the twentieth century? People think that even open complicity, public consorting with mass murderers has not spoiled the *œuvre* of figures like Lukács, Bloch, Brecht, Maiakovsky, Pound, Jünger, Heidegger, Gentile, Priestley, MacDiarmid or Upward. The common belief appears to be that these vices are private ones as in the case of other citizens – in other words, that intellectuals in their capacity as intellectuals are irresponsible. Is Merleau-Ponty excused for his shrewd and perverse explaining away, nay, advocacy, of terror trials and death camps in the Soviet Union because his books are of no consequence? I do not think so. We do not want to apply censorship to the writings of these distasteful men because we do not want to use censorship at all. We value freedom of speech more than intellectual honesty – about the criteria of which in this world of unbelief we are unable to attain consent. But if this is so, is moral criticism of such an awful exercise in self-debasement as Sartre's *Les Communistes et la paix* still possible? Are cultural relativists prepared to defend systems of centrally planned death by starvation as a *pur et dur* manifestation of something that is rooted in the contemporary third world, predicament, wicked or innocent? The answer still is: whatever the truth of the matter may be, *let them speak*.

Let us now for a moment invert the argument. Let us consider the intellectuals who, not caring a damn about anything said above, *do* feel responsible. Why do they feel like they do? I can approach this question only obliquely, through an example which has been puzzling me for a very long time. Everybody conversant with the intellectual history of this century knows that documents of communist remorse and self-criticism fill miles and miles of library shelves, while Nazis are in general unrepentant. Why? I said in my book, *L'Oeil et la main*, that this is because Nazis are sincere and Bolsheviks mendacious. What does this mean? Political ideologies like the two alluded to will enunciate a sort of Messianic promise. The communist promise is the successor of the Great Tradition: it is universalistic in its notion of unity, 'human self-identity' (to quote Kolakowski), in its repudiation of institutional or rational mediation, in its implied millenarist view of Man, redeemed effortlessly by a change in the nature of things, brought about by heroic action. One could and, I suppose with a shudder, still can be a communist with best wishes for everybody. And the Messianic promise of communism is not only some vulgar hope for happiness; it is about self-improvement, about community, about inner and outer freedom melting together in the kingdom of perfect mortal love.

The communist can be a misled fanatic – and, of course, a hangman, a bureaucrat, a cynic – but the Nazi most probably will simply be a scoundrel. National socialism suggests that everything will be all right for *us*, for *our kind*, that the rest have interests not worth respecting because they are others, *therefore* scarcely human; that you should cease to think, you should obey and serve and be terrible. This is an ideology for *Landsknechte*, not for intellectuals. The former, repentant communists demonstrate the truth of La Rochefoucauld's famous remark about hypocrisy, namely that it is the curtsey of vice to virtue. Remorseful ex-communists – however boring they might be in the end – bear witness to the social force of ideas. They feel that if some belief was a motive for evil deeds, one must be responsible, either because one has made an erroneous inference from a basically sensible idea, or because one has been idiotic enough to believe in an idea one should have seen through right at the beginning. Intellectual Bolsheviks thought that their failure to recognize demagoguery, murderous intent, wicked inner structure of a doctrine, that is, a *lack of intellectual honesty and skill*, was a matter to feel responsible – and ashamed – about.

This was not the sceptical, but the fanatical *epoché* or suspension of judgement: the voluntary renouncing of method, reasoning, argument, listening to the *altera pars* and so on. These people thought that penance was called for not only for the evil deeds themselves but also for the intellectual mistakes which made them possible.

Can we say according to what I alleged earlier on that their plea for assuming responsibility even for their words alone is gratiuitous, even meaningless? Can we say – ignoring their eventual passionate change of heart – that the great tempters and seducers are innocent? Can we discount this *experience* of responsibility as irrelevant sentimental moaning? I do not think so. Still, in this age of unmitigated Pyrrhonism it is deeply embarrassing. For those ex-communists who do penance are dogmatic (as opposed to sceptic) and think that there is a truth in the Great Tradition (the Graeco-Judaeo-Christian one) and that this truth has been betrayed. For they think that truth requires more than a mere proof or refutation; it requires *fidelity*: a loyalty of memory, of the remembrance of a truth already found, inherent in our European thought. It is rather forgetting, they apparently think, than just sheer methodological error which allowed some to mistake revolutionary socialism for the radical humanism it purported to have been. Well, infidelity is not considered any longer as *very* reprehensible; to keep faith where one is not constrained by clearly contractual obligations, is nowadays considered to be going beyond the bounds of strictly moral duty. Nevertheless, there could be a case for responsibility here, if only there really is or was something to be faithful to. Everything seems to depend on what our beliefs may be.

Communism, in contrast to fascism, did not intellectually break with the Great Tradition, thus it is not open to the heroic relativism of a Nietzsche or a Sorel. This is why it is liable to moral conversion, but it is at the same time why it is infinitely more dangerous in the long run: because, simply, it can be taken up by good men in good faith. And let it be remembered that what is at stake here are not trifling matters but cases even of genocide. This hypocritical and morbid fidelity enabled the disappointed and ashamed ex-communists to feel responsible. This ability of theirs was linked to a framework of moral thinking, to a strong faith supported by tradition which, when dramatically confronted with a distorted version of itself, proved strong enough to overcome specifically modern restraints and inhibitions. The capacity of feeling responsible rests on a moral choice embedded in tradition and faith. It permits us to renege, to denounce misdeeds when committed in a mental state compatible with the spiritual framework – of sacrilegiously polluted – when it is plain (*within* the inner structure of this tradition) that the actions did belie the words and even the words were satanically twisted; when the logic of this moral thought itself can show the 'interested error', in those inferences with the deadly results. *But not more*.

Those who thought that moral values are but a bulwark for cowardly knaves of the lower castes could not undergo a moral conversion. What they felt, their sins exposed, was naked defeat and unreflective despair – see Speer's memoirs or Malaparte's regrettable *Kaputt* or Jünger's *Strahlungen* or Benn's *Doppelleben*.

All this presumably means that our contemporary Pyrrhonism cannot sustain serious moral conflict. If Pyrrhonism is indeed the main characteristic of the modern intellectual condition, the guarantee against boorish intolerance and unjust persecution cannot be anything else but an extreme doctrine of freedom of speech, a doctrine absolving us from the responsibility of anything we might say and of the inferences drawn by ourselves and others from what we said.

But if we cannot assume responsibility for what we say what on earth can be the point in saying it?

14

Intellectuals and responsibility

EDWARD SHILS

I

No good purpose can be served by taking as our point of departure the proposition that intellectuals are and have nearly always been alienated from the centre of their society. There is no doubt that many, indeed many of the most eminent, and particularly in the past two centuries, have been very critical and even hostile in various degrees and ways to the centre or part of the centre of their respective societies. But it would give a false idea of intellectuals to begin by contending that it is an essential characteristic of intellectuals to be alienated from, or hostile to, or critical of, their own societies. The view sometimes asserted and more often implied, that the very nature of the activity of an intellectual inherently requires undifferentiated and undiscriminating alienation from traditions, authorities and institutions, contains a small amount of truth. Taken as it is stated, however, it is false and obstructs our understanding of the nature of intellectual activity and of the relations between intellectuals, their culture and the society in which they live.

The generalization which asserts that intellectuals are 'alienated' is a misrepresentation of the intellectuals' sense of responsibility for institutions; it is also a misrepresentation of their sense of responsibility to intellectual traditions. The generalization about the pervasiveness of alienation fails to appreciate the significance of intellectual traditions for intellectual activity. Any person who is alienated from primary intellectual traditions could not be an intellectual; he would have no starting place except his own genius. A genius would have to be very great indeed to re-invent language, genres, prosody, themes, etc., from the very beginning, all more or less at once, and entirely by himself. Even the most antinomian intellectuals, if they want to create an intellectual work, have to submit to intellectual traditions to a considerable extent. Even those intellectuals who wish to destroy intellectual traditions are held in the grip of intellectual traditions.

Traditions are made up of symbolic configurations, i.e. bodies of intellectual works, bodies of knowledge, standards of assessment and of the ideals and ends of intellectual activities; they would never have been formed and transmitted if intellectuals had not, without knowing that they were speaking prose, taken the responsibility for those traditions. In doing so, productive intellectuals and recipient and interpretative intellectuals have not necessarily felt an explicit sense of responsibility for those traditions; they have ordinarily taken their obligations to the traditions for granted. They have grown up and been active in the medium formed by the acceptance of those traditions by many of their antecedents and contemporaries. They have, where there has been a plurality of traditions, as there nearly always has been, chosen more or less knowingly, to affirm and observe one or more of these traditions as their own, but they seldom put their choice and adherence into the idiom of 'responsibility'.

These intellectuals have not been principled traditionalists, explicitly devoted to the maintenance of traditions in all spheres of life. In the sphere of intellectual life in which they were active, the tradition, especially the main works of the tradition, presented them with a concretely embodied standard which their own aspiration to create as good a work as they could caused them to respect. In performing their intellectual activities they have thus been responsible to the particular tradition which they have accepted as their own. They have created theological and philosophical works which postulate the far-reaching substantive validity of these traditions while at the same time departing from them; they have judged particular received works and newly created works in accordance with the criteria or standards which have appeared to discerning minds to be inherent in these traditions. They have created literary works within the patterns made available to them in these traditions and they have judged them by the standards embodied in the best of these works; they have produced scientific and scholarly works within the substantive framework set by these traditions and they have assessed these works by the standards embodied in the best of them. They have assessed and repudiated works which did not appear to conform with these standards.

In accepting the standard of achievement for their own striving to create works, whether they be poems about a well-established theme and subject-matter – like the numerous variants of *The Iliad* – or about agriculture, or scientific works, or whether they be works of historiography, or biographies and autobiographies or works of philosophy, theology and mathematics, intellectuals have had before themselves a standard to which they have conformed. In this respect, they have possessed or acted, without independent reflection, in a way which implied a positive response to the presented standard. They tried to live up to the standard and to exceed it; they have accepted responsibility to the standard.

In their intellectual-practical activities as civil servants applying propositions of economic analysis to problems of fiscal policy, or as research workers conducting 'applied research' in industrial laboratories, or as engineers in industrial plants, or as publicists attempting to influence public opinion and the opinion of the political, ecclesiastical and economic powers of their respective societies, they have adhered to or conformed with the intellectual traditions which they accepted from their elders and contemporaries. As physicians and surgeons and as judges and lawyers, they have conformed with the appropriate traditions which they have acquired in the course of their studies and which have been reinforced in them, in the course of their practice, by the common acceptance, by their elders and colleagues, of those traditions.

Their acceptance, *de facto*, of the responsibility for the maintenance of those intellectual traditions has usually not been put explicitly into words. Except on ceremonial occasions, traditions and responsibility to them are usually not spoken about. This does not mean that they are disregarded or that conduct is not influenced by them. A person might act responsibly without thinking that he is doing so; he is in his own view, simply doing what ought to be done. They have acted in accordance with those traditions mainly because they have appeared to them to be self-evident. They have not avowedly or deliberately argued for the validity of those traditions; they have simply acted on them, as postulates not in need of explicit arguments.

By exerting themselves to produce a work which would be as good as they could make it, judging its goodness by the standard which they have accepted from their tradition, they have enriched their tradition. Nevertheless, the enrichment of the tradition has not been their primary objective. What they have striven for has been to produce a work satisfying to themselves and to their imagined audience, which is expected to apply the standards embodied in the tradition of works which they have come to know.

This is not always so. Sometimes authors or artists or scientists have argued explicitly for their traditions as such, particularly when confronting alternative or rival traditions. Intellectuals give expression to a sense of responsibility towards the substantive belief they already possess. Again, they do not often put it in terms of 'responsibility' but should we not regard the often passionate reaffirmation of their own individual beliefs and even more the beliefs which they hold as members of some community of belief, especially in matters of religion and politics, as expressions of a sense of responsibility to certain transcendent norms or values?

Scientist-intellectuals have a strong sense of responsibility not only to make their own scientific discoveries conform with the standards or norms of their scientific community but also to the wider range of scientific propositions and about 'science' as an ostensibly unitary body of ostensibly rigorously demonstrated beliefs. There is, indeed, intermittently, an explicit declaration among scientists of responsibility to the integrity of scientific knowledge and for maintaining among the laity confidence in the moral and intellectual value of scientific knowledge and scientific activity. In recent years, scientists seem to speak more about the responsibility of scientists for the practical application of scientific knowledge than was the case previously.

The sense of responsibility intellectuals feel for adherence to the tradition of the intellectual works they have received is not usually aimed at the maintenance of the tradition exactly in the state in which it was originally received by them. Sometimes religious intellectuals have seen their responsibility for improving these traditions as incumbent upon them by virtue of their membership of a particular religious community, which is defined by the

common acceptance of the corresponding tradition. These intellectuals have believed themselves to be responsible for reaffirming
and reinforcing the validity of their tradition against criticisms by
those who have not shared them. Their sense of responsibility for
the integrity of the body of beliefs of their religious community
and for the maintenance of the community itself is heightened by
the belief that if they do not respond to these criticisms by showing
that they are invalid, it will be concluded that the works or
doctrines criticized are not able to meet these challenges and are
hence defective and invalid. This sense of responsibility to the
fundamental articles of faith and for the religious community may
underlie the effort to draw out implications which are ostensibly
logically contained in the traditional beliefs which they defend.
They fulfil the responsibility which they have accepted to their
tradition and for its defence, not by what is regarded as innovation
but rather by demonstrating that the tradition already implicitly
contained the novel propositions which they draw from it.

In modern science, the situation is not wholly different; one
difference is that the scientists who attempt to improve their
tradition, when they follow new lines opened up by new observations which do not fit into the received traditions or when they
discover new problems which were not at all or barely foreseen in
the traditions which they had received, do not claim that they are
simply drawing out what was already contained in their earlier
theories.

That intellectuals act often out of a sense of responsibility to a
tradition without any open acknowledgement of their responsibility to do so is evident in the case of literary men and women,
especially in modern times. Their sense of responsibility to the
tradition in which they are working is most frequently only
implicit. In most instances, the responsibility they feel to the
tradition appears primarily in the fact that they produce their
works within their own tradition. They are usually perfectly
content to leave to literary critics the responsibility for protecting
their tradition against derogation and rejection. Their sense of
responsibility is for their own work; they regard themselves as
responsible for drawing something 'original' from its inchoate state
in their own minds. By 'original' they mean something distinctive
which will be different from what their minds expressed before in a

literary work and which will correspond to a pattern which is forming its tradition. Originality is not a primary object of striving; the objective is to do justice to the requirements of the work as they are discovered by the authors or artists in the course of composition.

Modern literary men or women ordinarily have a dual sense of responsibility, one to the tradition, the other for nurturing and disciplining their own potentiality to create a distinctive work of high quality. It is the latter which is often the more explicitly avowed responsibility. It is to the tradition of full expression in the genre in which they are working that they regard themselves as being responsible but the explicit avowal is not so common.

Serious intellectuals have an urgent sense of responsibility for their intellectual work. That, indeed, is the mark of a serious intellectual. Those intellectuals who are not serious about their intellectual work have little sense of responsibility for the quality of their achievement; they are interested in money, deference, fame. Of course, seriousness and a high sense of responsibility do not always result in work of a very high quality. Other virtues are required for the attainment of a high level of achievement. Similarly, unseriousness and a lack of sense of intellectual responsibility does not invariably result in poor work. By and large, however, there is a rough but significant correlation between the quality of intellectual work and the sense of intellectual responsibility of its author.

It should be said very emphatically that intellectuals are not equally devoted to those internal traditions of their profession which place great weight on truthfulness. Journalists in the broad sense do not always have a strong sense of responsibility to conform with the rule of truthfulness. Professional advancement, or a sense of responsibility for certain political ends, might be in conflict with responsibility to truth; the former are often given prevalence over the latter. This also occurs in the composition of literary works, especially novels.

2

Plato's views about philosophers as kings are ambiguous. What is not ambiguous is the assertion that very few kings have been philosophers or any other kind of intellectuals. The same is true of presidents and emperors; few of them have been intellectuals. Cabinet ministers, senators and legislators likewise include very small numbers of intellectuals. Even where a leading politician was once an outstanding intellectual, his intellectual activities are usually parts of his past before he attained high office. Thomas Masaryk was the author of a number of important works of intellectual history and sociology but his production ceased when he became president of Czechoslovakia. Woodrow Wilson had long ceased to be an active intellectual by the time he became president of the United States. Winston Churchill's years as an author were those in which he was in opposition or a 'backbencher' or even before he entered politics at all. Disraeli and Gladstone wrote works of literature and scholarship but I think that they were not produced during their respective prime ministries. Clémenceau's writings likewise were not produced during the period when he held high office in the French Republic. Turgot's intellectual achievements are somewhat equivocal in their bearing on the question of intellectual production during incumbency of very high office. His work on the philosophy of history was done well before his entry into government service. His economic writings were done mainly during the tenure as a civil servant – *Intendant* of Limoges – but during his brief period as Comptroller General, his writing consisted mainly of memoranda on matters of policy.

The tasks which must be dealt with by a professional politician in office are much less compatible with intellectual activities than is oppositional political activity or at least of being out of office. The latter roles leave some time for reading, thinking and writing which are difficult to combine with the activities of a leader in a government. Of course, even a leader of an opposition movement or party must accept responsibility for activities which are not intellectual but that still leaves time for intellectual activities for which must less time can be found in the schedule of a politician in office. Intellectuals who attain governmental office practically cease to be intellectuals as long as they are in office. Sometimes the intellectual-turned-politician ceases to be an intellectual, i.e. he ceases to perform intellectual activities, even when he leaves office.

There have been intellectuals – mainly but not always academic intellectuals – who have acceded to very high offices of government. To cite some random instances: Thomas Jefferson, Woodrow Wilson, Henry Kissinger and Daniel Patrick Moynihan in the United States; Isaac Disraeli, Sidney Webb, Hugh Gaitskell, Richard Crossman and Anthony Crosland in Great Britain; Theodor Heuss and Ludwig Erhard in the Federal German Republic; Luigi Einaudi and Amintore Fanfani in Italy; Léon Blum in France; and Saburo Okita in Japan. The list could be extended beyond this handful of figures but it would still not be very large.

In the long, often broken, line from Emperor Asoka to Jawaharlal Nehru and Sarvepali Radhakrishnan, there have been very few intellectuals among India's rulers. Nehru and an old friend Krishna Menon were among the few intellectuals who held high office in India; this is noteworthy since the first generation of the politicians of independent India had been in opposition. There were, of course, very long periods when India was ruled by foreigners, so that most public political life in India occurred only in the last half century of British rule. In that situation, except for a very brief period in the 1930s, Indian public political life was wholly oppositional. The Indian movement for independence, justified by an ideal of nationality, was supported by some Indian intellectuals and although he was a very artful oppositional politician, Mahatma Gandhi was also an intellectual. He acquired his principles of non-violence from Tolstoy and Thoreau and his arguments on behalf of an economy based on handicrafts from Ruskin. He was an author of many books of principles or doctrine and his autobiography bears a title which suggests that the quest for truth was his main preoccupation. His intellectual activities were made possible by the fact that he was the leader of an oppositional movement. (He also resembled many other intellectuals who have been interested in politics in that having been in public life for three decades, he did not want to hold a responsible office, once his political agitation turned out to be successful.)

Active political activity which requires responsibility to be taken for the maintenance or attainment of given policies is uncongenial to intellectual activities; as a result intellectuals in politics are found predominantly in oppositional parties. This is in the nature of the activity of being a politician; a politician has to do many things which are not intellectual and, with many of those things, intellectuals have little sympathy. In addition to lacking a taste for the routines and compromises of the exercise of political authority, intellectuals have since the nineteenth century – coincidentally with the development of public political contention – tended to be critical of, and even inimical to, reigning political authorities, oligarchical or democratic. They have cast their suffrage for the parties of progress, frequently socialistic parties, which have usually had a larger intellectual, indeed theoretical, component in their platforms than the ruling, relatively less progressivistic parties.

There are other factors which create and maintain the breach between political activities and intellectuals. In political life, such as it was under absolute monarchs and emperors, great influence and high office were often reserved for the kinsmen of the ruler and offspring of the aristocracy and great landowners, as well as for eunuchs and courtiers in the favour of the ruler. Intellectuals were usually in marginal positions. Court poets were not uncommon and court historiographers were likewise fairly common. Court astrologers, court physicians and other persons in the near margins of the centre of authority were also almost invariably present. Such positions usually required flattery or silence on the affairs of state. There were occasions where one or another of these court intellectuals might gain some influence on matters of high policy – perhaps court physicians were more likely to do so than the others – but they were rather rare. Their influence was very jealously regarded by the aristocrats, courtiers and eunuchs who had a more secure tenure derived from kinship or intimacy with a member of the royal or imperial ruling family. The court intellectual ordinarily had nothing but his knowledge and talent to guarantee his continuance at court.

Intellectuals as advisers, invited by the ruler or recommended to him by a powerful person, had more disappointing experiences than the intellectuals who were appointed for the performance of specialized services, although the latter too could fall foul of courtiers and officials who regarded them as rivals. (The misfortunes of Ssu-ma Ch'ien show that abstention from attempting to exercise political influence was by no means a guarantee against hostility and mistreatment; the fate of Long Shang at the hands of the successors to his patron was even harsher. In the West, Seneca was at least allowed to commit suicide.) Plato's disappointment in Syracuse and Clarendon's relegation by Charles II were the mildest of discomfitures. These difficulties have left an imprint on the traditional images held by intellectuals about their experiences at the hands of the mighty. The fickleness and obduracy, the wilfulness and prejudice of rulers have become persistent features of the conceptions of rulers which are contained in the traditions available to intellectuals.

Nevertheless, the frustrations and limitations of intellectuals in the service of rulers – from the margin of the centre – have not discouraged them from overlooking the unhappy fate of their predecessors and taking up appointments to advisory posts. Great aggregations of authority are very fascinating to human beings, not least to intellectuals. It is not easy for them to turn their minds away from the powerful; intellectuals have a greater than ordinary propensity to direct their minds to remote and central events and they are gratified by being in the presence of the ostensible instigators of such events.

Despite the phantasy intellectuals harbour about themselves, living in obscurity, disregarded by the powerful, many rulers have shown a *faiblesse* for intellectuals and wished to have a few of them in their presence as instruments or as ornaments. Intellectuals despite their tradition of distrust have been gratified by the prospect and the realities of proximity to power.

In the twentieth century and particularly since 1940, the appointment of academic intellectuals as advisers, or counsellors, or experts has become nearly universal. Even in countries with well-established and proud civil services such as Great Britain and (Western) Germany this has become very frequent. In the United States, which has no such tradition of a highly esteemed professional civil service – although it did in fact have a permanent professional civil service despite the obstacle of political patronage and the 'spoils system' – intellectuals were drawn into advisory or consultative functions on a large scale well before this happened in Great Britain and Germany. In totalitarian societies where the lines dividing rulers and rules are much sharper than in liberal democratic countries, rulers do not entirely spurn intellectuals who are politically unblemished by liberal or democratic views. In such societies where the rulers justify themselves by the invocation and propagation of some doctrine or 'ideology', officially appointed custodians of the propagation and reiteration of the ideology are called upon to serve. Totalitarian rulers are not indifferent to intellectuals even though they dislike and distrust them. But intellectuals from outside the boundaries of party and ideology are seldom summoned as counsellors or advisers. The passage between the universities and the highest circles of the party which dominate government seems not to be so frequent.

The political life of most democratic societies, especially the system of competing parties, is on the whole not very attractive to active intellectuals; it is, at least, as it is seen from the outside, too turmoilsome and too demanding of attention to small matters. There is too much compromise with too many unworthy interests, too much association with boring and 'low types'. There are too few 'great issues', especially for the members of a governing party. There is too much need to appear to agree with views and policies to which one is not fully committed. It is, furthermore, very strenuous, very demanding of time and, even if successful, has only very insecure tenure. Of course, intellectuals like gossip and intrigue but they also wish to do intellectual work which they would have to renounce if they were to go in for parliamentary politics. Intellectuals usually dislike the trivial rough-and-tumble of party politics. Nevertheless, they are preoccupied with the centre of society and particularly with the political centre; they want to be near it and to influence it.

The bearing of these observations on the problems entailed in the 'responsibilities of intellectuals' is rather ambiguous. One thing might be said: intellectuals when they are interested in politics do not relish the 'responsibilities of office', particularly of elected office. It is my impression that they prefer to influence the exercise of authority or to exercise it themselves but they do not like to be responsible to the electorate or to an elected legislature for their accomplishments in it. They prefer to influence the exercise of authority as advisers, experts, consultants or publicists. These latter roles have numerous features which are congenial to intellectuals. They bring them into the presence of the mighty; they enable them to observe politicians at close hand; and they enable them to influence the use of power without having to be responsible for the consequences of their actions, or to answer for what they do. These advisory and publicist roles also permit them to act out of a sense of responsibility to the ideals which they wish to serve but they do not wish to serve those ideals as participants in an occupation which involves exclusive devotion to it. Intellectuals in politics tend to have a sense of responsibility to ideals rather than a sense of responsibility for particular consequences.

3

The world-historical map of the sense of civil responsibility among intellectuals is very uneven. It also varies markedly among the different sectors of the intellectual category (or stratum) within the same epoch and the same society. Imperial China from about the fifth century BC up to the nineteenth century AD and Great Britain in the nineteenth century and the first half of the twentieth century were exceptional in this respect.

In China, Confucius and Mencius were quite clear about the responsibility of the person educated in the classics (the 'four books') for the guidance and service of rulers and for governing the state in accordance with the Tao. When Confucianism became the state religion of the Chinese Empire and when the examination system was established, the service of the emperor and the governing of the empire in accordance with Confucian teaching became the responsibility of Confucian intellectuals. A person educated in Chinese classics was led to accept as a matter of course that the service of the emperor in the role of a civil servant was an ideal of the Confucian conduct of life. There were, of course, many Confucian intellectuals who were not civil servants because although they had studied the canon and had submitted to the long and arduous course of examinations, they had been unsuccessful in gaining appointments. Others who did not have to support themselves preferred to be responsible for the cultivation of the ideal of study and reflection on Confucian teachings.

Some Confucian intellectuals, providing the staff of the Han-lin Academy, rose to positions higher than the executive branch. As the bureau of academicians, they had the 'duties of drafting, research and advice for the Emperor and Council of State'. From the bureau of academicians, Confucian intellectuals might be drafted to membership in the council of state which was the highest organ of policy, just below the emperor in dignity and often in fact more powerful than the emperor himself.

In addition to the Confucian intellectuals who had sat for the examinations and either failed or passed but never received an appointment – many distinguished literary men were in these categories – there were also other kinds of intellectuals in China. There were Buddhist scholars and Taoist philosophers, who had a different conception of responsibility to the emperor and the government of the empire; they did not wish to have responsibility for the maintenance of order, the raising of revenue, for coping with famines and floods and for maintaining the effectiveness of the armed forces. The Buddhists sought and, from time to time, gained considerable favours at court but they did not aspire to serve the government and to share in ruling the empire. Their objective in seeking the favour of the highest earthly powers was to maintain and increase the benefits which the Buddhist 'church' might enjoy through the favour of the imperial house or its courtiers and advisers. These included freedom from registration, supervision, confiscation, restriction of numbers of Buddhist monks, etc. The Taoists had a more disinterested neutrality. They commended indifference to or contempt for the things of this world; they disapproved of the rewards of earthly ambition and they disapproved of earthly ambition itself. Power was of no interest to them but they were aware that other intellectuals were interested in it and they censured them for it.

In the empires of the ancient Near East scribes were nearly the sole possessors of literacy. They had less power than the most powerful Confucian intellectuals. Yet they too were educated for the service of the state. It was from the great surrounding empires that the Israelite principalities learned about the scribal institution. Judaism being a religion formed around a sacred text, the scribes in the employment of government were not the only intellectuals. Priests stood alongside scribes as intellectuals of high prestige and probably, unlike scribes, they aspired to supreme power in a theocratic polity. The priests were performers of ritual rather than specialists in doctrine; they seem to have been more ready to be responsible to Jahweh and an ideal sacred order than to be responsible for the ruling of the secular parts of Israelite society.

In India Brahmins performed rituals at the royal or imperial courts; their responsibility was to the transcendental realm. They also less commonly were advisers to rulers. They became officials, i.e. civil servants, only relatively late in Indian history. Under the Moghuls, although government appointments were, in principle, reserved for Muslims – this was one reason for conversion from Hinduism to Islam – such were their talents and conventions, that they occasionally became very high officials in the government of the Moghul Indian Empire. When the Moghul Empire began to break up and was to be replaced by resurgent Hindu kingdoms or principalities and by the East India Company, Brahmins became advisers and officials in the secular sphere. They did not lose this privileged status with the ascendancy of the East India Company. They served the Company not only in judicial functions but also as tutors to the British officials of the Company in Sanskrit and Hindu law.

Some of the British officials of the East Indian Company became distinguished as scholars. Perhaps the greatest was the judge Sir William Jones who was one of the founders of Indological studies. The government of India which was the successor to the East India Company also employed many persons who, alongside their professional administrative duties produced important scholarly works during their service. The same was true of the provincial civil services. General Sir William Muir, James Beames, George Grierson, Malcolm Darling were only a few of these avocational intellectuals in the Indian governmental services; these and others like them were intellectuals who accepted responsibility for practical consequences in society.

4

Most regimes with elaborate administrative institutions have called upon intellectuals to serve them. They have been successful. The ancient British universities, particularly Oxford University, have, ever since the reform of the civil service in the mid-nineteenth century, regarded it as one of their responsibilities to guide some of their better graduates into the home and imperial civil services. As in China, the study of classical texts was regarded as superior qualification for governmental service. The examination for entry into the career of the higher civil service was designed for persons trained in classics as well as other academic subjects. As in China, many of those who pursued it successfully were intellectuals not only by their training and culture but also by their productive intellectual activities. Many scholarly and literary works have been produced avocationally by intellectuals who bore heavy practical responsibilities in the higher civil service in Great Britain.

In Prussia and then imperial Germany, the higher civil service drew on university graduates as it did in Great Britain but unlike Great Britain and China, in Germany, the study of classical texts was not regarded as the appropriate preparation for the administration of a powerful government of a large country. Instead, the intellectual preparation was intended to be substantively related to the tasks of administration. *Kameralistik*, later *Finanzwissenschaft, Verwaltungslehre* (or *-wissenschaft*), political economy of a descriptive historical sort, *Rechtswissenschaft, Staatslehre* – these were the subjects which a candidate for appointment to the higher civil service had to have studied. The avocational production of intellectual works was less common among German civil servants than among their British counterparts.

France after the revolution and restoration attempted to follow the principle of 'la carrière ouverte aux talents', at least to some extent, and this entailed appointing persons to governmental offices on the basis of their merits appropriate to the tasks to be performed. Patronage – especially royal favour – and the 'venality of offices' diminished as the modes of appointment by criteria of technical qualifications and prospective proficiency increased. The certified completion of a specified amount of education became more important. Completion of the course of study at one of the *grandes écoles*, and, most notably, the Ecole polytechnique, became more important for appointment to the governmental service. It was not thought that there were any problems of a deficient sense of responsibility among them; it was mostly accepted that study at a *grande école* would form in the student a sense of obligation to serve the government and hence society. It was believed that officials without special training and who held their offices through primordial claims or purchase or personal connection would not have a comparably strong sense of responsibility.

The service of government on foreign missions has also had some attraction for intellectuals. The diplomatic and consular services of Great Britain have also employed many intellectuals. I mention at random James Bryce, Charles Eliot, George Sansom, Harold Nicholson. The French diplomatic service was more hospitable to productive intellectuals than the civil service. Chateaubriand and Jusserand were a great writer and a distinguished scholar respectively and a tradition of avocational intellectual interest and production already existed in the French diplomatic service prior to the establishment of the Ecole libre des sciences politiques after the military defeat in the Franco-Prussian War. The Ecole libre reinforced the tradition from a side other than the literary one but the two most notable intellectuals in the French foreign service were Paul Claudel and St John Perse, both of whom were literary men.

It was not the intention of the Chinese or British governments to reward intellectuals by granting them sinecures. The presence of so many advocationally productive intellectuals in the British home and Indian civil services and in the British colonial and diplomatic services was an unintended consequence. Governments have done this by the award of sinecures and grants of land and money long before the Arts Council in Great Britain and the National Endowment in the Humanities in the United States. Recruitment of intellectuals to the civil service was intended for the more efficient, honest and loyal service of the government; the appointment of educated persons on the basis of their intellectual training and examinations to test their mastery of what they had studied was regarded as a better assurance of efficiency, honesty and loyalty than appointments on the basis of kinship, personal connections, membership in powerful families, purchase of offices, etc. The fact that some high civil servants and diplomats were productive and influential intellectuals was no more than a by-product of the belief that the discipline, pursuit and acquisition of knowledge was a desirable qualification for posts of high responsibility. It was also thought that such education contributed to the formation of strong character which would be capable of accepting large responsibilities and carrying them out effectively.

It was also thought that quite apart from the substantive knowledge bearing on the tasks to be dealt with by high administration and diplomacy, the discipline of the mind would be furthered by a stringent course of intellectual study.

There was never any question of the sense of responsibility of these intellectually trained persons appointed to their tasks and to the government of the day. Harold Laski once asserted that British civil servants, originating as they did preponderantly from the middle and upper middle classes would fail in their responsibilities to a Labour government. This never happened. In the 1940s as 1950s and 1960s, a small number of British officials – well connected in intellectual circles – were discovered to have been spies for the Soviet Union. Although their treasonous conduct might have been injurious to British interests, their number was small. Nor were most of them active avocationally as intellectuals. The fact that at least one of them was a productive intellectual and others frequented intellectual company has been cited to intimate that intellectuals tend to be disloyal to their government when employed as officials; so it was in the United States in the 1940s and 1950s when it turned out that a number of scientists – all British or German and Italian refugees in Great Britain – had been spies for the Soviet Union and a suspicion of the loyalty, i.e. irresponsibility, of scientists to their own government was from time to time suggested.

The intellectual culture of the German civil service, unlike that of their British and Chinese counterparts, was not shared with the members of the educated classes who were not civil servants; they had somewhat closer connections with university teachers of the subjects required for entry to the civil service. There were some exceptions, from Wilhelm von Humboldt at the beginning of the nineteenth century to Harry Graf Kessler and Arnold Brecht during the period of the Weimar Republic. Apparently among the Germans, there was no such close relations of an important civil servant like Edward Marsh with artists and writers of eminence in Great Britain. In imperial China and Great Britain the civil servants quite often remained active, productive intellectuals which was less the case in other countries. The loyalty of intellectuals in the intellectual-practical civil service was never impugned. Even where there was no frequent social intercourse between the civil service and intellectuals outside the civil service there was no distrust on the part of the latter towards the former.

Academic intellectuals particularly in the social scientific subjects, and perhaps also in the humanistic disciplines and natural sciences, admired those specialized practitioners of intellectual-practical professions in the civil service for their acceptance of the responsibilities of governmental service. The German academic intellectual world was generally proud of the German civil service; some even said that the training of civil servants was the main task of the universities. They shared a fundamental common culture with them; they belonged together to the educated classes. They admired them for their acceptance of the *Pflicht* or *Verantwortung* to serve the state.

Max Weber had a more qualified view. He was one of the most severe intellectual academic critics of the German bureaucracy. He seemed to have no doubt about its sense of responsibility to the state and to German society or about its efficiency; he regarded its probity as questionable. He thought, however, that the traditions of the civil service and the kinds of tasks normally dealt with hindered the formation of that higher sense of responsibility which avoids rigid attachment to particular objectives and which achieves flexibility without falling into characterless opportunism. Weber perhaps more than any other writer of the nineteenth and twentieth centuries made responsibility in action into one of the first obligations of intellectuals. The *Verantwortungsethik* was at the heart of Max Weber's view of society.

Within the service of government, there are some posts which are more intellectual than others. In large monarchical states there have always been court astrologers, court poets and court historians. Increasingly in modern times governments have employed trained scientists to provide useful scientific and technological knowledge, e.g. geologists, chemists, physicists, demographers, statisticians and economists; these scientists have usually not been administrators. They have had a dual responsibility – to truth, and for the promotion of the practical solutions sought by government. This implies more than strictly cognitive responsibilities.

5

We may conclude from the foregoing pages that there have been distinguished intellectuals who have had a strong sense of responsibility for the affairs of the political community and have attempted to give expression to it through their activity in roles which required responsibility for what they did before governments and legislatures. Some have attempted to make political careers but these have been relatively rare.

A successful political career, i.e. one which culminates in the attainment of high office, is often a distraction from intellectual activity; that might be one of the reasons why intellectuals have not aspired to such careers. However, even if they desired to make such a career, before the age of public politics, it would have been very difficult for a person who was not born into the higher classes of society to enter on such a career. Since the emergence of public politics with electoral contention and publicity, the prospect of the wear and tear of political contention has deterred persons who otherwise would like to hold public office. Both in absolutist regimes and in liberal democratic regimes, a deterrent to the acceptance of responsibility on political roles has been the intellectuals' distrust of the powerful, based partly on the tradition of the misfortunes of intellectuals in politics. This should not be overemphasized. More important in the West ever since the end of the eighteenth century and in Africa, Latin America and Asia in the twentieth century has been an aversion to the centre of society. This is a complicated matter. The aversion has not been universal as is evident from what has been set forth earlier in this paper. Furthermore, it is not free from a very deep ambivalence. The aversion to the centre is mixed with preoccupation with the centre. This has been especially marked among literary and artistic intellectuals. In the nineteenth century and in the first half of the twentieth, this was more uncommon among the academic intellectuals.

6

The social sciences as they developed first in German, French and Italian universities in the nineteenth century and then in American and to a lesser extent in British universities were regarded by their proponents as properly having the task of training young persons for administrative posts, social service and the investigation of the condition of society with the intention of improving it through public enlightenment and the improvement of governmental action. The development of *Kathedersozialismus* and the activities of the Verein für Sozialpolitik and parallel organizations in Great Britain and the United States introduced a serious quest for reliable knowledge which could be useful in the 'solution of social problems'.

Thus, although the ideal of gaining objective knowledge for cognitive ends was never disregarded, it was thought that this ideal could be pursued alongside of the fulfilment of responsibilities to society. By and large, the acceptance of the responsibilities to the existing society was conjoined in some institutions with the obligations to the discovery of the truth about nature, man and society. In continental countries, the universities were maintained by the state; in some of them, university professors had the legal status and obligations of civil servants. In Great Britain, where the universities were not institutions of the state, and in the United States, where there were both private and state or public universities, the same responsibility was accepted to truth and for training young persons for practical intellectual professions and in skills which would be useful to society.

Universities as corporate bodies never declared the 'criticism of society' to be one of their chief obligations; and until recently there were probably not many academic intellectuals who thought that their task was criticism of society. They thought it was their task to discover and transmit the truth about the subjects in which they had studied and in which they had reliable beliefs. Where the representations made by governmental and other earthly or transcendental institutions did not correspond with what academics discovered from their research, it was an obligation of the academics not to allow themselves to be dissuaded from their scientific and scholarly views by the assertions made by politicians, officials or priests. To tell nothing but the truth as far as they could determine and to adhere only to that was their first obligation. They had no responsibility to come into public contention with those authorities but if it happened that contention broke out, then they had an obligation to be steadfast.

There were also some scholars who thought that their study of the evolution of society disclosed to them the right lines of policy. They concluded that they were responsible for persuading governments and public opinion to act in a way which conformed with their norms.

There were, of course, some academics who did criticize their governments. When they did so, from within the range of views which were accepted by the centre of society, they usually did not run into difficulties with the external authorities. Authorities were, however, not always willing to be tolerant even of conventionally accepted standpoints. Sometimes when the criticisms, or even the factual assertions fell outside the conventional limits, in theology, economics, religious history or social science or geology, there were conflicts between academic intellectuals and the earthly powers and academics usually resented and criticized the intrusions of the external, earthly or ecclesiastical authority. But academic freedom as it was usually conceived did not include – although it also did not exclude – any responsibility for the criticism of governmental actions or social conditions.

7

Despite the tangible evidence of the sense of responsibility manifested by a considerable number of intellectuals for serving conscientiously the reigning authority, this has by no means been the sole or even predominant attitude of intellectuals, least of all since the French Revolution.

Free-lance intellectuals have not shared this sense of responsibility to the same extent. They came from a different tradition and the hardships of the career of the free-lance intellectual made for a greater degree of detachment from the existing society and a consequently greater unwillingness to acknowledge the same kinds of responsibilities for what went with it as were to be found until the French Revolution among the practitioners of the intellectual-practical professions and the academic intellectuals.

A very critical attitude towards reigning authority has been common among literary and artistic intellectuals. A refusal to share in the responsibilities borne by governments and other institutions of their society has also been common. This has often included a rejection or evasion of any responsibility for sustaining or participating in an affirmative way in the existing institutions of authority, such as government, army, university, church and even family. The attitude is the very opposite to that of the civil servant–intellectuals referred to earlier.

These critical and antinomian attitudes are very complex. They are not homogeneous within any individual. There is often a very obstinately held although unacknowledged and intermittent patriotism – perhaps it would be better to say a surge of nationality, occasionally breaking out into nationalism. In addition, although hostile to authority in their own society, many literary and artistic – and nowdays, academic – intellectuals have been very deferential to absolutist, repressive and brutal authorities in other countries or to political parties or movements which are submissively loyal to such absolutist societies.

Despite these irregularities there is one recurrent theme in the criticisms of authority in modern societies, namely the denial of the legitimacy of authority in these societies.

According to this view, since authorities are illegitimate, they have no valid grounds for calling on those to whom they are superordinated to respond positively to their commands or proposals. Responsibility for authority in their own societies is not accepted by those of whom it is sought on the ground that the authorities themselves have in their turn refused to acknowledge responsibility to a higher law. The legitimacy of authority is acknowledged only when it is thought that it is conducting itself responsibly to a higher law – divine or natural.

There have been intellectuals who have accepted responsibility for actions on behalf of societies other than their own with the intention of damaging their own society. We need not look further afield than Great Britain between the 1930s and the 1970s – such figures as George Blake, Guy Burgess, Donald Maclean, Anthony Blunt, Alan Nunn May. (Klaus Fuchs and Bruno Pontecorvo were traitors who were not of native British origin although they have acquired British nationality before they committed treason.) Alger Hiss and Whittaker Chambers were in the same category in the United States, although Chambers later renounced his earlier responsibility for the world-wide triumph of the Soviet Union and replaced it by a sense of responsibility to the Roman Catholic

Church and to the United States. These instances of treason are relatively rare among intellectuals, as they are in the wider body of citizens.

8

Those artists who proclaimed the battle-cry of *l'art pour l'art* could not turn their minds wholly from their contemporary society and its politics. They were invariably aware of them. The proclamation *l'art pour l'art* was simultaneously an avowal of the prizing of artistic activity as superior to any other and a rejection of society and politics. It was a declaration of the inferiority of society and politics to art; it was a declaration of the precedence of responsibility to art over responsibility to society and government. It was a refusal to accept any responsibility for what happened in bourgeois society. To the extent that they did have a sense of responsibility to any ideal other than the realm of art, they usually associated themselves with political movements seeking to transform society in accordance with an ideal fundamentally at variance with contemporary society.

The work of artistic intellectuals in the nineteenth and early twentieth centuries in European and later in North American societies was inserted into a pattern of life which had no necessary empirical or logical connection. Young plastic artists and to a lesser extent young literary artists lived in a culture of refusal to conform with the norms of bourgeois society. There was less hostility against aristocracy, even though the French Revolution which had decimated the aristocracy, was regarded very appreciatively by intellectuals in France and England and Germany when it was occurring and long afterward. Freedom of expression in art and literature, freedom from the burdens of traditional institutions like the family, commercial firms, the church, the army, the monarchy and the laws were the intellectuals' heritage from the French Revolution of 1789. Romantic emancipation from the constraints on creative expression received a dynamic infusion from the French Revolution. Although some intellectuals later turned against the revolution which they had enthusiastically greeted when they were younger and although some had been against the revolution from the very beginning, in the main, the inheritance from the revolution coupled with romanticism lived on, repeatedly renewed, in many variant forms. The upshot was a proud unwillingness to accept any responsibility for the centre, or for the performance of any roles in it – or if that was done, to do so in a melancholy, unhappy way (for example, Beyle and Vigny).

This rejection did not occur uniformly, continuously or all-pervasively throughout the intellectual classes of the Western world. Intellectuals like Flaubert who disdained and despised the French society of his time were profoundly disturbed by the military defeat of France at the hands of Prussia in the war of 1870–1; in the Second World War Paul Valéry who seems never to have thought about politics or the national standing of France except with refined disdain, became enthusiastic when the bombers of the United States Air Force flew over Paris presaging the defeat of the Germans and the political rehabilitation of France.

Intellectuals did not succeed in freeing themselves from the tradition of nationality; neither the conservative intellectuals who regretted the destruction of the *ancien régime*, nor the emancipatory intellectuals who looked forward to a redeemed and free mankind, nor the sardonic and detached intellectuals who saw themselves as free from every illusion and superstition could emancipate themselves from the tradition of nationality.

There were, of course, intellectuals who thought that the European societies of their time were at a high point in the progress of the human race. Nevertheless, among the greatest men of letters and artists, the latter views did not gain the ascendancy over those which rejected responsibility to or for their society. It was the outlook of the latter which gained the suffrage of literary and artistic intellectuals in most European countries. The degree of vehemence varied from individual to individual and from country to country. The degree of vehemence and even bitter hatred of the bourgeoisie and of bourgeois society was perhaps most pronounced in France. France with its overpowering prestige in literature and art laid out a pattern which came to appear normal for many literary men and women and artists throughout Western societies, including Eastern Europe. Yet, this pervasive rejection of social and political responsibility was not political or revolutionary radicalism. It was rather an apolitical, aesthetic, scientistic, sometimes religious, often agnostic, rather than anti-political attitude. It did, however, present an 'opening to the left', an increasing drift towards sympathy and sometimes affiliation with revolutionary or at least far-reachingly alientated political sects. After the Russian Revolution of 1917 which was regarded by many liberals and aesthetics as an event long overdue, the dislike of their own bourgeois societies led to a great increase in sympathy with the Communist Parties. Many of them yielded to 'the totalitarian temptation'. They are still drawn to it. Nevertheless, not only in European societies and North America but in Eastern Europe and Asia as well, many intellectuals, critical though they were of their own societies, resisted that.

9

This support of tyranny outside one's own society and on such a large scale is probably unprecedented in the history of the political relations of intellectuals. It is not that intellectuals were indifferent to foreign countries before modern times. After seamen and merchants, intellectuals knew more about foreign countries than any other groups in their societies. They found things to admire in these other societies, just as the Greek intellectuals admired the wisdom of Brahmins and magi. They might also appreciate an alien society as the birthplace of their own, as Romans thought of Troy. Intellectuals prior to modern times were often eager to acquire the culture of foreign countries, as Japanese intellectuals were desirous of learning Confucianism and Buddhism from Chinese intellectuals. But this knowledge of foreign societies and their culture and admiration for one or another element of those foreign societies and cultures did not result in such a comprehensive xenophilia as occurred among intellectuals in the West, and as the Orient too manifested towards the Soviet Union. This xenophilia was not confined to artists and literary men. It was also to be found among natural scientists and to a lesser degree among humanistic scholars. It was, moreover, present in combinations with the cultivation of the idea of *l'art pour l'art*, with bohemianism and a staid, more or less, civil outlook.

The Francophilia which was raised to a high point by the outbreak of the Great Revolution in France in 1789 was certainly widespread among intellectuals in Italy, Great Britain and Germany but it did not last as long, nor was it on such a large scale as was the enthusiasm for the Russian revolutions of October 1917 among intellectuals in Western Europe, North America and South and East Asia. It still survives but in an attenuated form. In the case of the centrality of France for intellectuals from all over the world, it was not only 'the ideas of 1789' but the genuinely superior achievements of French scientists, scholars, writers and artists for much for the nineteenth and twentieth centuries which made for the Francophilia. Even now when the latter achievements of French intellectuals have diminished, the enthusiasm for Derrida, Foucault, Althusser and Lévi-Strauss represent such an attribution of intellectual centrality to France.

The enthusiasm of non-Russian intellectuals for the Soviet Union resembled the Francophilia of intellectuals for France from the eighteenth century onwards, and has in part nurtured the repugnance which many intellectuals have felt for the authoritative institutions of their own societies. The Soviet Union was admired because it opposed the system of private property in the means of production, bourgeois democracy, and party politics, hedonism and individualism. The ideal alternative, even more vaguely and unrealistically delineated than the distored image of their own, existing societies, was a utopian *Gemeinschaft*. The Soviet Union seemed to many intellectuals to embody this ideal or to be on the way to embodying it. After seventy years, when well-documented experience has shown that the ideal alternative is not embodied in Soviet society, there is still a powerful propensity to believe that it contains that potentiality and that it is therefore closer to the ideal than are their own societies which they view with a disapproving and purblind eye.

10

The uncivil, anti-bourgeois, anti-political attitude has become attenuated, to some extent in the period since the end of the Second World War. The belief that art should be cultivated for the sake of the intrinsic value of the product and the activity – 'art for art's sake' – has not lost its hold. Artists are less fervently inclined to regard art as part of the struggle against bourgeois society.

There is probably still a dormant desire that a revolution will purge society of its evils; the exhilaration of the student disturbances of the 1960s and early 1970s and the excitement which was ignited among intellectuals by the 'the glorious days of May' in Paris in 1968 are a sign that the reconciliation with their own society of the intellectuals who yearn for an ideology does not rest on very deep foundations. If the hope for revolution has been nearly abandoned by intellectuals who are not members of the sectarian *groupuscules*, the war against bourgeois society and culture still goes on. It is now, however, joined by sectors of the intellectual stratum who had previously been indifferent to it.

The radical 'politicization' of the academic humanities is a rather novel phenomenon in the history of universities. Academic humanists – classical scholars, historians, students of national languages and literatures and orientalists – had often not conducted their studies as parts of a political programme under the influence of an ethical and political ideal but at the same time they adhered to a strict loyalty to the ideal of critically assessed evidence and painstaking documentation.

The social scientists, seeking to be scientists, espoused a similar ideal of objectivity, of strict reasoning and careful observation, whether it entailed a study of printed and unpublished sources or field work by direct observation and interviewing of the persons being studied or the interrogation of 'informants'. Of course, many social scientists had strong political convictions, whether they were utilitarians, socialists, liberals or conservatives. Yet they also believed in the possibility of objectivity and they tried to keep their political preferences distinct from their observations and analyses. They knew that it was difficult to do so but they had little doubt that it was, in principle, possible to do so and they tried as scrupulously as they could to subject themselves to the discipline called for by the ideal of objectivity.

This too has changed in the past quarter of a century. It is frequently asserted that 'evaluative neutrality' in social scientific research is a phantasm. Some go so far as to say that it is a 'bourgeois' fiction, promulgated to fortify the power of the ruling classes. It is a view widely asserted that objectivity or 'evaluative neutrality' is impossible. Of course, this view is incompatible with the scientific aspirations of many social scientists but such has been the force of current opinion that they affirm the view to which they do not adhere in practice.

This view is asserted by many social scientists who are very far from being revolutionary in their beliefs and sympathies. But they do believe that social science should be engaged with political authority – both in opposition to it and in its service – or both simultaneously as is often the case among 'policy scientists'.

Since social research has now become much more costly than it used to be, it has become more dependent on financial support drawn from outside the regular budget of universities. These external sources are primarily government and private philanthropic foundations. Both of these patrons wish their funds to be spent not primarily for the support of the advancement of knowledge as such but for the support of the advancement of knowledge which will contribute to the welfare of the society for which the officials regard themselves as responsible. In adapting themselves to this situation, social scientists have accepted the obligation to conceive of their work as serving a 'social' end, i.e. as supporting or opposing a particular practical policy – usually a governmental policy. This is a minimal form of political responsibility and it is quite compatible both with the objectivity of knowledge and with a civil attitude.

Nevertheless, the entry of Marxism in one variant version or another into academic social science is a sign that the 'civil' acceptance of responsibility by academic social scientists has not by any means replaced the radical incivility, i.e. the refusal – so prominent several decades ago – to accept responsibility for working within the framework of constitutional political activity. The two attitudes coexist, often in the same mind.

The natural sciences have also become more politicized in the sense that academic natural scientists have become much more political than they used to be before governmental financial support of research in the natural sciences became as predominant as it is nowadays. In liberal democratic countries, government and politics are much more prominent in the minds of scientists than they were. It could not be otherwise since scientists are now very aware of the extent to which the magnitude of financial support for their research is dependent on governmental decisions. But quite apart from this, scientific knowledge having entered so penetratingly into governmental decisions, both domestic and international, natural scientists have become very much more interested in politics. The importance of the knowledge which they create in the decisions of governments has given some of them a sense of responsibility for its application.

<h2 style="text-align:center">I I</h2>

Between the extremes of subservient acceptance of responsibility for the purposes of authority and the insistent claim to arrogate responsibility for guiding and counselling if not actually ruling, between the extremes of utter indifference to any responsibility for the well-being of society and the rancorous and aggressive rejection of any responsibility and indeed a hatred which would obliterate any sense of responsibility towards the prevailing society, there is a large and various set of attitudes and actions. There is a large and variegated intellectual population which participates in none of the extremes. At any one time, nearly all of these attitudes, extreme and civil, have been present among the intellectuals of modern societies. Their relative preponderance or recessiveness varies. It seems to me that the more extreme attitudes have been more prominent among intellectuals in modern societies than they have been in the past, but none of the extremes has ever enduringly dominated the outlook of the majority of intellectuals in those societies.

The civil attitude has not often been articulately or dramatically expressed either in theory or in practice; it is more often expressed in practice than in theoretical formulation. It has not been negligible, but it is often underestimated because it is not melodramatic in its rhetoric, and is not attended by such events as assassinations, *coups d'état*, huge demonstrations and processions, violent altercations and random brutality. It has not entered much into the discussions of intellectuals.

It is certainly important to acknowledge and to investigate the high degree of rejection by intellectuals, in their conduct and in declarations, of responsibility for the society in which they live. The investigation should, however, attend equally to the intellectuals of civil demeanour and conduct and those whose political interests are lacking in intensity and are very intermittent as well as to those whose attitudes – and, sometimes, conduct – are closer to the extremes.

One significant factor in the increased prominence of the attitude of civil irresponsibility is the increase in the size of the intellectual stratum. The intellectual stratum has increased in size in all countries. Both those engaged in specifically intellectual activities and those engaged in intellectual-practical activities have increased. The number of those who engage professionally, i.e. full-time and for remuneration, in intellectual activities has increased as probably have those avocational intellectuals who engage in intellectual activities while practising other occupations, whether they be intellectual-practical activities or wholly practical activities with a relatively small degree of intellectual content and qualification for entry. The fraction of intellectuals engaged professionally in intellectual activities conducted in institutions such as university teachers, advanced secondary school teachers, scientists and scholars working in research institutions, journalists, television authors, etc., has grown greatly in absolute terms. The fraction who perform specifically intellectual activities as amateurs, i.e. as dependent for their incomes on inherited wealth or wealth they themselves have accumulated by their own efforts in non-intellectual activities, has undoubtedly decreased, although their numbers in absolute terms might not have decreased. In any case they occupy a less prominent place in the intellectual life of most countries than they did in earlier centuries. Independent or free-lance authors have also increased in number in consequence of more widespread literacy, greater leisure and higher purchasing power – all of which have increased the readership of books.

One of the most important features of the intellectual stratum of the present day, as compared with earlier periods in the West and in the Orient, is that only a very small fraction of it consists of civil servants and ecclesiastical officials, priests, parsons, monks, deacons, bishops, etc. The fraction of intellectuals who are not maintained by their service of church and state has increased enormously. Whereas in China until the nineteenth century, most intellectuals were in the civil service or had acquired the culture required for appointment to the civil service; this is not the case any more even in communist China and it has not been the case in the West since the eighteenth century. The size of civil services has increased in all societies relative to the total population but the contribution of this growth to the growth in the size of the intellectual stratum has been incommensurate and indirect; the increased number of university graduates fostered by the increased opportunities for appointment to the civil service on the basis of educational qualifications and examinations of intellectual content has increased the reservoir from which intellectuals are drawn.

The slower expansion of the avocational intellectual stratum in the service of state and church has been more than merely overtaken by the growth of universities and the corresponding growth in the number of university teachers. The number of university teachers has grown greatly but it has done so not only because of the increased demand for university education as a function of increased opportunities for appointment to the civil service. Increased literacy and leisure and more curiosity about the world and the more realizable desire for entertainment have increased the audience for the products of the journalistic literary professions, working through television, radio and printing press, and they have thus made it possible for more persons to gain their livelihood as free-lance writers. There are more novelists and probably even more poets in many of the richer countries and perhaps in the poorer ones, too, than there used to be. Increased wealth, the preoccupation with health – and belief in the curability of illness – and the increase in occasions of conflict over respective rights and obligations have increased the numbers of lawyers and physicians, some of whom are intellectuals; intellectuals have always lurked in the interstices of the intellectual-practical professions. The increase in the opportunities in the latter professions has also contributed to the increase in the demand for more teachers in universities.

The belief in the intrinsic and practical value of scientific knowledge has also contributed to the increase in the size of the intellectual stratum. Scientists and applied scientists have increased greatly in number and in the fraction which they make up in the entire intellectual stratum.

The growth in the size of the intellectual stratum ran along two lines; these were lines separating persons who did not from those who did sell or try to sell their intellectual products in the market and who had to live from the proceeds of those sales. The first column of the first line was that of the intellectuals who taught in schools and universities, who interpreted and transmitted the results of past intellectual activity while in varying degrees they also produced intellectual works of their own. These academic intellectuals were supplemented – in some countries, they were overshadowed or outnumbered – by amateur and avocational intellectuals. This second column of intellectuals comprised persons of private means or beneficiaries of private and princely patronage who held no official positions or only sinecures, and persons who followed other occupations – practical-intellectual, mainly – judges, lawyers, journalists, civil servants and scribes, librarians, physicians, astrologers, etc.

A third column in this first line of institutional intellectuals was formed of religious intellectuals – monks, priests, ecclesiastical administrators; except for teachers in theological seminaries, their tasks were primarily not intellectual as the religions were dominated by sacred books and doctrines, there was often an inclination towards intellectual activity on the part of some of the persons who had been admitted to the practice of these activities.

All of the intellectuals in this first line were distinguished by the stability and regularity of their income. Many of them were employed by governmentally maintained institutions. Others performed their intellectual and practical intellectual tasks in privately maintained institutions, such as churches and research institutes. (The boundary is not a disjunctive one, nor is the classification exhaustive.) There were intellectuals who were not maintained by institutions but who, more than many who were so maintained, were enabled to devote all their energy to intellectual work since their livelihood was guaranteed by the steady flow of income from their own private property.

The modern age has seen tremendous growth in the second line; this is the line of the free-lance intellectuals, who supported themselves or tried to support themselves from the sale of their intellectual 'goods and services'. Itinerant bards and singers of epics – itinerant because there was not sufficient wealth for their continuous maintenance in any one locality – were paid in hospitality and in kind and by small uncovenanted sums producing sufficient payment to maintain them. There were also teachers, itinerant and sedentary, who gave lessons for remuneration.

In Occidental antiquity, in most of the Orient and in Islam, this second line of intellectuals working for payment was very scantily populated and not particularly esteemed; in fact, teachers who taught privately for monetary remuneration were disparaged. Furthermore, the audience willing to pay and capable of paying in money or kind for the entertainment and instruction provided by these kinds of intellectuals was relatively small; the institutional apparatus and tradition of oral communication likewise limited the size of audiences. China was an exception thanks to the early invention of block printing which meant that multiple copies of a work could be reproduced in a fairly short time. As a result there were authors who drew some income from the sale of their writings earlier than anywhere else in the world. Nevertheless, as compared with later developments, the second line in the growth of the intellectual stratum remained relatively small even in China in comparison with the first line.

An immense increase in the size of the intellectual stratum in all societies in modern times has occurred in both the first and second lines. The increases have not by any means been uniform. Within the first line, the second column of rentier or amateur intellectuals has diminished relatively and probably even absolutely. The third column – the column of religious intellectuals in Western liberal democratic societies and in totalitarian societies, which are aggressively atheistic or at best simply hostile to religious belief and practice – has decreased in absolute numbers and percentage, the latter much more than the former. In prominence too, religious intellectuals have receded.

The proliferation of intellectuals of the second line has been one of the most important features of the past three centuries. The appearance of the role of the *freier Schriftsteller*, the free-lance *homme de lettres*, the 'man of letters' who lives from his pen or his voice is not unique in world history but it was a very restricted activity until the beginning of modern times. The 'free-lance author', the person who seeks to gain a livelihood through the income from the writing or speaking of books, poems, literary journalism – once spoken, then almost entirely printed and now also printed and broadcast – does not perform his other intellectual work as a member of an institution, either intellectual-practical or intellectual. Such intellectuals do not live under institutional authority in the conduct of their intellectual work and they do not have stipulated salaries. Of course, they do not live entirely independently of institutions. Being human, they have lived in families. They are citizens, or at least subjects in political communities and they must observe the laws of the society in which they live. If they are active members of organized political parties, they are bound in varying degrees by the leaders and officials of their respective parties. If they are serious in their religious beliefs, they are members of religious communities and their beliefs and conduct are bound by the discipline required by membership in those communities.

In their intellectual activity they are dependent on publishers to arrange for the printing and publication of their books and for the payment of 'advances' and royalties. They have been dependent on bookshops for the distribution of their works to readers; they have been dependent on newspapers and journals for the notice and review of their works. (If they live in societies without intellectual freedom, even though they work on their own and depend on the sale of their intellectual products for their income, they are restricted too by institutions such as censorship and writers' unions and 'academies'.) And, of course, they have almost always at one time been pupils in schools through which they learned to read and write and through which they first were enabled to come into contact with literary and other intellectual traditions, however widely they might subsequently have departed from those 'scholastic' literary traditions.

Yet at the heart of their intellectual activities, they were outside the reach of institutional authority. That was what they desired. They were independent intellectual entrepreneurs.

Independence of institutions in the practice of literary or artistic creations is an ideal with a long history. It began as an ideal in the fifteenth century in the Italian city-states where painters and sculptors were dissatisfied with the requirement that they organized into guilds. They thought that artists did work similar to the work of scientists; they were not handicraftsmen ornamenting and decorating buildings. Their insistence that the roots of artistic creation lay in the higher mental faculties was readily combined with the idea of genius untrammelled by institutions. The life of a writer or artist had therefore to be free of the constraints of everyday social life. But it was an ideal the pursuit of which was obstructed by hardships, especially in its earlier stages. No income was guaranteed; the future was therefore full of uncertainties. Only a small fraction of those who entered on such careers were able to live tolerably satisfactorily; not many more than a handful became rich from the income from their writings or paintings or sculptures. For the others who survived the course, the life was always a hard one. Many fell by the wayside, ceased writing or painting following other occupations or they gained an exiguous livelihood by hack journalism or some other surrogate.

The hard life of independant literary men and women was sometimes associated with a Bohemian mode of existence. Insufficient and unpredictable income made marriage and an orderly domestic life difficult. Sexual connections without marriage were therefore part of this mode of life. Necessity and the ideal coincided at this point. The ideal of a 'free spirit' required, just as impecuniousness and unpredictability encouraged, departure from the rules and conventions of bourgeois society; 'respectability' became a manifestation of a lack of imagination and of disregard for the highest values. Bohemia was an island fortress within the engulfing bourgeois society. Separated from bourgeois, philistine society, Bohemia was a realm into which the outlook of bourgeois society could not penetrate. There writers could live freely, if impecuniously and uneasily.

The two currents of thought which ran into the formation of Bohemia were both, on the face of it, apolitical. Neither the idea of genius nor that of art being of the same dignity as science contained any political attitude; there was nothing explicitly political in these two ideals. Nevertheless, in the nineteenth century, the hardy after-life of the 'ideas of 1789' and the expansion of the socialist criticism of bourgeois society and of the alternative ideal offered in socialism led, in the setting of public, visible politics, to the development of a Bohemian political attitude. It was an easily made extension of a denial of the claims of authority in the personal – or private – and artistic and literary spheres to hostility against existing political authority which was in any case associated with the bourgeoisie with its repulsive vulgarity in matters of aesthetic taste and moral sensibility.

Bohemian culture came to be regarded by those who participated in it as having an affinity with the outcasts of society, prostitutes, thieves, homeless persons, lumpenproletarians, etc. There was, indeed, such an affinity. The outcasts, as a result of misfortune and inclination, rejected responsibility to and for bourgeois society; they did not regard it as a responsibility to respect the laws and rules of society; they would accept no responsibility to live in and to respect the style, implicitly and explicitly, demanded by the Philistine, 'bourgeoisified' part of society. They had no responsibility for the maintenance or gradual improvement of the society as a whole. They refused to see such activities as falling within the boundaries of their responsibility. In so far as they had any responsibilities, it was to the ideals of literature and art. It was not a great leap of the imagination for Bohemian intellectuals to discover a community of outlook with anarchists and revolutionary socialists in Germany, France and the United States, and even in England, to the extent that England had a Bohemia in the last part of the nineteenth century.

Of course, a great many literary men and women of the second half of the nineteenth and the first decades of the twentieth centuries were not Bohemians. There was a writers' style of life; it was not Bohemian but it was also deliberately not philistine.

Not all literary men and women and artists, even those who were Bohemians, slipped into this confederation with anarchists and revolutionary socialists. Some who did not join this confederation held themselves aloof, nonetheless, from all contaminating sympathy with the political and economic centre of society although they were also not Bohemians in their pace and mode of life. They too disavowed any responsibility for the concerns of bourgeois society and they even found gratification in portraying its dissolution; Thomas Mann and John Galsworthy represent this type. There were also literary men and women who lived, morally and intellectually, more or less in harmony with bourgeois society; some of them not only participated in it and enjoyed to but also affirmed it; but the latter action was rather rare. (The affirmation was more an affirmation of grand bourgeois and aristocratic conviviality. Proust and Thomas Mann represented the former; Arnold Bennett the latter.)

Nonetheless, the influence of the idea of the writer and painter as an artist and as a genius, coupled with ideals of social justice and with images of the moral drabness and insensateness of bourgeois society did not lose strength. The penumbra of these secondary proto-political traditions surrounding the substantive traditions of literary and artistic creation precipitated an image of the human world in which there was a cleavage between artistic endeavour and dedication on the one side, and the impassive acceptance of responsibility for occupational tasks, domestic duties and political obligations on the other.

There had never been anything like this before in Western civilization. Plato knew that tyrants, even when they were the protégés of philosophers, would be obdurate to their counsel. Aristotle expected no great spiritual leaps forward by statesmen, nor did Cicero. Augustine knew that the City of God was not the city of man; Hobbes knew that rulers were apt to be disregardful of the conditions under which they could keep themselves in office and power. Confucius and Mencius, Shang-Wang and Wang-an-Shih and Kautilya knew that rulers were weak reeds and wayward ones as well but they all knew that they had to be counselled, supported and guided, if society were not to descend into chaos. Machiavelli knew as much. Confucius and Mencius and those who espoused and revised their views never doubted that society must be under earthly authority, that earthly authority was indispensable; the only question was whether the earthly authority ruled wisely and was respectful towards the spirits of ancestors and the spirit of the Heavens and whether for this to happen, the service and counsel of good men, learned in the classics, were necessary.

There were, of course, philosophers in China and elsewhere in the ancient Occidental and Oriental worlds who expected nothing from rulers; they had, naturally, to be very prudent in expressing such views. They thought that the actions, objectives and ideals of earthly rulers were worthless and that human beings should turn away from them but they did not espouse revolutionary programmes. They did not propose a forceful abolition of the existing institutions of authority and their replacement through violent action which would establish another, better society. Criticisms of the injustice visited on the poor and weak by the rich and powerful have been common to the ancient Mesopotamian civilizations and to ancient Israel. But these criticisms usually did not praise rebellion.

The promulgation of ideas of ideal or ethically superior political and social arrangements has long been a feature of religious and philosophical reflection. It has been especially pronounced from the time of the Israelite prophets. Islamic and Christian philosophers have offered comparable ideals. But the continuous and detailed confrontation between ideals and the conduct of authority was absent. The concrete knowledge of particular social and political events, which is characteristic of modern societies, was lacking in societies with high rates of illiteracy and official secretiveness. The practice of continued and detailed confrontation was left for modern Western intellectuals and then following in their footsteps, intellectuals in Latin America, Asia and Africa.

12

Many years ago, observers (e.g. Max Handman, Walter Kotschnig, *et al.*) pointed out the dangers of a large body of 'unemployed intellectuals' to the order and peace of society. It was not a baseless observation. What has been more striking has been the hostility of free-lance literary and artistic intellectuals – later, other types as well – to their own societies and their moral encouragement to those who would replace them, through the use of violence, by far better, problemless societies. The ferocious rebellions led by Huang Ch'ao in the late Tang dynasty, and its successors in the tenth century, the rebellions in the middle period of the Northern Sung and in the later Ming, and, not least, the Taiping Rebellion of the nineteenth century drew some of their leadership and their bitterness from men who had taken the examinations and failed to gain the desired degrees. These were 'unemployed intellectuals' trained in Confucian classics and then made into 'superfluous men'. They were the first 'unemployed intellectuals' who turned into the revolutionary path. Karl Marx thought that a certain socialist movement of which he disapproved drew its support from lawyers without briefs, physicians without patients, students who specialized in billiards. Unemployed intellectuals might indeed be a danger to social order but it is not they who have generated the outlook and the tradition of revulsion from bourgeois society.

How did this particular sector of the intellectual stratum become so prominent? One thing above all must be mentioned in accounting for their prominence. Among them, there were geniuses whose great works were able to command attention and appreciation by many persons who did not share their 'critical views'. Yet it was not by their genius alone that free-lance or independent intellectuals have been able to acquire so much prominence in intellectual life. They did so because they expressed an outlook which worked on the incipient moral restlessness of young persons with intellectual – above all, literary and artistic – aspirations.

There had emerged, a long time before, a belief among romantic literary men that they were prophets, 'acknowledged legislators of mankind', seers and sages. In societies which were losing their belief in the validity of the doctrines formed from revealed religions, there remained among quondam believers a need for some surrogate for the connection with sacred truths. Vatic literary men supplied some of this surrogate. They set forth, or assumed, a transcendental standard by which they judged their own societies. They believed that they must be heard and, by their assertion of their righteousness, they succeeded in gaining an audience which took them at their word.

There was much else which enabled writers of outstanding achievements, who shared much of the Bohemian outlook if not its mode of life, to acquire prominence in the educated classes and in other sectors of the intellectual stratum, especially among journalists and teachers. (Both of the latter were megaphones which amplified their voices and focussed the attention of the wider public.)

There were other factors as well which should be taken into account to tell how and why it was that the romantic conception of the special moral calling of the literary and artistic intellectuals and particularly their fundamental disavowal of any responsibility for participation in the existing order of society were able to gain a sympathetic reception.

There have always been misgivings among intellectuals about the conduct of earthly affairs by those who rule society. The great Confucian intellectuals, who were said by Max Weber to have accommodated themselves most fully to the existing social order, were in fact very alert to deviations from the conduct required by the Spirit of the Heavens and by traditions and rites. Perhaps among those whose practical interests preponderated over their intellectual interests, the stringency of the Confucian ethical assessment of the ruler's conduct became attenuated. Nevertheless, they never were entirely dissipated over the course of Chinese history. They only rarely verged on such thoroughgoing rejection of their regime.

When at the end of the nineteenth and the beginning of the twentieth centuries, Chinese intellectuals – academic, publicists as well as free-lance intellectuals – became bitterly critical of their tradition they turned to Western progressive intellectuals like Herbert Spencer; later they found their way to the writing of Western socialist intellectuals. Their aim was to rehabilitate their country and to restore it to its earlier preeminence; they were willing to extirpate all the formative traditions of China in order to do this. The May 4th Movement was in part a by-product of the antipathy of Western intellectuals towards their own bourgeois society.

13

The free-lance intellectual's concept of the world and of his response to it has undergone a notable expansion in the present century. It has expanded into the outlook of institutional intellectuals and it has expanded into the intellectual strata of societies without sovereignty or colonial societies or societies peripheral in other respects.

Whereas for much of the history of the intellectual stratum in Western societies and well into the twentieth century there has been a fairly high barrier between the first and second lines, i.e., between 'institutional' intellectuals and 'free-lance' intellectuals, the barrier has become lower since the Second World War. It is not easy to say why this has happened. The loosening of the bonds of sexual puritanism, the change in sartorial conduct and the abrogation of the distance between educated speech with its proprieties on the one side and colloquial slang and obscene speech on the other has diminished. The great expansion in the size of universities, indicated by the increased numbers of teachers and students, meant that the expansion at the junior levels of the teachers brought into universities the modes of speech and dress and the view of sexual matters of the younger generation. The universities have, moreover, come more intimately and more directly and immediately into contact with the society outside them. The university has not been able or it has not wished to keep itself unmarked by its closer connection with the outer, non-academic world. By the time that the barriers between institutional and free-lance intellectuals have been lowered or made more porous, the free-lance intellectuals added a political facet to their derogatory view of bourgeois society. This latest combination entered the academic world and brought with it on its entry the distrustful hostile attitude towards the intellectual's own society and its political order.

A paradoxical situation has arisen. On the one side the universities and university teachers have become much more intricately connected with government and with private business firms than they used to be before the Second World War; on the other side, university teachers have become much more hostile to government and to private business than they were before the Second World War. (There are, of course, many qualifications to those made in the latter statement: the reanimation of traditional individualistic liberalism and the greater appreciation of the market economy is a movement contrary to the trend referred to but the contradiction is confined largely to economists and a very small number of social scientists.) Among physical scientists, the anti-governmental and anti-capitalistic tendency is very strong; it has become that way in the humanities as well. Other institutional intellectuals, the journalists of the printed press, radio and television, have moved in the same direction. (The producers of informational and interpretative programmes should be included among the journalists; they too have moved in the direction of the free-lance literary and artistic intellectuals.)

What is the upshot of these changes with regard to the acceptance of responsibilities? Intellectuals have remained by and large concerned to observe their responsibilities towards their own disciplinary intellectual traditions, except for some of the humanistic subjects. This concern for their own disciplinary tradition has, however, been adulterated by the infusion of political beliefs to a greater extent than before. With regard to the acceptance of responsibility for the institutions at the centre of society, there are

contradictory tendencies. Incumbent governments are more dis-
trusted and denounced by the intellectuals of their own society
than they were a century ago. At the same time, more intellectuals
are entering the service of governments in the performance of
'mission-oriented' research and of 'contract-research' as well as by
service in governmental research institutions and private industrial laboratories. The censorious attitude towards the centre does
not seem to be moderated by these developments. Antinomian
intellectuals are not less eager for governmental patronage than are
those who are not so hostile to government. Much of the antinomian intellectual activity is, of course, carried on in the name of
responsibility to a higher standard, or an ideal of emancipation
from obligations to traditional norms and institutions.

In communist societies, the problem of responsibility is set into
a quite different context. The critical or censorious attitudes of
intellectuals towards the authorities who rule their societies are
given much less freedom of expression and when they do try to
express themselves by the very limited public means which are
available to them, they are dealt with very severely. The situation
of dissident and censorious intellectuals varies from one communist country to another but only within fairly narrow limits.

The situation in communist countries illustrates the proposition
that the positive acceptance of responsibilities is possible only in a
society in which public liberties and public politics exist. This
does not mean that a sense of responsibility is entirely lacking but
it is likely to deteriorate where there is no freedom to choose
between the acceptance of a responsibility and its rejection.

The situation of intellectuals' acceptance of responsibility and
their sense of responsibility in societies which lacked sovereignty,
and in which a foreign power ruled the society was in some
respects similar to that which prevails in totalitarian societies.
There were, however, rather significant differences. For one
thing, the size of the intellectual stratum, except in India, was very
small. There were not many indigenous journalists, and the
number of secondary school teachers was smaller; that of teachers
in higher educational institutions was even smaller. Expatriates
filled many of the posts.

Privately, Indian teachers resented the presence of the foreign
government and sympathized with movements to refuse co-

operation with it. Where there was some indigenous participation
in the higher reaches of the civil service, to which some native
intellectuals were appointed, there was a genuine sense of responsibility for the performance of their duties. Nearly all native
politicians were in opposition although the degree of opposition
was variable. There were very few free-lance intellectuals, even in
India, where, despite the high rate of illiteracy, there was a
considerable reading public and hence a small group of novelists –
and probably a larger group of poets in each of the major Indian
languages as well as in English. There were some Indian members
of the Indian civil service who wrote literary and scholarly works.
There were also intellectuals among the politicians, particularly in
the Congress Socialist Party (e.g. Nehru, Masani, Mehta,
Narayan, Patwardhan and Lohia); Gandhian intellectuals also
existed. There were in addition a number of very active intellectuals who were social reformers, mainly but not exclusively
members of the Servants of India Society. The small Communist
Party of India included in its ranks some intellectuals and it had
among its sympathizers several quite eminent university and
college teachers.

After Independence the picture changed quite markedly. There
was a great increase in the size of the intellectual class, quite
far-reaching freedom of expression and many more sorts for
Indians in the senior ranks of the major – almost entirely English-
language – newspapers. The journalists, at least in public, supported the government, partly because the government by its
advertisement of public announcements could affect the financial
well-being of the newspapers. The academic profession in India
was less ready to support the government, not because its
members disagreed with the domestic economic and foreign
policies of the government but because it did not make rapid
enough progress towards an improved standard of living for the
mass population and because it tolerated the deep inequalities of
Indian society. Politicians especially became objects of dispa-
ragement; it was said that they were lazy, corrupt and self-
indulgent in addition to being time-servers. In the first decades of
independent India, intellectuals, except for those in high positions
in the Union government, particularly the higher civil servants
who had continued from the Indian Civil Service and who met a

high standard of responsibility in their relations with the prime minister and his cabinet, became a carping, captious discontented lot who did not think very realistically about costs and consequences. Indeed Max Weber's critical views of the *Literaten* seemed almost to have been formulated with the Indian academic intellectuals in mind. The huge majority of the Congress Party, and the weakness of opposition parties, were discouragements to the formation of a sense of responsibility among Indian intellectuals.

Of the intellectuals of Black Africa, there is not much to be said apart from the large increase in their numbers. They soon fell out with their rulers and in many respects came to resemble the Indian intellectuals as they developed after independence. They did not fail to arouse the animosity of the politicians who reaped many of the benefits of independence, above all lucrative posts and opportunities for advantageous corruption. Many African literary men have had to take refuge in countries outside their own in order to escape from the persecution at the hands of the political rulers of the country. The succession of military usurpations aggravated the alienation of academic intellectuals – the largest body of intellectuals in nearly every African country – and reduced them to a sense of impotence and despondency.

In several of the Black African countries there had been institutions of higher education established before the attainment of independence. It was in these institutions that a greater sense of institutional responsibility developed in a small number of individuals as well as a sense of responsibility to the traditions of their respective substantive disciplines. The attachment to these traditions was not always firm enough to withstand the discouragements of civil responsibility and the power of primordial indigenous traditions. The latter caused tribal loyalties to outweigh intellectual responsibility within the institution. Since the objects of tribal and political attachment frequently coincided, the coherence of the institution and attachment to the substantive scholarly and scientific traditions had to pay the price.

The intellectuals of societies which until recently lacked a sovereignty, i.e. societies which did not form political communities more or less coterminous with the boundaries of the society, have had a special problem not shared with liberal democratic or communist societies. The problems arising from the relations of centres and periphery have been especially acute among the intellectuals of those societies.

Every society faces in varying degrees problems arising from the relations of centre and periphery. These problems reach an extreme point of aggravation in societies which are ruled from outside their boundaries or which have relatively recently been so ruled. One of the reasons for the aggravation is the modern culture of the society of which the intellectuals are the chief bearers.

There is a deep disjunction between the substance of the modern culture of the intellectuals and the traditional high culture of the society. Furthermore, the intellectuals of the particular society have been educated in modern higher educational institutions which are alien in pattern to the institutions through which the traditional culture was transmitted. Intellectuals of colonial or quasi-colonial countries have a strong, although unfocussed, sense of nationality – their sense of their own 'nationality' is ordinarily far stronger than it is in the rest of the society, except for some politicians for whom the proclamation of their nationality is a major device of political contention.

The sense of nationality of the intellectuals is sometimes experienced as being in conflict with their attachments to their modern culture. Their modern culture has its main focus outside their society; the source of their particular variant of modern culture is located in the country of their former rulers, to which, as nationalists, they have some antipathy. The subjective experience of ambivalence between their attachment to their own particular traditional culture and to their modern culture has often been exaggerated by observers; there are, nevertheless, instances in which the ambivalence is painfully felt.

Several other aspects of these multiple attachments are much more significant for the intellectuals of formerly colonial and quasi-colonial countries. One of these is the fact that the focus of the models of creativity of various parts of their modern culture lies outside the territorial boundaries of their own society. This generates in them a sense of being peripheral, which for them is a status of inferiority which is distressing to them and which impairs their own sense of responsibility for their own field of work. It is difficult for them to escape from this sense of incapacity to contribute noticeably to their subject. This condition is not so marked in fields of study of which the subject-matter is their own language, literature, history or society. In the former two fields, they do have to a much greater degree a sense of being central; a little less so in the latter two. In those subjects which are world-wide in cultivation or in which the territorial location of the data is irrelevant – as in mathematics or astronomy – the centre is clearly located outside their own territory. This results in a dampening sense of being unregarded and powerless.

There are many complicated consequences of this state of affairs. One consequence is censure from the politicians and publicists of their own society for being 'remnants of the colonial past' or for being subservient to the formerly colonial powers or for being outposts of 'neo-colonialism'. Defensive adoption of the accusation made against themselves, and aggressive denunciation of persons in the same situation as themselves, is one reaction. Another is subsidence into a sense of isolation and impotence. Other reactions are also to be found. All of them weaken the sense of responsibility for those of their intellectual traditions which are foreign in origin, and for political activity and public service in their own societies.

The hard economic straits of the Black African societies deepen the sense of impotence and hopelessness; alternatively they foster the withdrawal of attention from the public sphere. There had earlier been an excess of 'politicization' in the cases referred to; this has been followed by an attrition of any interest except a very cynical one, in the political affairs of their society. This is not compensated by a strengthening of the sense of responsibility for maintaining the intellectual quality of their disciplines and for improving it by their own contributions to it.

Something should be said here about the sympathy with revolution of intellectuals in societies which have recently gained sovereignty or in a country like China which never lost its sovereignty but in which sovereignty was encroached on by foreign powers. When in the nineteenth century, Asian intellectuals and the tiny number of Black African intellectuals became sensitive to the military, economic and political inferiority of their societies to the major European powers, they thought that if their societies could acquire the scientific and technological knowledge possessed by those foreign societies, the gap could be closed and their dignity restored. To varying degrees, they thought that their indigenous religious and philosophical traditions must be modified if not entirely jettisoned. The disavowal of their indigenous traditions did not come easily to them; there were many hesitations and misgivings among those who thought that their indigenous traditions were to be blamed for their inferiority to the European powers.

Until the First World War, this conflict, although often stated in terms which made it appear to be an irreconcilable one, was on the whole not very acute. Scattered individuals here and there felt it acutely but they were not numerous. Most of the small numbers of intellectuals entertained both traditions concurrently and did not see anything anomalous in it.

The Russian Revolution of 1917 and the formation of the Communist International changed this pronouncedly. As among Western intellectuals, and indeed through the Western intellectuals as intermediaries, intellectuals, some of high talent, others less, in Asia and in the colonial societies and in societies which had been colonies a long time ago saw in Marxism–Leninism a doctrine through which they could gain their national liberty and dignity. Through Marxism–Leninism, and through some sort of affiliation with or guidance by the Soviet Union, they could make the progress which they desired without having to be dependent on ideas or practices coming directly from the West. In variously adulterated forms, such an idea became infused in the educated classes of the societies in question.

This transmission of socialist and Communistic ideas occurred to a considerable extent through the migrations of students from the colonial or quasi-colonial countries who studied at the centre in Europe and to a lesser extent in North America. There the students from the colonial countries frequently gravitated towards socialistic and communistic circles because there they found the congenial company of persons who were antagonistic towards imperialism and who were less prejudiced against them on the ground of colour than the members of the host-population whom they encountered in the ordinary round of life. They did not always distinguish between socialists and communists; the important thing is that they became anti-capitalistic and critical of bourgeois and parliamentary politics. (Those who fell in with socialists did not add hostility to parliamentary politics to their anti-capitalistic attitudes.)

Intellectuals formed by studies abroad almost invariably became more nationalistic than they had been at home. They became aware of themselves as members of a national collectivity. When they returned to their own countries, imbued with nationalistic and socialistic or communistic beliefs, they became partisans of the political movements which were espousing similar ideas. They did not always publicly express their partisanship because many of them were appointed to governmental posts or were employed by firms owned and managed by expatriates from the metropolis. Those who became teachers also had to guard their words. But even if they had not to hide their sympathies, the nature of the political activities which could be carried on under colonial rule was such as to be a hindrance to the development of a sense of responsibility. Until the very last years of colonial rule, political activity was almost exclusively agitational; there was no likelihood of having a responsibility for governing. The sense of responsibility could scarcely be formed.

This has been a feature of the political life of those states and has been one of the factors which accounts for the high frequency of *coups d'état* in those societies. As far as the intellectuals are concerned the oppositional tradition has continued, reinforced by the belief that until a genuinely socialistic or at least thoroughgoing anti-capitalistic regime is established, the well-being and progress of society cannot be realized. This belief in the necessity of a total transformation is a great obstacle to responsible political action.

In Nigeria, for example, the outbreak of violent disorders, the massacre of Ibos in Northern Nigeria and the long and desultory civil war, with its succession of putsches, disordered the embryonic sense of responsibility of Nigerian intellectuals, turning them into an embittered, diffuse opposition and a small group who sought the favour of whatever government was in power and who were regarded as opportunists by those who were excluded from any voice or hand in the affairs of the government or from any of the perquisites offered by such subservience.

The preconditions for the sense and practice of responsibility are thus scantily provided by economic, political and cultural conditions in the newly sovereign societies of Black Africa. The primary or substantive traditions within which intellectuals live and work in those societies are problematic. The indigenous traditions are remote from the traditions of modern scientific and scholarly disciplines which are relatively recent implantations from the civilization and society of the late foreign ruler. Literary traditions draw more on indigenous traditions than do those of the scholarly and scientific disciplines. The genre of the novel is, however, an alien form although the subject-matter is much less so. The institutions in which institutional intellectuals work, and the poverty and illiteracy of the Black African societies, are obstacles to the emergence of a body of economically independent free-lance intellectuals; it is necessary for them to gain a significant part of their livelihood by working for the governmental radio and television systems, or as officials in the ministry of education or as school teachers.

The institutional intellectuals of Black Africa are for the most part acting within an alien intellectual tradition; this is often cited by their antagonists among politicians and publicists as evidence of their irresponsibility towards their own society and its indigenous traditions. The use of the language of the society of the former colonial ruler offers their critics another ground for accusations of irresponsibility. The novelty of the institutions, the scantiness of an older generation already deeply attached to the institutions and to the traditions of their subjects hinders the effective assimilation of newcomers.

The weakness of the substantive tradition, scientific, scholarly and literary, the faintness of the intellectual institutional traditions and the discouragement in the political sphere are combined obstacles to the formation of a sense of intellectual and civil responsibility among the intellectuals of Black Africa.

There are, however, scattered manifestations of a high sense of responsibility among African intellectuals. The most notable was a group of university teachers in Legon who very shortly after the overthrow of Kwame Nkrumah founded a fortnightly under the title of *The Legon Observer* which for a time was a model of responsible criticism and counsel to the new (military) government and then to the elected government of Kofi Busia, himself a reputable academic who was living in exile at the time of the military overthrow of the first government. All this was dissipated in the *coups d'état* which have followed.

14

What am I to conclude from this fragmentary and sketchy survey of the extent to which intellectuals in various civilizations and societies have accepted responsibilities? The most general proposition is that intellectuals have had more sense of responsibility for the maintenance of traditions of intellectual achievement than they have had for the well-being of their political or civil collectivities. But they have not been wholly without that either, even in the present situation of intellectuals in the world.

There is a conflict between the performance of intellectual actions and responsibility in civil or political affairs. In part, this is because of the scarcity of time and energy in the life of any individual. Political actions and intellectual actions are different kinds of actions and they cannot be practised simultaneously or even over longer stretches of time within the span of the adult life of an individual.

Being distinctive activities, and each having its own distinctive institutions, and patterns of life and judgement, there is bound to be some tension even under the best circumstances. In modern times in Western societies there have developed among intellectuals certain traditions which have aggravated the relationship. As Asian and African countries, each against the background of its own unique history, experienced the emergence of modern intellectual strata, they acquired through their overseas studies and through their attraction to Western centrality some of the prevailing Western traditions of the relations and responsibilities of intellectuals.

In my own view, the relations between intellectuals and their societies, including their politics, leave much to be desired. The question as to where the fault lies for the areas of unsatisfactoriness cannot be discussed here, although it would be fruitful to do so. It might be especially fruitful to do so as a precondition for answering the question: How can the situation be improved? Since answers to this question will be even more controversial than my analysis of the situation as it is and has been, the issue had best be left to another occasion.

Index of names